Bimal Jalan

Former Governor
Reserve Bank of India

This book by Tamal Bandyopadhyay, one of India's distinguished journalists, is truly fascinating. It is the story of a highly successful bank, written in a conversational style without any recourse to elaborate statistics or technical jargon. What Tamal has to say about the formation, staffing and the extraordinary services rendered by the bank, and its chief executive officer, is based on hundreds of hours of personal interviews with bankers, central bankers, policy makers, customers and investors in India and abroad.

In fact, the book is less about the bank itself and more about the people who, in the mid-1990s, conceived of setting up a first-class bank with a handful of staff and modest capital resources. They successfully realized their dream with a lot of hard work, imagination and innovative solutions to emerging problems.

Tamal's account of how all this was done is anecdotal, inspirational and entirely accessible to the lay reader. I highly recommend this book to all those who are interested in learning more about post-liberalization India and what we need to do to realize our full potential in the twenty-first century.

Praise for the Book

Deepak Parekh
Chairman
HDFC Bank

When Tamal Bandyopadhyay approached me with the idea of writing a book on HDFC Bank, I was a bit apprehensive, given that the bank was set up only in 1994 and commenced operations in 1995. To my mind, there was not much of a history to formally document. Nonetheless, Tamal was convinced there was a story to tell and I conceded. All I had to do was spend a few hours with him, explaining the philosophy behind the bank and its early days.

The book is a pleasant surprise. Books on banking and finance can often be drab, but this gripping book almost reads like a work of contemporary fiction, written in a lucid and informal style. His focus has been on the people behind the bank.

Tamal has already established himself among India's most respected financial journalists and is regarded for his incisive reasoning and analysis.

Despite knowing Tamal for almost two decades, I can say that a new side to Tamal's true talent has emerged. It is time to welcome the arrival of a new author who I am sure has just begun his new innings.

Praise for the Book

K. V. Kamath
Chairman
ICICI Bank Ltd and Infosys Ltd

This is even better than lunch with Tamal Bandyopadhyay, the fascinating piece that he would do while at his previous job! A fast-paced story, told in typical Tamal style: except this is a true story. Unputdownable. Well researched, well written and extremely readable.

When I received the book as a manuscript, I started to glance through it, then started reading it and ended up finishing the book in one sitting. My dinner had to wait. Tamal has managed to capture the earthiness of the institution he is writing about, and the people that run it, in full colour.

This book is a biopic of both the bank and its people, and succeeds in presenting a 360 degree view and chronicles the story from the day Deepak Parekh got Aditya Puri came on board to where it has reached today.

Along the way, Tamal captures vignettes one did not know about: like Aditya has no computer on his desk and wades through physical printouts of mails, and still manages to leave office at half past five in the evening. Well chronicled, an easy and enjoyable read.

Praise for the Book

Raju Narisetti
Managing Editor
The Wall Street Journal Digital Network

Tamal Bandyopadhyay's book is the ultimate insider story of a bank's birth and its coming of age, brought to life vividly in a sweeping and engrossing eighteen-year-long saga that could only have been retold by India's most respected and well-sourced banking and financial journalist. Many books have tried to give meaning to India's recent history, and put it in the larger context of a complicated and confounding society, but this effort stands out because it does something that has been difficult to attempt—retelling the story of modern India through the lens of business.

As corporate biographies and business autobiographies go, Tamal has produced a deeply intimate portrait of a bank through the people who envisioned it, the people who made that dream a daily reality and, more importantly, all the people that were touched in their everyday lives by an institution that was rooted as much in a clearly articulated profit-making motive as in its unstated, underlying, nation-building mission.

Tamal has brought to life, through his in-depth reporting and intimate familiarity with the subject and all the key players, an engrossing and sweeping tale of twenty-first-century India, in all its earthy foibles and charms. His HDFC Bank narrative will add immensely in understanding the work-in-progress that is modern-day India.

Praise for the Book

T. N. Ninan
Chairman
Business Standard Ltd

Banking can be a dull subject, but Tamal Bandyopadhyay has made the story of HDFC Bank a story about the people who gave birth to it and led it to its current stellar status—as the most valuable Indian bank, in less than two decades. Along the way, he has underlined a lesson that has been learnt at great cost in the banking centres of the world: Good banking is about keeping things simple, focusing on the basics and being cautious about risk.

Deepak Parekh gave birth to the bank and put together the initial core team, but it is Aditya Puri who has led it from then till now, and this is a story about him as much as about the bank. Aditya comes across as very different from your cookie-cutter model banker, and Tamal's sharp reporting instincts as well as eye for detail help him paint a profile that accurately reflects this.

Start-up successes are not easy in India, if anywhere, and nearly half the banks that started along with HDFC Bank don't exist anymore. The ones that have been built well will survive their founders. Deepak and Aditya are still there, but no one can be in doubt that what they have created will be around for a long time, as one of the pillars of the Indian financial system and as one of the strengths of the Indian economy. In the bank's success, there are lessons for other bankers, indeed businessmen in any field, to learn.

For that reason, this is a story that needs to be told, and Tamal has told it well.

Praise for the Book

U. K. Sinha
Chairman
Securities and Exchange Board of India

Building a world-class institution needs vision, leadership, professional expertise and empowerment, great passion, perseverance and discipline. This book by Tamal Bandyopadhyay has justifiably articulated the canons that led to the making of HDFC Bank as one among the top ten outlier companies of the world in terms of consistency in performance over the past decade.

Banking sector reforms in India, the entry of private and global banks and the increasing reliance on technology in the banking space have revolutionized the industry. The era of lazy and balance sheet-focused banking has given way to dynamic universal banking, focused on creating value for its stakeholders. In the process, some players have succeeded, some others have failed, and a few have succeeded only after merging with those already successful. Tamal has been careful enough to capture this broader context, even while telling the story of a specific bank.

The anecdotes on persons and personalities who drove the story of building the bank provide the necessary spice for making the book an interesting read. The book creatively tells the story of the making of HDFC Bank as a case study for building a business in a developing country. Tamal's efforts are visible in presenting substantive content in a very lucid style, making the reading a lively experience for readers.

I congratulate Tamal for bringing out the untold story of the making of a successful bank in India after economic liberalization.

A
BANK
for the
BUCK

A

BANK

for the

BUCK

THE NEW BANK MOVEMENT
& *the untold story of*
THE MAKING OF INDIA'S
MOST VALUED BANK

TAMAL BANDYOPADHYAY

JAICO PUBLISHING HOUSE
Ahmedabad Bangalore Bhopal Bhubaneswar Chennai
Delhi Hyderabad Kolkata Lucknow Mumbai

Published by Jaico Publishing House
A-2 Jash Chambers, 7-A Sir Phirozshah Mehta Road
Fort, Mumbai - 400 001
jaicopub@jaicobooks.com
www.jaicobooks.com

A BANK FOR THE BUCK
ISBN 978-81-8495-396-1

First Jaico Impression: 2013

Page design and layouts: Special Effects, Mumbai

Printed by
Gopsons Papers Ltd.
A-2 & 3, Sector 64
NOIDA - 201 301

To my parents

Contents

Chapter 1

One Day in Malaysia...1

> The next day, shortly after Deepak checked in at a hotel in Mauritius, the telephone rang. It was Aditya. 'I am on,' he said.

Chapter 2

Raising a Toast...21

> Hasmukh-bhai, by then chairman emeritus at HDFC, was blunt. 'We don't know anything about banking. Why do we need a bank?' he asked.

Chapter 3

The Dirty Dozen..41

> 'No salary hike, no foreign trips, back to your own home, how does that sound to you?' Aditya asked (Samir).

Chapter 10

> One fine morning, out of the blue, Rana (Talwar) called Deepak and offered to merge.

Chapter 11

> Had the senior person noticed the red flag that the system raised, it would have been a different story.

Chapter 12

> 'He gives the impression of being an extremely aggressive guy, but if you look closely his banking is as conservative as it can be.'

Chapter 13

> Once the market is opened to competition, people must be allowed the freedom. They are capable of delivering the best globally.

Foreword

The author, Tamal Bandyopadhyay, called me a month ago and requested me to write a foreword for his forthcoming book on HDFC Bank Ltd—a unique story of the evolution of a modern bank in India, woven from several interviews. I was happy to write a foreword from respect and affection for the author, and decided to write only about him in the foreword. While he said he would be comfortable with whatever I wrote, he urged me to read the full manuscript and then decide what to write. I can now say that I'm glad I had the pleasure of reading the book even before it came into the public domain.

I have known Tamal for about fifteen years—first when I was deputy governor, and subsequently as governor of the Reserve Bank of India (RBI). He impressed many of us with the background information that he acquired on the relevant subject, before attending press briefings and interactions with us on money and banking. He used to come fully prepared for a discussion, both on the analytics and on the contemporary relevance. His questions were very thoughtful and incisive. He was trusted for discretion and for respecting confidentiality with regard to background briefing. He combined responsibility with forthrightness.

From my former colleagues at the RBI, I gathered that Tamal is liked by them for his personal integrity and professional abilities. His writings are characterized by not only curiosity but also public interest. He manages to be provocative without indulging in sensationalism in his presentations.

I have been reading his columns regularly. The analysis in his writings carries impressive credibility, since his sources appear generally authentic, and is based on appropriate background work. Often, there is a lot between the lines to buttress what he states briefly. He is free, fair and frank and can differ without offending. I continue to be impressed by his sincerity and devotion to duty, while loving what he does. I believe that many of these qualities are reflected in this book.

While reading a book, it is normal for people to relate their own life and experiences to the narration. It is also not unusual for readers to gain insights into subjects that matter to them and occasionally draw lessons. Many interesting aspects have been brought out in this narration. What constitutes leadership? What are the possible different managements styles? How does a senior management team operate, which involves cooperation, dissent and acceptance of hierarchy? Is there value for austerity in some aspects of functioning and not in others? What is the importance of networking? How does it operate? How is a business culture created and nurtured? Is a peep into personal lives necessary to make narration more lively and more convincing?

The global crisis has brought into focus several issues related to banking. It is recognized that the financial sector is special and, in particular, retail banking is special. There is often a temptation for senior management to take excessive risks. There are often huge conflicts of interests in the functioning of universal banks. The alignment of shareholders' interest and management's incentives is important while loyalty of shareholders is desirable for all corporate entities. In some ways, these are alluded to in the narration.

An interesting statement of contemporary relevance for bankers all over the world is that a bank should not take advantage of the pain of customers, but try to alleviate it, if possible. In fact, traditionally bankers cherished the trust of customers, but bankers' trust has been increasingly undermined by the emphasis on transactions-based banking in preference to relationship banking. Defining core values that govern the functions of an institution is, therefore, important. Whether or not one agrees with the adopted core values is unimportant; what is important is that there should be some core values which take an over-riding priority over compulsions of day-to-day functioning at all levels.

I am happy to note that the first chairman of HDFC Bank was drawn from the RBI. In fact, he was in charge of regulation of foreign exchange in the RBI, a draconian regulatory regime. There is an important lesson here: the notion that regulators or professionals in the public sector may not have the leadership qualities essential for the private sector is misplaced. In fact, the government should encourage those working in public institutions to move to the private sector without creating obstructions based on mistrust. It is surprising that the leaders of the private sector active in business are trusted to be on the boards of public sector enterprises and institutions such as the RBI, whereas those who are associated with the public sector are often barred from moving to the private sector for some time, after retirement.

In the case of HDFC Bank, it had the benefit of having a senior RBI official, known for integrity and competence, as the first chairman, as mentioned in the book. He was succeeded by another respected official from the RBI soon after retirement. Perhaps, in the true spirit of public–private partnership, there should be a greater movement of professionals between public and private sectors in the best interest of the country.

The book makes references to two mergers in the banking system. In both cases, the RBI comes out as an enabler of mergers, which was most appropriate under the circumstances. It is also gratifying to note that the RBI levied penalties where it considered appropriate, and, even more important, that the institution concerned responded to the penalties not with denial, but with improvements. It is noteworthy that the RBI imposed penalties on the bank despite the fact that a former deputy governor of the RBI was the chairman of the bank. As the actions of the RBI and the response of HDFC Bank show, it is extremely important for bankers to exercise a banker's prudence in all transactions, including complying with 'know your customer' requirements.

This book starts a new trend in writing on the financial sector in India. It describes, with striking simplicity, the birth and evolution of a modern bank in which institutions, individuals, ideas and ideologies play a part in a mutually interactive manner. By and large, it reflects realities as recalled

Tamal Bandyopadhyay

by the major participants. Is it the whole truth? Obviously not, since it is difficult to capture all aspects. Is it nothing but the truth? Yes, since on all accounts it appears to be based on revealed facts.

The book is timely, when trust in the financial sector, in particular in banks, is at an all-time low in the modern history of global economy. Fortunately, there is no such loss of trust in banks in India, but the narration is still useful in the context of current interest in issuing new banking licenses. The importance of fit and proper criteria, which involves several judgements, is clearly brought out in the story.

I found the narrative fascinating since I could relate to many of the events, some of the issues and quite a few of the people involved. It is a sort of recent oral history of a financial institution. I hope others will be inspired by this narrative to write similar accounts of success, and perhaps failure, of major financial institutions in India. I do believe Tamal has set a new trend in the dissemination of knowledge about some aspects of the financial sector in India.

Y. V. Reddy
Former Governor
Reserve Bank of India

Preface

What one can do when one turns eighteen varies from country to country. In India, one can vote and get a licence to drive a car, but one can't drink in public places. In New Delhi, India's capital, and Mumbai, the commercial hub, the drinking age is twenty-five years. In China, the world's fastest growing economy, turning eighteen gives one the licence to drink.

If one goes by the date of incorporation, HDFC Bank turned eighteen on 30 August 2012. Has life since become very different for the bank's employees, customers and investors? I don't think so. It has been life as usual for the bank. The freedom of 'adulthood' hasn't changed its character—it won't probably do anything it hasn't done so far.

In some sense, this bank has been a precocious child; it has known pretty well from day one that as a bank what it doesn't do matters more than what it does.

It hasn't done many things that its peers have done or tried to do and so the past eighteen years have not been hugely exciting. There has been absolutely no volatility in its performance—it has announced its earnings with monotonous precision, quarter after quarter, higher than the industry average—something the investors love and swear by.

HDFC Bank does very ordinary things in ordinary ways, but that yields extraordinary results. With this book I have attempted to tell the story of HDFC Bank in the context of the overall banking space in India, which has been changing with freedom from regulations, introduction of new products and newer ideas. Since my focus is the story, I haven't used excessive data unless they help illustrate the story. Many of the anecdotes in this book aren't in public domain yet, and in that sense this book is the untold story of the making of India's most valuable bank.

I started reporting on the banking sector about a year after HDFC Bank was born, but I discovered several incidents narrated in this book only while working on this project. They have been impeccably sourced, even though in some cases the people involved don't want to be named.

This book is based on hundreds of hours of interviews with bankers, central bankers, policy makers, corporate executives, consumers and investors in different parts of India and overseas. Most of the interviews were conducted in person and a few on the phone. For the data, I depended on information available in the public domain such as stock market notices, documents filed with regulators in India and abroad and the bank's balance sheets.

Some of the conversations narrated in this book may not be exactly the way they happened because they were not documented; I depended on people's versions, recalled from their memories. I have lightly edited these in a few cases for effect, but by and large they are a faithful representation of what happened.

I have tried to maintain an informal style of narration. For instance, I have used the first names of people mentioned in the book unless more than one person has the same first name, as that would have created confusion. So, Deepak Parekh is called Deepak, but Deepak Maheshwari and Deepak Satwalekar have been referred to by their surnames. D. D. Rathi of the Aditya Birla Group is well known by his surname and hence I call him Rathi, but Ishaat Hussain of Tata Sons Ltd is Ishaat, and not Hussain.

The entire story is divided into thirteen chapters. They don't follow a chronology but rather a theme, as my objective is not to merely write the bank's history but to weave the story of the making of a successful bank in India after economic liberalization.

The first four chapters—'One Day in Malaysia', 'Raising a Toast', 'The Dirty Dozen' and 'There's a Baby on the Trading Floor!'— are about the making of the bank: how it was conceptualized, how the team was built and the fun of the initial days when many senior recruits wore helmets and supervised the brick and mortar work at the headquarters and the branches and held training sessions under a tree at a textile mill compound in central Mumbai.

The next four chapters—'Business Before the Shop Opens', 'Doing Ordinary Things in Extraordinary Ways', 'The Change in Course' and 'The Entire Pyramid'—discuss the business philosophy of the bank and how it is different from that of others. Chapter 6 is, in fact, the heart of the book. It talks about the things that make HDFC Bank different from others, in terms of business philosophy, product innovation, cost of funds, risk management and so on.

Chapters 9 and 10 are about two mergers, the first instance of a friendly merger through share swap and the biggest merger in India's banking history, respectively. Again, the emphasis is not on financial ratios and data but on how the mergers happened—the inside story. Of course, there are data but their use is limited to creating the context.

HDFC Bank, despite being a highly successful venture, couldn't escape the regulator's wrath. On two occasions, the bank was penalized by the RBI. Chapter 11—'Warts and All'—dissects what went wrong with the bank, how it got into a mess and the safety valves it created to avoid such incidents. The next chapter—'The Common Sense Banker'—tries to analyse the Puri magic, what makes Aditya Puri, the longest-serving chief executive officer of any bank in India, different from his peers.

Finally, the last chapter—'Whose Bank Is It Anyway?'—looks at why this bank has been successful. It's not that it hasn't had problems—in terms of the occasional boardroom fights with the promoter on policies and minor egotistical skirmishes among senior people—but despite these it has succeeded because it's nobody's bank.

The key lesson from the HDFC Bank story is that freedom for professional managers, non-interference by the board and the promoter and passion for success are more important than ownership. HDFC Bank illustrates this formula better than anybody else—something that the new set of private banks opening shop soon can imbibe.

If you like the book, my dear reader, it's because the story of the bank is compelling. If you find it boring, blame the storyteller.

Tamal Bandyopadhyay

Acknowledgements

Writing acknowledgements for a book is like giving an Oscar acceptance speech. Experts say one should ask oneself three questions before giving any sort of an acceptance speech: Whom are you thanking? What are you thanking them for? What did their gift of time or expertise mean to you?

When Jaico Publishing House approached me with the idea of this book, my first reaction was muted, for two reasons. First, the transition from writing a 1,000-word weekly column in a financial daily to writing a book is like a T20 cricketer going in to play a test match; it's a very different discipline. Second, I wasn't sure how HDFC Bank, and its promoter Housing Development Finance Corporation Ltd (HDFC), would react to the idea of a book on the bank.

Jaico believed this would be a valuable story not only for business school students to learn about how a bank of this class can be set up in India, but also for new players to learn from the HDFC Bank experience, as after a decade India's banking regulator—the RBI—plans to open doors to a fresh set of private banks.

Jaico's commissioning editor Poornima Swaminathan's persuasion made me rethink and I decided to give it a shot after Deepak Parekh, chairman of HDFC, and Aditya Puri, managing director of HDFC Bank, promised to extend all their help. I thank both organizations, and their executives (present and past), for their unstinted support. I am not naming every individual I met from the organizations as the book is, after all, about them.

I thank Akash Shah, publisher of Jaico, and Rayasam H. Sharma, chief editor of Jaico, for the idea of this book and for their trust in me.

I thank *Mint*, where I work, for giving me a two-month book leave and allowing me to take up this assignment with Jaico even though the paper has its own publishing wing in partnership with another reputed publisher.

I thank Y. V. Reddy, former governor of the RBI, for being extremely kind and encouraging in writing the foreword to this book.

Several bankers, policy makers, corporate executives and investors I met while researching for this book spoke to me off the record, and many others spoke on record. I cannot name those who prefer anonymity. Here, I name only those who are not currently part of the HDFC family. All of them took time off to tell me stories about the bank and explain their perspective. I wish to thank them for their contributions to my knowledge and all the help they lent in creating this book.

They are Bimal Jalan, former governor of the RBI; S. P. Talwar, former deputy governor of the RBI; D. R. Mehta, former deputy governor of the RBI and ex-chairman of the Securities and Exchange Board of India; K. V. Kamath, non-executive chairman of ICICI Bank

Ltd and Infosys Ltd; Arun Maira, member of the Planning Commission; Ravi Narain, managing director of National Stock Exchange Ltd; Samir Arora, founder of Helios Capital Management Pte Ltd; Anil Ahuja, head of 3i Group in Asia; Satpal Khattar, chairman of Khattar Holding Pte Ltd; Shirish Apte, co-chairman of Asia-Pacific banking at Citigroup Inc.; Piyush Gutpa, chief executive officer of DBS Group Holdings Ltd and DBS Bank Ltd; Shailendra Bhandari, managing director of ING Vysya Bank Ltd; Neeraj Swaroop, chief executive officer of Standard Chartered Bank PLC in Southeast Asia; Ishaat Hussain, finance director of Tata Sons Ltd; D. D. Rathi, director of Grasim Industries Ltd; C. N. Ram, group chief information officer of Essar Group; Luis Miranda, chairman of the board of advisors of Centre for Civil Society; Samir Bhatia, former managing director and chief executive officer of Equifax Credit Information Services Pvt. Ltd; Deepak Satwalekar, former managing director of HDFC Standard Life Insurance Co. Ltd; Keki Mistry, vice chairman of HDFC; Renu Sud Karnad, managing director of HDFC; S. S. Thakur, first chairman of HDFC Bank; Ranjan Kapur, country manager of WPP India; Rashesh Shah, chairman and chief executive officer of Edelweiss Capital Ltd; Vinod Yennemadi, director of Shamrao Vithal Cooperative Bank Ltd; Samit Ghosh, founder and managing director of Ujjivan Financial Services Pvt. Ltd; Hemendra Kothari, an investment banker; and Amit Judge, a serial entrepreneur and a former director of HDFC Bank.

I thank my friend B. G. Shirshat for data support and three young students — Dakshini Bhattacharya, Kinjal Chheda and M. Srinivasan—for transcribing the interviews conducted while researching this book.

A special thanks to Manoranjan Goswami, an associate professor, for offering me complete privacy in his house to write this book and to Saurav Mondal for playing the role of a major-domo, helping me in every way from fixing computer problems to buying tea for me.

The cover photo and author photo credit goes to my photographer-colleague Hemant Mishra.

Last but not the least, I thank Somnath Dasgupta, a friend and former colleague, the first reader of this book. His incisive questions and valuable suggestions have helped make this book interesting.

Finally, I thank my wife Rita, for tolerating all my idiosyncrasies. I left Mumbai for two months in search of privacy to write this book, leaving everything behind for her to look after. But for her support I would not have been able to take up this project.

Chapter 1

One Day in Malaysia

On a Thursday morning in February 1994, the telephone rang at Citibank House in Jalan U-Thant, a tony neighbourhood dotted with the world's embassies in Malaysia's capital Kuala Lumpur. Amrita, the eight-year-old daughter of Aditya Puri, the chief executive officer (CEO) of the Malaysia operations of Citibank N. A., answered the telephone. The caller was a man gaining tremendous influence in India's financial industry. He wanted to speak to her father.

'Papa, a Mr Parekh is on the line,' Amrita yelled. Aditya had just finished his breakfast and was adjusting his tie. He was rushing for a meeting with Shaukat Aziz, head of Citibank's Asia-Pacific region and another man of tremendous clout who would, a decade later, become the 15th Prime Minister of Pakistan in General Pervez Musharraf's government.

But he had to take this call.

Deepak Parekh was an old friend. He was more than an

old friend. He was the chairman of Housing Development Finance Corporation Ltd (HDFC), India's lone mortgage company founded by his uncle Hasmukh Thakordas Parekh, a veteran banker. Aditya had known Deepak since his days as a management trainee with automaker Mahindra & Mahindra Ltd, his first job after graduation. Aditya's buddy Bharat Shah, later a colleague at Citibank, was Deepak's cousin.

Bharat had a group of close friends with a common passion, bridge. These included investment banker Hemendra Kothari, builder Dilip Thakker, Aditya, Deepak and a few others, all power houses who would meet for dinner every fortnight and often go over to each other's homes. 'As a young kid, Aditya used to fix our drinks and stand behind the bar,' Deepak told me.

Aditya got to know Deepak better while he was heading Citibank's institutional banking business for India, Sri Lanka, Nepal and Bangladesh, based out of Mumbai.

After a brief exchange of pleasantries, Deepak told Aditya he would be in Kuala Lumpur that weekend, and invited himself over for dinner. Deepak was, in fact, going to Mauritius to attend a board meeting of the Commonwealth Development Corporation. The normal course would have been to fly from Mumbai (then Bombay) to Singapore and from there to Mauritius. Instead, Deepak decided to make the detour from Singapore to Malaysia. 'I told him I'm coming but I didn't tell him why,' Deepak said. That would have to wait until dinner.

Citibank House in Jalan U-Thant is a sprawling old bungalow, built before Malaysia got its independence, spread over one and a half acres and decked with a swimming pool and a volleyball court. Forty-something Aditya was a rising star at Citibank—one among fifty executives worldwide chosen by the bank's chairman and CEO John Shepard Reed. This 'gang of fifty' would be critical for the US bank's future. The chosen ones were given options, separate from the usual equity options—golden handcuffs, as they would privately say.

Aditya's Mercedes drove Deepak and buddy Bharat, who had tagged along from the airport, to his house in the evening. They sat by the poolside, sipping single malt, and Aditya's wife Smiley, like a good hostess, made sure the *kebab*s were succulent and the *papads* crisp despite the liberal sprinklings of shredded onions and green chillies.

Deepak was there to tell Aditya that HDFC was shortly going to get a licence from the Reserve Bank of India (RBI) to run a bank. And that he was looking for a CEO.

Before approaching Aditya, Deepak had spoken to Bharat, who was working in Singapore. Bharat used to report to Aditya in Citibank in India. But they weren't boss and subordinate; they were friends forever.

Whenever Bharat travelled to Malaysia on work, he would invariably stay with Aditya and spend the evenings by the pool. Aditya did the same whenever he was in Singapore. Deepak wanted Bharat to help him rope in Aditya as the new bank's CEO.

Deepak had decided that Aditya was the one capable of building his vision of a world-standard private bank in a newly liberalized India, an institution comparable with the best global banks. Aditya, of John's gang of fifty, would be his man.

Bharat told Deepak to speak to Aditya directly. But he offered to accompany Deepak to Malaysia. At Citibank House, with Bharat by his side, Deepak eased into his pitch: 'You run around the world a lot,' he told Aditya. 'Now come back to the country, do some real work, build a bank.'

Aditya was by no means gullible. He was earning about $100,000 annually, about ₹31.5 lakh, a tidy sum in those days. Then, there were the bonuses, the regular options and the special options he was entitled to as one of John's chosen fifty.

Their conversation at the poolside continued:

'What bank?' Aditya asked Deepak.

'We are getting a licence to set one up.'

'That will be your bank.'

'No, it will be your bank. I won't even be on the board. It will be run by professional management and you will head that.'

'Do you know how much I get here?' Aditya asked Deepak.

'*Arre baba*, you have earned enough. Now, do something for the nation. You've worked enough for foreign companies. *Abhi aake desh ke liye kuch karo.*'

'Come on Deepak,' Aditya insisted. 'You need to tell me what's in it for me.'

'You will build an institution,' Deepak told him. 'I can't match your salary. But we will give you stock options. You will do well and earn much more than what you are earning.'

Smiley was curious about the unusually animated and earnest discussion among the three men. In one of her rounds while topping their plates with *pakoras*, she finally got the drift, 'You three will run a bank!' she exclaimed.

Tamal Bandyopadhyay

After some more of Deepak's hard persuasion, Aditya agreed to consider the offer, provided he was promised a good share of the stocks. His math was simple: If the bank was successful he would make good the losses he would suffer by leaving Citibank, and he would have built an institution.

There was another reason perhaps to return to India—to be with his father, Tapishwar Puri, who had been the aide-de-camp to India's first air marshal, Subroto Mukherjee. Aditya's dad wasn't getting any younger and returning to India would allow him more time with his father.

Aditya asked Smiley whether she wanted to go back to India. She was and still is his confidante.

Aditya first met Smiley at a party in Delhi when he was doing his chartered accountancy articleship. She was a student in Miranda House, the distinguished residential women's college of Delhi University. They lost touch with each other since and went their separate ways. When the time came for marriage, Aditya went looking for Smiley and, within a week, proposed to her.

Before heading its Malaysia operations, Aditya was in Hong Kong looking after credit and market risk for Citibank in North Asia. He had worked in Saudi Arabia before that, returned to India, and again taken a job abroad. He knew that if he returned to India this time, it would be for good. His teenage son Amit was already in India, studying at Mayo College in Ajmer. Amrita was studying in the American School in Kuala Lumpur.

'I am surprised you are asking me this. Go by what your heart says,' Smiley replied.

Deepak told Aditya he was on the board of trustees of the famed Bombay Scottish School in Mumbai, and getting admission for Amrita would be a cakewalk. Deepak even promised to escort Amrita to the school at Mahim.

'I want complete freedom to run the bank,' Aditya told Deepak. 'No interference.'

'You will get it,' Deepak told him.

Aditya asked for twenty-four hours to make a decision. The next day, shortly after Deepak checked in at a hotel in Mauritius, the telephone rang. It was Aditya. 'I am on,' he said.

Elsewhere in Uganda

Months before Deepak met Aditya in Malaysia, in late 1993, he made a call to S. S. Thakur, former controller of foreign exchange in India. Thakur, after a long stint with the RBI, had joined the United Nations' International Civil Services as a senior advisor, and was deputed from New York to Zambia to advise that country's central bank.

Deepak told Thakur that he was soon going to get an in-principle approval from the RBI to set up a bank and that he wanted Thakur to be the bank's founder-chairman. Deepak explained that he wanted a high level of corporate governance and regulatory compliance at the bank, and that he believed Thakur was the top candidate for the job.

Thakur had played a key role in formulating India's Foreign Exchange Regulation Act (FERA) and was involved in implementing it in national and multinational companies. FERA, enacted in 1973 by the Indira Gandhi government, imposed stringent regulations on certain payments that dealt with foreign exchange and securities and transactions involving the Indian currency. Its purpose was to regulate payments to conserve India's precious foreign exchange resources.

Many dubbed the Act draconian. Its first victim was the American icon The Coca-Cola Co., India's leading soft drink until 1977. Coca-Cola decided to leave India after the Janata government, citing the new law, ordered it to hand over its formula—a trade secret held in a bank vault in Atlanta for decades—and dilute its stake in the Indian unit.

Coca-Cola, and its closest rival PepsiCo Inc., also American, would return to India sixteen years later in 1993, after India opened up its economy.

As controller of foreign exchange at the RBI, Thakur knew Deepak well. He knew Deepak's uncle H. T. Parekh even better. Thakur had helped HDFC immensely during its early days in getting bulk deposits. Not many people were willing to take home loans as it was a new concept in the late 1970s, just after HDFC was formed. Even more were reluctant to deposit money with it. The first public issue of the shares of HDFC bombed and the mortgage lender found it a headache to get a capital of a mere ₹10 crore.

It was during this phase of disquiet that the World Bank Group's International Finance Corporation (IFC) stepped in and picked up a 5% stake in HDFC, and even offered it a loan of $4 million. But it was quite the tease, adding a rider that it would release the money only if HDFC could arrange matching deposits in Indian rupees. In other words, HDFC had to mobilize the rupee equivalent of $4 million to draw IFC's line of credit. Although not a big sum as a dollar used to fetch around ₹8.75 in 1978, HDFC found even this extremely difficult to mobilize.

Retail deposits were out of question in those days. In fact, in the first decade of HDFC's existence, till 1988, while hundreds came to borrow no one trusted the company with their money. HDFC had to depend on bulk deposits. There were many FERA companies—locally incorporated companies with foreign equity holdings in excess of 40%—that raised money from the market but couldn't remit the funds as the RBI was never prompt in clearing their applications. HDFC sensed an opportunity there.

Hasmukh-bhai, as the founder of HDFC was widely known, got himself a list of tea companies in Assam that had raised money from the public and were sitting on the funds, as the RBI was being slow in clearing their applications for remitting the money overseas. He wanted these companies to deposit their monies with HDFC till the RBI gave its nod. But there was a hitch. By the rules of the book, these companies were allowed to keep their funds only with banks, not with mortgage companies. Thakur, convinced by Hasmukh-bhai's argument, changed the rule and allowed these companies to deposit their monies with mortgage companies as well. And that's how HDFC started getting FERA deposits and, more importantly, was able to draw from the IFC loan.

Deepak knew the story well, and thought it a good idea to have an ex-RBI insider as his bank's first chairman. He got

Thakur's number in Zambia from a contact in the RBI and called him. 'Mr Thakur, I would like you to come to Bombay. I will send you the ticket. Can you come for a couple days?'

Thakur flew to Mumbai and met Deepak. He heard him out. It was a bold and tempting offer. But to resign from the prestigious United Nations' job was a tough call, especially when he was earning a handsome tax-free package.

Deepak offered Thakur shares of HDFC. Thakur eventually agreed to the offer, though not because of the shares as, in those days, not many really cared for HDFC's stock. 'I took up the assignment in spite of the monetary loss', Thakur told me, 'because it was a challenging task and they were very sincere in their approach.'

Thakur joined HDFC Bank Ltd as founder-chairman on 2 January 1994 at Ramon House in downtown Mumbai, where the mortgage company is headquartered even today. He occupied the cabin of H. T. Parekh on the fourth floor of Ramon House after Hasmukh-bhai passed away in November 1994. At the time of joining, Thakur was in his early sixties. 'A couple of months later, the RBI issued a new rule which said that if a bank has a managing director, its chairman must be a non-executive chairman. [I had] no regrets,' Thakur, now eighty, told me at his office in Express Towers at Nariman Point, Mumbai's financial district. He is now a public interest director on the board of MCX Stock Exchange Ltd. 'I was the chairman [of HDFC Bank] till 2000.'

The Pune Warrior

Deepak's third choice was not a banker but a corporate executive and a close friend, Vinod Yennemadi. Vinod had worked with at least half a dozen companies, local and foreign. Deepak got to know him while doing his chartered accountancy in London in the 1960s. Deepak was a regular visitor to the YMCA Indian Student Hostel, at 41 Fitzroy Square in London, where Vinod was staying.

After completing his chartered accountancy, Vinod joined Shell International—at Burmah-Shell Oil Storage and Distributing Company of India Ltd—in 1971 at a princely salary of ₹2,000 a month. He worked with the group till it was nationalized in 1976 (and renamed Bharat Petroleum Corporation Ltd the next year).

Vinod's next job was with the RPG Group. He became the finance director of a small firm of the RPG Group, a subsidiary of Asian Cables Ltd. Following this, he joined Mather & Platt, a company that produced fire protection systems and submersible pumps, as its finance director.

Manohar Rajaram Chhabria of the Dubai-based Jumbo Group bought over Mather & Platt and took an instant liking to Vinod, but Vinod did not like the new owner's ways. He left the group to join Baba Kalyani—known for his auto parts company Bharat Forge Ltd—as finance director of Kalyani Steels Ltd in Pune in 1992. And that's where Deepak met his old pal Vinod after years.

On a Sunday morning in the first week of February 1994, Deepak told Vinod that HDFC was applying for a banking

Tamal Bandyopadhyay

licence and he was reasonably sure he would get it. 'What are you doing in Pune? Come back to Bombay and join me and set up the bank,' he told Vinod.

Vinod wasn't keen. 'From 1971, I have been on the other side of the counter, asking for money,' he told Deepak. 'I have never been a banker myself. What will I do with your bank?'

Deepak didn't buy his argument. After all, Deepak hadn't been in the housing loans sector before he joined HDFC. He had worked with Ernst & Young, Precision Fasteners, ANZ Grindlays Bank and Chase Manhattan Bank—none of them a mortgage company—in New York and Mumbai until his uncle brought him to HDFC in 1978.

At the age of thirty-four, he took a 50% cut in his Chase Manhattan salary to join HDFC as a deputy general manager.

'You needn't worry, you'll learn,' Deepak told Vinod.

On 4 April 1994, Vinod joined the bank. He was the first employee on the bank's payroll. Thakur had joined the bank before him, in January, but he was on a contract. Vinod didn't want to join on 1 April, All Fools' Day, and as 2 and 3 April covered the weekend, he had to wait a few more days. HDFC had a five-day working week.

Testing the Waters

Before taking the plunge, Aditya decided to send his wife Smiley and daughter Amrita to India for a month to test the waters. Deepak had taken care of Amrita's school admission but Aditya wanted to see whether his wife and daughter would find it easy living in Mumbai—a lively and spirited city but also humid and difficult—after having lived privileged lives abroad. He didn't want to have to regret the move later.

After a month, when Aditya came to India to see how they were doing, at Smiley's sister's house at Bandra's Pali Hill in Mumbai, he was hugely relieved to see Amrita grooving to the popular Raveena Tandon song *'Tu cheez badi hai mast mast'* from the Hindi film *Mohra*. For her, that was possibly a practice session. Later, Amrita would act in Anil Kapoor's *Aisha* along with Sonam Kapoor, Mukesh Bhatt's crime thriller *Blood Money* and UTV's *Kai Po Che!*

Citibank was not willing to accept Aditya's resignation till he firmly told Shaukat he would not change his mind. He got no official farewell. He took a Singapore Airlines flight to India and, from the airport, drove straight to Ramon House to meet Deepak. By then, Thakur and Vinod were already on board and the key elements of the first team that would run the bank were in place.

For Deepak, half the battle was over. He had got the people he wanted—a bright young banker with a vision, a former central banker who knew the rules and regulations of banking like the back of his hand, and a trusted friend who was thorough with the intricacies of the corporate world. 'This bank cannot fail,' Deepak told himself the day Aditya landed in Mumbai.

What's in a Name?

There was still one detail nagging Deepak. He was not comfortable with the idea of lending the 'HDFC' name to the bank, as that would mean anyone running the bank would also have to be an ambassador of the long-nurtured HDFC brand. Will they stand for the value and ethos HDFC symbolized? He was worried that if the bank didn't do well, the HDFC brand would get sullied.

A conservative Deepak had one name in mind: The Bank of Bombay. His logic was faultless. The bank was the only one among a group of ten new private lenders allowed to have its headquarters in Mumbai. The others were asked to have their registered offices outside the large metro cities, keeping in sync with the RBI's focus on spreading banking services across the nation through the slew of new private banks. ICICI Bank Ltd had its registered office in Baroda, Gujarat; Centurion Bank Ltd in Panjim, Goa; Global Trust Bank Ltd in Hyderabad, Andhra Pradesh; IndusInd Bank Ltd in Pune, Maharashtra; and UTI Bank Ltd (later renamed Axis Bank Ltd) in Jaipur, Rajasthan.

But the acronym for Bank of Bombay—BoB—clashed with an established public sector bank, Bank of Baroda. As an afterthought, Deepak suggested Bombay Bank. Neither name worked for the others.

Thakur prepared a list of two dozen names. His personal favourite was Everest Bank of India, to symbolize the height the bank would reach one day. Other suggestions included Greater Bank of Bombay and Bombay International Bank, many of them revolving round 'Bombay'. But the majority wanted the name to be 'HDFC Bank'.

HDFC was already a household name in India. Its board was not sure how effectively the bank would function and they didn't want to risk their reputation by officially adopting the new entity. There were many brainstorming sessions to break the deadlock.

Deepak Satwalekar, managing director of HDFC, was possessive about the HDFC brand. After all, the bankers were all outsiders. How would they view the value system at HDFC and its brand? 'Until their credentials are established clearly, I am reluctant to lend the name,' he told his colleagues in private.

'Why don't we call it Bombay International Bank?' Satwalekar suggested to Aditya over lunch one day. 'You can call it that,' Aditya told him, 'but I will catch a flight and go back to Kuala Lumpur. I am not interested in any Bombay International Bank. If it's HDFC Bank, I am here. Otherwise, forget it.'

Aditya got support from his chairman. Thakur reasoned that the Unit Trust of India (UTI), the Industrial Development Bank of India (IDBI) and the Industrial Credit and Investment Corporation of India Ltd (ICICI) had lent their brand names to their banks and if the HDFC brand name were not given to the bank, it would require a lot more effort to build the bank's brand. Hasmukh-bhai saw the point and, finally, so did Deepak and Satwalekar. The outsiders had the final say.

The HDFC insiders had one condition, though: If HDFC's shareholding in the bank dropped below a certain level, the mortgage company could ask the bank to change its name. The final agreement on the name doesn't have any clause on charging a royalty for lending the brand name, something that the diversified Tata Group does with its many subsidiaries.

Plan B

The shrewd strategist that Deepak is, he didn't leave anything to chance. He drafted a plan B, as he does for any situation—the reason why, along with Aditya, Deepak was also in talks with Mehli Mistry, another long-time Citibanker, for the top job.

Mehli was with Citibank in Saudi Arabia but quit the job and returned to Mumbai when Citibank decided to pull out from a Saudi Arabian bank named Samba, the acronym for 'Saudi American Bank' (the name was changed to Samba Financial Group in 2003). It was established in February 1980 with the takeover of Citibank branches in Jeddah and Riyadh, in accordance with a local law that forced all foreign banks to convert their branches to affiliates with Saudi nationals acquiring at least 60% ownership. Mehli was heading Samba at the time.

Mehli informally agreed to the proposal and Deepak even told one of the new recruits, Harish Engineer of Bank of America Corporation, to update Mehli on RBI regulations. Harish did have a few sessions with Mehli at Ramon House but he could not come on board because of taxation issues.

Mehli was a US citizen. This meant he would have to pay taxes on income both in India and in the United States and HDFC Bank was not willing to pick up the tab. Deepak kept him on hold for a few weeks till he was convinced that John's blue-eyed boy Aditya would agree for the top job.

The parting with Mehli was amicable and there was no bad blood. Mehli went on to become the head of Grindlays' India operations, which was sold to Standard Chartered Bank PLC in 2000.

Deepak declined to be on the bank's board, despite being closely involved in creating it, primarily because he was on the board of a number of blue-chip companies that any bank would want to do business with. Had Deepak joined the bank's board, HDFC Bank could not have done business with these companies as India's banking laws prohibit a bank from lending money to a company whose director is on the bank's board. Simply put, Deepak could not remain on the boards of the blue-chip companies and the bank at the same time.

It was a prudent decision to give up directorship of the bank and remain on the boards of Glaxo India Ltd, Siemens Ltd, Hindustan Unilever Ltd, Indian Hotels Co. Ltd, Mahindra & Mahindra Ltd and Castrol India Ltd. He could use the relationships with these companies to the bank's advantage.

The RBI still doesn't like the CEO of one finance company to be on the board of another finance company as that may create a conflict of interest. There is no written law on this, though.

Three representatives of HDFC were nominated on the bank's board: Deepak Satwalekar, Nasser Munjee and Keki Mistry.

Deepak chose not to be on the board but Thakur, Aditya and Vinod could always lean on his broad shoulders. In the initial stages, he was the bank's face to the regulator, investors and even consumers. Nobody grudged that. Banking is in Deepak's genes. His grandfather, Thakordas Parekh, was the first employee of the Central Bank of India. His father, Shantilal Parekh, had spent about forty years in the same bank till he retired as a deputy general manager. And before founding HDFC, his uncle, Hasmukh-bhai, had headed ICICI, the development finance institution that spawned ICICI Bank, HDFC's closest private sector rival.

Deepak is not on the board of the bank but he does not miss a single meeting—always attending as a special invitee.

Initial Package

One can well imagine why Aditya had strong reservations about taking up this assignment if one takes a look at his initial package at HDFC Bank—₹1 lakh per month, plus ₹20,000 dearness allowance along with actual medical benefit and ₹50,000 leave fare concession.

Thakur's salary was ₹15 lakh per annum.

A company-leased accommodation, a car—a Premier NE-118—for official use, gas and electricity, ₹2,500 a month as entertainment allowance, ₹1,500 for servants and gardeners, ₹1,500 for soft furnishing, ₹1,000 for books and periodicals and two club memberships were common for both. While this was better than packages at public sector banks, it was nowhere near what was paid to Aditya's counterparts at foreign banks, which would be HDFC Bank's main rivals.

Money would come their way as the bank and the stock did phenomenally well. But at that point none of them had any fantasies about compensation, only dreams about creating a bank with a difference.

Chapter 2

_____

Raising a Toast

The idea of floating a bank came to the HDFC bosses in 1987, a few years before the banking regulator decided to open the sector to private companies. For the mortgage company's tenth anniversary on 17 October 1987, Satwalekar, then its general manager for finance and planning, prepared a paper for the board on non-mortgage opportunities for HDFC.

Satwalekar, who would eventually climb the ranks to become the managing director of HDFC and later head its life insurance venture when India opened up that sector, was convinced that a pure-play housing financing business alone would not fully justify the strengths and capabilities of HDFC.

He listed a number of businesses HDFC could venture into: commercial banking, mutual funds, insurance, property funds and private equity. Satwalekar wanted HDFC to begin securitization of home loans as well. He believed banking was a critical building block for any business that may want to grab the opportunities that would arise *whenever* (not *if*) India chose to open up her constricted economy.

In principle, the board agreed that HDFC needed to get into these activities. When the RBI began discussions on allowing new private banks to open up, after the P. V. Narasimha Rao government liberalized India's economy in 1991, the HDFC top brass was very excited. On 22 January 1993, the RBI finally issued guidelines on the entry of new private banks.

For over two decades, since the nationalization of fourteen large banks in 1969, followed by another seven in 1980, no private bank had been allowed to set up shop. During this period, public sector banks had expanded their networks extensively, adding numerous branches, often in remote areas at the behest of political bosses, and catering to the socio-economic needs of the masses in a highly regulated industry where the central bank dictated interest rates and directed credit flow.

Within two decades of nationalization, government-owned banks accounted for 91% of the bank branches in the country and 85% of the total business done by the sector. The rest was shared by a handful of foreign banks and old private banks. 'A stage has now been reached when new private sector banks may be allowed to be set up,' the RBI, India's central bank, said in its historic declaration in 1993.

Down with Lazy Banking

The RBI's objective was to introduce competition in the sector and force banks to be efficient and more productive. Bank employees—from tellers to managers—were in great demand in the marriage market in those days. A girl's father would pay any price to hook a banker son-in-law, though one from the Indian civil service cadre remained the top choice. A bank job gave a person status and dignity, though banks had nothing much to do in the tightly regulated industry. Technology and product innovation were unheard of. A bank's primary job was to mobilize money from individuals and lend most of the money to companies. Of course, 40% of the loans would go to the so-called priority sector of farmers and small-scale industries, a rule that stands even today.

Those were the days of lazy banking. Banks could, of course, blame the regulations, which did not allow much scope for dynamism. Because of the very high pre-emption in the form of the cash reserve ratio (CRR), or the portion of deposits that commercial banks need to keep with the RBI, and the statutory liquidity ratio (SLR), or the compulsory investment in government bonds, bankers were left with very little money to lend. Besides, no bank was listed and so there was no pressure from investors to perform.

In this seller's market, the concept of customer care did not exist. A branch manager was happy being confined to his or her glass cabin, where promoters of companies and corporate professionals would come to pay their homage. Barring a few exceptions, most bank chiefs saw their primary job as making sure the balance sheets grew every year. RBI guidelines made it clear that allowing the entry of private banks was a part of the financial sector reforms to provide competitive, efficient and low-cost financial intermediation through the use of technology. The new banks were to have a capital of at least ₹100 crore and their shares had to be listed on the stock exchanges.

A little before this, India had introduced new asset classification norms as part of its prudential regulations. Banks could no longer get away with accumulating bad loans—which were piling up as a result of poor credit appraisals and monitoring as well as political pressure to favour certain industrial groups. Then, there were the so-called loan *melas*, or waiver for loans given to farmers, again dictated by politicians.

Banks now had to set aside money to make up for any such souring assets. Of course, this resulted in some early glitches. The provisioning requirement eroded the profitability of many banks and the government had to step in and infuse capital in phases to keep them alive. All for the better, though.

Simultaneously, Parliament amended the Banking Regulation Act of 1949 to lower the government's absolute ownership in state-run lenders to 51%, despite resistance from the powerful trade unions that controlled the industry in those days. The RBI, on its part, arranged a hefty World Bank line of credit for upgrading technology in select public sector banks. India's banking industry was on the edge of a re-invention.

'Why Do We Need a Bank?'

It wasn't easy for Deepak to convince the board of HDFC to take the plunge into banking. Hasmukh-bhai, by then chairman emeritus at HDFC, was blunt. 'We don't know anything about banking. Why do we need a bank?' he asked.

There were more questions. 'Why do you want to start a bank?' 'What do you know about banking?' 'Who will run it?' 'What kind of liabilities are we going to create?'

'Applying for a bank licence doesn't mean that we are getting it, but what's the harm in trying it out?' Deepak argued. He hired Atul Sud to prepare a draft application and that was the clincher. Atul had just left American Express Co. after serving thirteen years as its India head for commercial and investment banking and treasury.

The RBI received 113 applications, many of these from large industrial houses. It asked noted economist-bureaucrat Sharad Marathe, the first chairman of IDBI, to review the applications.

Sharad, who was also the alternate executive director representing India on the International Monetary Fund and the economic advisor to the Government of India from 1964 to 1968, had been on the boards of several Indian and multinational companies, including Glaxo India where Deepak was a director. While reviewing the applications, Sharad didn't discuss anything with Deepak, but after the RBI released the licences, he told Deepak that HDFC's application was the best.

HDFC Bank was incorporated on 30 August 1994.

On 5 January 1995, Deepak got a call from RBI governor C. Rangarajan's office. The licence was through.

Roughly one in every eleven applicants was given a licence, making it ten overall, including Development Credit Bank Ltd, an old cooperative bank that was allowed to convert itself into a full-fledged commercial bank.

Four of the new entrants were floated by established financial institutions. HDFC apart, development financial institutions ICICI and IDBI got licences. So did India's oldest mutual fund, UTI, which teamed up with state-run life insurance behemoth Life Insurance Corporation of India.

Some finance professionals were also given licences to set up banks. Ramesh Gelli, former chief of ING Vysya Bank Ltd and a Padmashree awardee, got the nod to set up Global Trust Bank Ltd; Darshanjit Singh, son of Inderjit Singh, former chairman of Punjab & Sind Bank, to set up Bank of Punjab Ltd; and Devendra Ahuja of the non-banking finance company 20th Century Finance Corporation Ltd to set up Centurion Bank.

A few group companies of the Hindujas, backed by the Sindhi diaspora, got a licence for IndusInd Bank Ltd and the Jains of Bennett, Coleman and Co. Ltd, which runs India's largest media house and publishes the *Times of India* newspaper, got a licence for Times Bank Ltd.

'Are We Risking Too Much of Our Money?'

The RBI was all right with a capital of ₹100 crore, but Deepak wanted to have double that amount in capital to make the bank solid. The board of HDFC was not comfortable with the idea as the mortgage company's capital base was just ₹100 crore at that time. There was an intense debate on how much money HDFC should put on the table.

The RBI had capped promoter holding in a bank at 40%. For the ₹200-crore capital Deepak was insisting on, a 40% contribution meant bringing in ₹80 crore into the bank, an amount equal to 80% of the capital of HDFC. This was not a joke, certainly not for the board members. 'Are we risking too much of our money?' the board asked.

It was an illustrious board with directors such as former RBI governor M. Narasimham, who wrote two seminal reports on financial sector reforms, industrialist Keshub Mahindra, bureaucrat and former chairman of the State Bank of India (SBI) D. N. Ghosh and former capital market regulator S. A. Dave.

The board also insisted that since HDFC was new to banking, to mitigate risks its bank would need a foreign partner as early as possible, essentially an investor. A foreign partner was also a necessity because HDFC Bank was an unknown entity in the global banking world. It needed someone who would not hesitate to give it lines of credit. Unless it got these lines of credit from foreign banks, or at least from its foreign partner, it would not be able to grow and help Indian importers who needed dollar funds. The final decision was to sell a 15% stake in the bank to a foreign bank, and keep 25% with HDFC.

The NatWest Misadventure

In search of the ideal foreign partner, Deepak went to London to try his luck with the National Westminster Bank PLC, better known as NatWest, a very large UK bank with a looming presence over the city, literally. It had built the tallest office block in London, the NatWest Tower, in the 1970s, when it overtook Barclays PLC to become Britain's largest commercial bank.

Deepak's itinerary was not thoughtfully designed and was more a toss of a coin: Whom did one know and what was the first available flight to get to them. Deepak had been introduced to Robert Alexander, NatWest's chairman, through somebody. Alexander took him to meet Derek Wanless, group CEO of NatWest. Deepak spent a day with them in London.

His next stop was New York, where Deepak called on Bankers Trust, a big American bank. Deepak was on its international advisory board. The day was well spent with the head of international and foreign exchange divisions at Bankers Trust and Charles Steadman 'Charlie' Sanford, chairman of the board and CEO. They were quite excited about the new Indian bank.

From there, Deepak flew to Singapore to talk to DBS Bank Ltd (earlier known as the Development Bank of Singapore Ltd). The DBS Group was interested but, eventually, it could not go ahead with the plan as the Indian banking regulator made it clear that if the DBS Group were to hold a large stake in HDFC Bank it would not be allowed to set up a branch in India, something the Singapore bank was keen on doing.

Both NatWest and Bankers Trust were willing to pick up a stake in HDFC Bank. The final choice was NatWest as the response from London came first.

Bankers Trust put pressure on Deepak, whom they knew well.

'Come on Deepak, you can't let us down,' Charlie said.

'The only way I can let you come in is by asking NatWest to share their stake with you—7.5% each,' Deepak responded. He would have been happy to allow both the banks to come in as HDFC Bank then could have had a British and an American association.

Bankers Trust tried to negotiate with NatWest but the UK bank refused. It wanted a piece of India, as the economy was opening up and the balance-of-payment crisis had receded. There was big-bang liberalization. By that time, HDFC was sixteen years old and growing at a healthy pace as middle-class Indians had started to dream about owning a home.

So NatWest Markets Ltd, the corporate and investment banking arm of the NatWest Group, became HDFC Bank's partner. The shares were offered at par. But when Deepak and Aditya went to London to seal the deal, they found NatWest had one worry: who would be accountable if there was a run on the bank?

The NatWest Group had had problems in Australia when one of the banks it had invested in suffered a liquidity shortage. Depositors chased the group to London and asked it for money as it was one of the promoters of the Australian bank, though a minor one.

'We will pick up a 20% stake but don't want to be called a promoter,' NatWest told Deepak.

HDFC could still own a 25% stake in the bank—below the RBI's 40% limit for promoters—and allow NatWest to pick up a 20% stake now that the UK bank had declined to be classified as a promoter. Had NatWest agreed to be a promoter, it could not have taken a 20% stake, as that would have increased the combined promoters' stake to 45%, beyond the permissible threshold.

Today, almost everybody in the HDFC Group admits that NatWest didn't add much value, but in the initial days the partnership was a great selling point for the new bank. A multi-part launch campaign milked the partnership in every possible way.

Half-page advertisements in the nation's leading financial dailies in January 1995 positioned HDFC Bank as 'The Action Bank' and said NatWest Markets was the 'Window to the World'. Along with the parentage ('The HDFC Advantage') and commitment to customer care ('Customers Are Really Everything'), the campaign said the alliance with NatWest Markets gave the bank a unique international edge.

'North, South, East, NatWest'

The ad copy proudly laid down information on the NatWest Group: that it was present in forty locations in seventeen countries, had an asset base of at least $250 billion, was one of the largest foreign exchange players in the world, and ran daily transactions of at least $45 billion.

There was also a joint ad campaign by HDFC Bank and NatWest Markets in February 1995—'North, South, East, NatWest'. Among other things, it said, 'NatWest Markets has now formed a strategic alliance with HDFC Bank to provide a unique service to clients in India. Together with HDFC Bank, NatWest Markets is dedicated to providing clients in India a truly international edge.'

The calling cards of HDFC Bank executives also mentioned the strategic alliance with NatWest Markets, just in case they were to meet foreign bankers for credit lines.

NatWest did not give HDFC Bank the international edge it so coveted because the UK bank did not really have a large international presence. It had about $12 billion in assets in the Asia-Pacific region and employed nine hundred people in nine countries, with Hong Kong as its regional headquarters. In 1994, NatWest Markets helped to arrange $3 billion for Asian nations.

From the day it signed the agreement with HDFC Bank, NatWest was worried and did not want to get into a mess similar to that it had faced in Australia. It did not want to put in a penny more. HDFC Bank had to struggle to increase the limits for letters of credit and foreign exchange dealings.

The relationship lasted less than three years as NatWest got involved in a major scandal of mis-marking interest options in London, having dabbled in complicated derivative products it did not fully understand. In 1997, NatWest Markets revealed a £50 million loss. That sum exploded to £90.5 million after investigations, deeply eroding the confidence of its investors and shareholders.

NatWest decided to sell its 20% stake in HDFC Bank—part of its larger strategy to pull out of equity investments in Asia after the Southeast Asian crisis in 1997. The bank's management told HDFC Bank that it had to sell its investment as it needed money. At that time, shares of HDFC Bank were trading at around ₹54 apiece, almost five and a half times the price at which the UK bank had bought them. 'I was not a fool to buy back the shares by paying so much more than what I'd begged them to put in just two and a half years ago,' Deepak told me.

A Mistake

HDFC Bank instead found another investor to replace NatWest.

'That was a mistake. We could have raised our stake to 40% by buying at least 15% of their holding,' Deepak says in hindsight, candid in his admission.

NatWest had a long but not-so-exciting history in investment banking. It had made a series of small but costly acquisitions. In November 1995, it bought Gleacher & Co., an American boutique investment bank specializing in mergers and acquisitions. It followed this with the acquisition of Greenwich Capital Markets Inc., a bond house, Gartmore Investment Ltd, an asset management company, and Hambro Magan Corporate Finance, a UK mergers and acquisitions company.

There was a protracted legal battle until finally, in February 2000, NatWest's shareholders accepted a takeover offer from the Royal Bank of Scotland PLC, a fellow UK bank but much smaller in size.

'It was not the greatest [banking group]; [they] had no clue about running a bank in India—what was the point of the partnership?' reminisces Satwalekar about the NatWest tie-up. Even technology-wise, HDFC Bank was superior to NatWest. The UK bank made a cool ₹220 crore on an investment of ₹40 crore in a short span without adding any value.

'We should be extremely careful about partnerships as at some point in time our needs and their needs will diverge,' Satwalekar said, making a larger point. He is quite sceptical about a foreign partner's intentions. The only reason a foreign entity wants to come to India, according to him, is because it needs a foothold in the fast-growing economy.

Historically, most joint ventures in India—particularly in the financial services space—have not succeeded as the foreign partners either wanted bigger stakes in the Indian entities or aspired to have a full-fledged presence on Indian soil. A case in point is the partnership of Goldman Sachs Group Inc. with Kotak Mahindra Group for investment banking. Goldman Sachs stayed with Kotak Mahindra till it understood the

Indian market. ICICI Bank's investment banking arm, ICICI Securities Ltd (I-Sec), faced the same fate and had to part with its foreign partner J. P. Morgan & Co.

Kotak Mahindra bought Goldman Sachs' entire 25% stake in its investment banking and securities outfit in March 2006, fourteen years after the alliance, as Goldman Sachs wanted to be in India on its own. J. P. Morgan & Co. pulled out of I-Sec in March 1998, five years after forming the joint venture with I-Sec with a 39.6% stake.

Eleven days after getting the licence and forging the strategic alliance with NatWest, HDFC Bank opened its first branch on the sixth floor of Ramon House, the headquarters of HDFC, on 16 January 1995, with fewer than a dozen staff, including Vinod, his secretary Goretti Soares (whom he brought from Mather & Platt) and an administration person who came from Bayer India Ltd.

Deepak inaugurated this apology of a branch, which for all practical purposes was nothing more than an extension counter. T. Chandrasekhar, the loveable property manager of HDFC, did the interiors for the sixth floor. He also organized an elaborate Ganesha puja for the inauguration. That idol of Ganesha—the Hindu god revered as a remover of obstacles and the preferred god to seek blessings for any new beginnings—now adorns Vinod's drawing room at Khar, a western suburb of Mumbai.

A month later, on 18 February 1995, Manmohan Singh, then finance minister and the chief architect of India's financial sector reforms, opened the bank's corporate office at Sandoz House on Dr Annie Besant Road, Worli.

Coincidentally, it was also the birthday of Bharat, one of the early recruits.

Deepak Goes to North Block

With a general election round the corner, the bank couldn't have a big function involving Singh to announce its arrival. The finance minister, in fact, was reluctant to come. Hasmukh-bhai knew Singh well but he was not there to invite him. His nephew went to North Block on Raisina Hill in New Delhi—where the finance ministry is housed—but the finance minister told Deepak he would not be able to make it because of the upcoming election.

'In that case we won't have any function and won't call the press. You come, cut the ribbon, and have tea with us,' Deepak told him. Singh was also aware of the illustrious members of the HDFC board. He agreed to cut the ribbon, walk around, have a cup of tea, but said no to lunch, dinner and the press.

RBI governor C. Rangarajan and his deputy D. R. Mehta, who later became India's capital market regulator, were the other dignitaries.

Aditya took Singh around the office. The locker section was in the basement; the banking hall and the information technology (IT) hall were on the ground floor; the dealing room was on the first floor. The corporate office, on the second floor, was not fully ready yet.

Singh's brief speech focused on why the government

wanted to introduce world-class Indian private banks, the need for more competition and employment and the need to expand banking activities across the nation, a need now referred to by a fancier term called 'financial inclusion'.

Singh was very impressed with the training facilities. 'Accent on training is going to be very important to sustain the banking activity,' he said.

As the first branch was already opened at Ramon House, Aditya could actually show the finance minister how the transactions were done—fetching account details from a server and checking a customer's signature. He also explained why a centralized approach was superior to 'branch banking'. In this system, a customer banks with a bank and not with any particular branch—something unheard of in the state-run banking industry at that time. A customer's signature is registered centrally and any branch can call up the signature on its computer when required for a transaction.

The finance minister was also shown the security features. By that time Deepak had already opened an account and Aditya could show Deepak's signature on the screen and explain how the system of remote access and centralized banking would work.

Singh was mighty impressed by the computers in the dealing room and the way Luis Miranda, HDFC Bank's head of foreign exchange business, explained the trading system. C. N. Ram, the bank's technology head, showed off the automated teller machines (ATMs) to Singh and Rangarajan, who had been his professors at the Indian Institute of Management, Ahmedabad (IIM-A). ATMs were still a novelty in those days.

The bank had prepared dummy ATM cards in the names of Singh and Rangarajan. While demonstrating how an ATM worked, Ram inserted the card with Singh's name into the machine and punched in the keys. The ATM instantly flashed a message indicating insufficient funds. 'You are not the central bank; you can give the FM some money. What's the big deal?' Rangarajan's joke got everyone laughing.

The laughter got louder in the evening. Next to Sandoz House, on the terrace of architect I. M. Kadri's office, the bank threw a party to celebrate the launch. Deepak knew Kadri well. Sharad Pawar, then chief minister of Maharashtra, joined the party. Corporate India raised a toast to the birth of a bank that changed many established norms, created new ones, did very ordinary things in extraordinary ways and discovered the distinction between real and perceived risks.

Chapter 3

The Dirty Dozen

ICICI Bank, India's largest private lender, and HDFC Bank, the second largest in terms of assets but ahead of ICICI Bank in terms of market value, are as different as chalk and cheese in their approach to banking. ICICI Bank is flamboyant, innovative and quick as a flash when it comes to seizing an opportunity. HDFC Bank is staid and waits for opportunities but emerges a winner at the end of the day.

In many segments, HDFC Bank learns patiently from the experiences of others before it steps into a new business, whereas ICICI Bank loves playing the pioneer. The ICICI Bank stock is volatile; HDFC shares are range-bound. The same applies to earnings. ICICI Bank is often unpredictable, both surprisingly and shockingly. HDFC Bank is monotonously predictable on most financial parameters.

But there is one similarity between the two: K. V. Kamath, who succeeded the legendary N. Vaghul at ICICI, drafted the vision for ICICI Bank in 1996 while he was still in Indonesia heading the Bakrie Group; Aditya drew the blueprint for HDFC Bank in Malaysia while he was on a three-and-a-half-month exit notice at Citibank.

Aditya's vision was to create an Indian bank that could compete with the best on global parameters. India's economic liberalization, he believed, would give the new bank a fantastic opportunity. Public sector banks, with over 90% of the branch network in India, had the advantage of distribution; foreign banks had the products. Aditya wanted to combine the products and services of foreign banks with the relationships, funding and distribution networks of state-run banks.

Also, technology and telecommunications were on the cusp of an unbelievable change and outsourcing had become a possibility. A disruption was emerging worldwide. Aditya saw in that a lifetime opportunity.

He gave the chosen twelve employees—the dirty dozen—the freedom to bring their own people to the bank, people who would share the same dream and passion. But he had one caveat—not too many people could be hired from any particular bank, as this would make it difficult for HDFC Bank to evolve its own culture.

So Aditya, perched on a broken chair at Sandoz House, in an office still being done up, declared to those being hired that they would be working in the best bank in India. His men, the dirty dozen, shared that vision. People in the industry laughed at and ridiculed them. Aditya told his team they had no choice but to succeed, as that was the only way they could make any real money. He could not afford to pay them great salaries, but made up by way of stock options. And if the bank did well, so would its shares.

Thakur, the bank's chairman, was the first to join. His role was to frame the policy guidelines, including audit and compliance regulations. Vinod joined the bank in April 1994. The day he joined, Vinod called Goretti, secretary to the managing director of Mather & Platt, where he had worked, to join him at the new bank.

Goretti was only too happy to say yes. She thought it a golden opportunity to be able to return home every evening by half past five to look after her children. She had done her due diligence—HDFC had a five-day week, unlike Mather & Platt, and she would not have to work on Saturdays. On 1 June 1994, she entered an empty office at Ramon House as the bank's third employee and asked Vinod where she would sit. 'The whole place is yours,' he told her. However, she was not correct about the five-day week. Indeed, HDFC had a five-day week but not the bank.

By July, the office resembled a Mumbai railway station— new employees were pouring in from all over India and abroad and they were all handing Goretti their bills and tickets for reimbursements. Goretti was also busy typing appointment letters—some on HDFC's letterhead and a few on plain A4 paper.

While still in Malaysia, Aditya would fax the telephone numbers of prospective candidates to Vinod. Deepak, too, was continuously scouting for the right talent.

'Who Will Pack Our Furniture?'

Harish too was an early catch. He was in London on a three-month assignment. Deepak called him to come back to India and work for his bank. 'What bank? Aren't you an HFC [housing finance company]?' Harish asked him.

'Come on, I have got a licence now,' Deepak told him.

Harish knew Deepak and many others at HDFC because he was a relationship manager with Bank of America, where he had spent twenty-six years. Although he was a corporate banker, his role in Bank of America was quite diverse. He had been sent to London to fix a problem for the bank in relation to business brought in by non-resident Indians (NRIs).

By sheer coincidence, the day Deepak called him, Harish also got a call from his country manager Ambi Venkateswaran.

'Harish, why don't you take up an assignment in London and stay there for five years?'

'Had I wanted to stay overseas, I wouldn't have come to London from Los Angeles. I will have to go back to India,' Harish retorted, already sold on Deepak's idea.

Harish resigned and Ambi agreed to let him go on one condition: Harish had to hire his replacement in London. He did that in two weeks and took a flight to Mumbai.

In the earlier part of their lives, Harish and Aditya used to fight for business as corporate bankers. They were working in the same market in India, with the same idea of either displacing the other or introducing new products. Bank of America and Citibank shared a healthy rivalry in the late 1980s and the early 1990s in the top-tier markets.

Harish joined HDFC Bank on 12 July 1994 as its corporate banking head. His wife Sudha thought he had lost his head to leave a high-paying job and a well-settled career. 'Why do you want to start all over again?' she asked him. Sudha used to work at Bank of America, where Harish and she met and fell in love.

Harish was forty-nine years old then, and a father of two. He lived in the Shanu Deep building on Altamount Road in Mumbai. He called Thakur, Aditya, Deepak and Vinod home on a Sunday to help ease Sudha's worries. In their presence, Sudha lost her nerve and asked some silly questions: 'Who will pack our furniture? Where will we stay?'

Aditya promised to take care of everything and told her that when Harish retired, he would have a better house. Eighteen years later, Harish would live in a bigger flat at Breach Candy, an up-market neighbourhood in South Mumbai, overlooking the Arabian Sea.

Harish-bhai, as he is popularly known in the bank, and Anil Jaggia, chief information officer, constitute the baldies club in the bank.

'Hang on, Somebody Wants to Talk to You'

The second of the dirty dozen was Ram, an expert on information technology, also from Bank of America, in Chennai. Sometime in May 1994, he met Satwalekar, Vinod and Thakur at Ramon House. He met Deepak the next day.

'You know what', Deepak told Ram during the chat, 'I was going to meet a colleague of yours this morning, and I thought it might be very embarrassing for you if he found you here. So last night I called him and asked him to come in the afternoon.'

'What really struck me was that the chairman of HDFC appreciated the fact that I might be embarrassed if my colleague saw me in his room. It's a fantastic organization,' Ram says.

He went home convinced about working with Deepak, and a formal offer letter followed. The job also presented him an opportunity to return to India's financial capital after a three-year stint in the sleepy southern state of Tamil Nadu.

By that time, Ram had spent twelve years with Bank of America, having been its first IT employee in India. His assignment was to establish the systems—grow the organization, set up the connectivity, plug in India-specific banking systems and, later, migrate them to the mainstream global banking systems.

Bank of America at the time used the BankMaster software that was connected to home-grown mainframe-based systems used by it worldwide. It had data centres in Singapore, Hong Kong, London and San Francisco.

An electronics engineer from the Indian Institute of Technology (IIT) in Chennai, Ram began his career as a graduate trainee with Tata Iron and Steel Co. Ltd (Tisco; now Tata Steel Ltd) in Jamshedpur. He left the company to study at IIM-A before joining Bank of America.

The job was exciting as Bank of America was planning to set up a retail business. It didn't have a retail presence anywhere outside the United States. The bank's India manager,

Vikram Talwar, had coaxed the management into doing retail in the country, given the vast potential of the market, and had lobbied intensely for the mandarins in the Bank of America headquarters in Charlotte, North Carolina. But by the time Ram and his team could put the systems together, the project had to be scrapped.

The project had envisaged home banking, a precursor to Internet banking, and a complete suite of products based on the experience of running those systems in America. The idea was to bring those products to India and customize them.

It took the team three years to construct the systems, but as the project neared completion, Bank of America acquired Seattle-First National Bank of Washington, which had a big retail presence in Asia. This meant Bank of America's retail business in India would fold into that organization. The bank found it would be too expensive to run Thailand, Manila, Hong Kong and Singapore with the same software while leaving out India. So it scrapped the tech project worth $25 million and decided to look for a system that would suit the entire region.

The HDFC Bank offer for Ram came through a placement agency, Personal Search Services Pvt. Ltd of the Clarence–Lobo PSS Group. 'I decided to give it a try as I was fresh out of a project and knew exactly what was needed to be done,' Ram said.

'I Just Want to Have a Chat with You . . .
I Can't Reveal My Name'

One day, while at work in the Bank of America office in Chennai (then Madras), Ram got a call from Vinod who merely told him somebody wanted to speak to him, but didn't tell him who.

'I just want to have a chat with you,' the caller on the other side said. 'I am going to join the bank and just thought we could have a colleague-to-colleague chat. I can't reveal my name at this point as I am still serving in another organization. But you and I will be colleagues in HDFC Bank.'

It was a long chat, mostly about Ram's vision for IT and how the new bank could use technology innovatively.

Ram's vision was clear: Banks had to reach out to customers and automate more to improve their efficiency and effectiveness. The process, rather than being inward, had to be outward. Most banks at the time were automating to improve their own efficiency and any benefit to the customer was only incidental. The banks were thinking about themselves—their consolidation, their risk appetite, their dashboards.

At that time, the telecom sector was the virtual monopoly of Mahanagar Telephone Nigam Ltd, Videsh Sanchar Nigam Ltd, the Department of Telecom Services and the Department of Telecom Operations; the latter two were central government divisions that merged in October 2000 to form Bharat Sanchar Nigam Ltd. There was no other option but to apply to a telecom operator, wait for the link to be commissioned and then hope that the line would be up and running. And there had to be a backup in the form of 'dial-ups'. But clearly the opportunity was to leverage technology not merely for operational efficiency at the back end but to provide customers greater convenience and superior high-quality service.

Ram told the caller that the way to look at IT was to see how HDFC Bank could make a difference to its customers. He believed that banks should look for more and more products even if it meant doing a lot of the work customers were expected to do.

Ram didn't know he was speaking to Aditya. Neither did he know Aditya would be heading the bank.

Ram first met Aditya in 1985 as a rival banker at the Siemens office at Worli in Mumbai, where he had gone with Harish to meet the business personnel and explain what IT could do for their cash management systems. Bank of America had a treasury management software that it had deployed in South America. It had imported the software to India and was looking for customers who could use the terminal to automate a lot of their banking work.

Harish introduced Ram to Aditya. Ram found him rather a flamboyant fellow—the way he carried himself, the swagger—very distinctive.

That was almost ten years ago. Ram saw Aditya at Ramon House a few weeks after he joined HDFC Bank. 'We were sitting at a table and the architect was showing us designs of the future office at Sandoz House. Aditya was there but I wasn't introduced to him at that time. I still didn't know he would be heading the bank.'

Joining the Bank Was
Rajan's Quickest Decision

Another catch from Bank of America was A. Rajan, its head of operations in Delhi. A science graduate from Bombay University (now University of Mumbai), he had spent almost twenty years with the bank. When he got a call from HDFC Bank in July 1994, Rajan was overseeing a project on business process re-engineering for Bank of America—a process that mimics building a bank from scratch.

Rajan's first meeting with Vinod didn't go that well and he found Vinod a bit daunting. Aditya followed up with a call to him after about two weeks. Rajan didn't know him personally but was aware of the fact that Aditya was one of the three pillars of Citibank during his days in India heading corporate banking, the other two being A. S. Thyagarajan, head of treasury, and Jaithirth 'Jerry' Rao, who was handling retail.

'Aditya came on the landline and bluntly said he was ready to take me as head of operations and asked me whether I had any questions. I was taken aback,' Rajan told me.

Rajan had been given stock options at Bank of America, a special privilege at that time. As a senior president at the bank, he was eyeing an overseas posting. Naturally, he couldn't make up his mind immediately about joining the new venture. He insisted on the lowdown on the new bank, how it would work, its mission and so on.

Aditya didn't have the patience or the time to explain it all. 'All these things can be explained later, for now just tell me whether you're interested.'

Rajan told Aditya he would join. 'That was my quickest decision ever,' Rajan recalls.

Rajan's boss at Bank of America, Louis Pratico or Lou, was a seasoned banker. He tried his best to persuade Rajan to stay as he was anyway learning how to start a new bank as part of his assignment on business process outsourcing.

Ambi, Bank of America's country manager, trying to dissuade Rajan, told him there were two kinds of banks in India—the big multinationals, such as Citibank, the Hongkong and Shanghai Banking Corporation (HSBC) and Standard Chartered, that had deep pockets and the technology, and public sector giants, such as SBI. 'So', Ambi asked Rajan, 'from where would this new bank get its business?'

But Rajan had made up his mind, based on a leap of faith. By that time, Harish and Ram had already left Bank of America for HDFC Bank.

During his days with Bank of America, Rajan used to stay in South Mumbai. Vinod, the practical man that he is, identified some flats at Gamdevi in central Mumbai for Rajan, not an address that would make any banker proud. Vinod himself used to stay at Santa Cruz, a western suburb in Mumbai.

To Vinod's dismay, Rajan rejected his choices and moved into a flat on tony Napean Sea Road. 'You foreign bankers are all tough and have high expectations,' Vinod told him.

Aditya had not joined yet. It wasn't until a few months later that Aditya entered the Sandoz House office, which was still being renovated. He was given a table and a makeshift partition separated him from the others. Almost immediately, he asked Rajan to make a list of everything a new bank would require. That was Rajan's first task.

For Shailendra, It Was like Tossing a Coin

The next to join the bank was Shailendra Bhandari, who eventually went on to head ING Vysya Bank. He was with Citibank then, running one of its subsidiaries—Citicorp Securities & Investments Ltd. A head-hunter called him but Shailendra was not interested in leaving his job. Two weeks later, Aditya called him from Kuala Lumpur and persuaded him to meet Deepak.

Deepak told Shailendra that he would not be on the board of the bank but would fully support it. His intention was to scout for the best talent from the market. Shailendra had worked with Aditya in Citibank in Delhi in the mid-1980s, when Aditya used to handle corporate banking and Shailendra, treasury and markets. He never worked for Aditya at Citibank, but they knew each other well.

After meeting Deepak and chatting with Aditya over the telephone, Shailendra showed some inclination to join the bank but changed his mind, as he believed Citibank was too good to let go of. Aditya advised him to take some time and think it over. He also wanted to talk to Shailendra's wife Reena.

Shailendra and his wife were clear about one thing—though this venture could turn out great, there would definitely be a great deal of hard work and uncertainty. Aditya told Reena this was an opportunity of a lifetime and Shailendra should grab it. 'I remember telling Reena that the whole issue was like tossing a coin: staying with Citibank was fine and going with HDFC Bank was also fine. We simply had to decide which option to choose,' Shailendra said.

One of the things that eventually influenced him to join the bank was a little fact Aditya let slip in: '*Bharat* [of United Bank of Switzerland AG or UBS] *bhi aa raha hai.*' Shailendra knew Bharat well. He joined the bank in mid-August, around the same time that another Citibanker came on board—Paresh Sukthankar.

Shailendra joined as head of treasury but was apprehensive about how well he could run a bank's treasury from midtown Worli, where HDFC Bank planned to have its corporate office. Most banks in those days were located in South Mumbai, close to the central clearinghouse of RBI at Fort.

But the Fort area was expensive, with the rent going at ₹200–250 a square foot while the rate at Sandoz House was about half of that—₹120 a square foot. Shailendra was worried. Bharat, who was on garden leave at the time, along with Aditya, addressed Shailendra's concerns over a cup of coffee at the Oberoi.

It was decided that a small branch of the bank would be kept at Ramon House to remain connected and oversee processing of high-value cheques; Shailendra could manage the operation sitting at Sandoz House.

Paresh Took a 20–30% Pay Cut

Somebody from the bank, and not a head-hunter, called Paresh in July 1994. An MBA from the Jamnalal Bajaj Institute of Management Studies in Mumbai (incidentally, ICICI Bank's fourth managing director and CEO Chanda Kochhar also graduated from the same institute and both of them were toppers—Chanda in 1984 and Paresh in 1985), Paresh had been hired by Citibank through campus recruitment in 1985.

Thakur and Vinod explained the opportunity to Paresh. Paresh had worked with Aditya at Citibank in a couple of roles—once when Aditya was the corporate bank head of western India and Paresh was a relationship manager, and another time when Aditya was heading Citibank's institutional banking business in India and Paresh was part of the credit risk management team.

The job profile at HDFC Bank was the head of risk management. The offer letter was not on company letterhead but on a sheet of A4 paper with a neatly typed line on the top—'HDFC Bank (proposed)'—and signed by Vinod, the bank's chief financial officer (CFO).

'It is disturbing when you are taking this sort of risk. You could justify it if you were being compensated liberally but this was not the case here. I took a pay cut of about 20–30%,' said Paresh, who rose to be the effective No. 2 at HDFC Bank as one of its two executive directors. 'We were told that we will get some stock options and the bank will do well. But at that time options was a new concept. And it was a start-up bank.'

So why did he join? 'I felt that there was an opportunity to create something special and that we could make a meaningful difference to the way banking had been done in India . . . We were not born entrepreneurs but we were sure that we would build something world class over a period of time. We wanted to set a benchmark in terms of technology, service levels, risk management and others—world class, not better than others only in the Indian banking industry.'

Sporting a handlebar moustache, Paresh is down to earth and drives a peach Skoda Superb. He is more like a professor of mathematics than a banker, and loves to explain things to his colleagues instead of simply making a statement. As the bank's chief risk officer, he had once said: 'HDFC Bank is what it is not only for the things it has done but also for the things it has not done.'

Paresh reaches office sharp at 9.20 a.m. every morning. He gets off his car on the other side of the road and legs it across to save the time taken by the car to make a U-turn to the office entrance.

His role now has gone beyond risk management—finance, human resources, investor relations, corporate communications, information security and corporate social responsibility. Paresh, who many believe to be Aditya's heir apparent, drives most strategic initiatives and handles analysts' conferences. In the bank, he is the favourite sounding board for decisions across businesses and functions as he always brings a different point of view—he is brutally frank, but never abrasive. His other qualities, insiders say, are a great feel for numbers and a strong sense of fairness.

Mr Cool in times of crisis, Paresh also leads the way in the annual ritual of blood donation, organized by Bhavesh Zaveri, the bank's group head for operations.

Bharat, Deepak's cousin and Aditya's chum, was one of the early recruits. He wanted to stay in Singapore with UBS at least for six more months to complete his assignment but Aditya said a firm 'no' as Bharat would need to help them out with hiring people.

He returned to Mumbai in December 1994. Even though he didn't join the bank immediately, Bharat got involved in the project while serving his notice period in India. His wife, a doctor in Singapore, was not unhappy with the move as they had been planning to come back, though after a year, to be with their aged parents. Bharat was made the head of human resources and retail.

Luis Just Wanted to Work for an Indian Company

Luis Miranda, an alumnus of the University of Chicago Booth School of Business (then Graduate School of Business, University of Chicago), famous for its cutting edge research in economics and finance, had worked with most of the gang— Bharat, Shailendra, Paresh and Aditya, in his Citibank days between 1989 and 1992, till he joined HSBC.

He hadn't enjoyed his jobs with the foreign banks for the simple reason that the big decisions were taken either by people sitting halfway across the world with barely a clue about what really was happening in India or by expats who had a vastly different view of the world and the local realities.

Luis was keen to work for an Indian organization, but the problem was that professional outfits did not pay a decent salary in those days. And those that paid a decent salary were not professional in their approach.

A head-hunter from Personal Search Services told Luis about the new bank being created. (Later, it became a contentious issue as immediately after the head-hunter spoke to Luis, Bharat too called him and the head-hunter never got paid!) Bharat was still with UBS in Singapore and Aditya with Citibank in Malaysia.

At Ramon House, thirty-three-year-old Luis met Thakur, Vinod, Harish and Ram. Later, when Aditya called him, Luis was quite candid in saying that he wasn't looking at the salary as much as at working for an Indian company. That was the incentive to come on board.

Another attraction was the people he would be working with. Aditya was someone with whom he had had the occasional fight when they were at Citibank, but Luis always found him interesting. On 16 August 1994, he joined the bank.

His wife Fiona met Deepak before Luis joined the bank, at a farewell party for Gerald Clive 'Gerry' Dobby, CEO of HSBC India. The music was loud and nobody could hear what they were saying.

'Don't you think your husband is mad?' Deepak asked her.

'Why?'

'He's leaving a job with HSBC to join a start-up bank! When I left my job at Chase Manhattan to join HDFC, my mother and wife didn't talk to me for a very long time.' Deepak was teasing Fiona.

Fiona assured him that she wouldn't stop talking to her husband even for a day. 'He and I talked about all these issues before we got married. We knew that work would be a roller-coaster ride because there are so many opportunities and one wants to gather experience along the way,' she told him.

From Bandra, Luis and Fiona moved into an apartment on Malabar Hill that Bharat had arranged for them. It wasn't ready yet and Fiona had to go to Spain for a friend's wedding.

While she was away, Luis had just one room for himself with a mattress to sleep on. The kitchen was not ready yet and so, on his way to work, the new vice president in charge of foreign exchange at HDFC Bank would stop at Café Ideal on Marine Drive to have *bun maska*—oven-fresh buttered bread buns— with scrambled eggs and tea. He would be the first person in the office, arriving at around eight o'clock every morning.

After reaching the office, Luis would top off his breakfast with a *vada pav*—the hugely popular Maharashtrian street food—outside Ramon House. Being the first person to arrive, he would collect the newspapers and open up the office.

After reading the newspapers, Luis would spend time learning to use PowerPoint as there was no work in the early days. Showing off his new skill, Luis created the first presentation on HDFC Bank. Many years later, though a lot changed, slides from that first presentation were still being used to explain the business model and philosophy of the bank.

The father of one of Luis' friends, who was related to Aditya, once told him that they could be building a great Indian bank but their main motivation was money. Luis didn't buy that. 'Yes, we were given stocks, but look we never imagined even in our wildest dreams where the stock prices would go.'

Luis hadn't negotiated his compensation package. His only passion was to work for an Indian organization. The bank found in him a good ambassador and asked him to influence others to join the team. But it wasn't an easy task. 'It was quite difficult; no one readily wanted to leave their jobs at foreign banks to join a nascent venture. Also, a private bank in India had never really taken off.'

Luis hates hair on the head but is liberal with facial hair: he is the third member of the baldies club.

'No Salary Hike, No Foreign Trips'—How Did That Sound to Samir?

A career Citibanker, Samir Bhatia was familiar with Aditya's work–life balance—coming to office at half past nine in the morning and leaving at half past five in the evening. Aditya was a sharp guy with a phenomenal grasp of things. He could work with great speed, clarity and understanding.

Samir had never worked with Aditya but knew a lot about him. 'Aditya would go through every credit proposal with an x-ray vision and pick out just a few things that were absolutely necessary. There would be no paper on the table.'

In August 1994, Paresh, with whom Samir had worked in the risk management unit at Citibank, asked him whether he would like to have a chat with Aditya. By then Samir had put in his papers at Citibank and accepted an offer from ABN AMRO Bank N. V., but had not joined there yet.

'*Kya kar raha hai aaj kal?*' Aditya asked him at their first meeting at Ramon House.

'*Aaj kal toh main corporate banking mein hoon.*'

'*Kya karna chahta hai?*'

'*Main khush hoon*, I'm happy doing what I want.'

'Would you like to build a new bank?'

The prospect of creating a new bank was thrilling. Aditya told him there wouldn't be any foreign trips in a long time because they were building a domestic bank. He also said, 'Once you join, I can't give you a salary hike. Whatever salary you were getting, I can at best match that.' So much for selling a job to a potential recruit!

Aditya also asked him where he was staying.

'*Warden Road mein rehta hoon,*' Samir told him, in a Citibank flat.

Aditya told Samir the bank wouldn't be able to allot him a house and he would have to find his own. Samir had a family home in Santa Cruz where he used to live before moving to the Citibank flat.

'No salary hike, no foreign trips, back to your own home, how does that sound to you?' Aditya asked him.

Maybe it was Aditya's charm, maybe it was his way of communicating, maybe it was just the excitement of working with a start-up bank—Samir was convinced. 'Done. I'm on. But what am I going to do, what's my job?' he asked Aditya.

'First you come and build the bank and then we'll decide

kya karna hai. Right now, we need people to work and you simply come on board.'

A company flat on Warden Road and extensive travel to Africa and Eastern Europe—all gone in minutes. But Samir's wife Neela, who used to work for American Express, was fine with it.

Samir was around thirty-one years old then. 'It seemed a completely new thing to do and clearly there was a huge opportunity because there was room in between the foreign banks and the government banks—a massive vacuum in terms of speed of response, the ability to decide faster, fewer restrictions, branches . . . It was like something big was being built and one simply had to be a part of that excitement,' Samir told me.

Samir joined the bank in September 1994—the day Aditya formally came on board. 'I saw Aditya walking in . . . I had heard about his fabulous office in Malaysia overlooking the ocean, and here there was no cabin as such and only one toilet was functional.' A unisex toilet as Goretti was also a part of the team!

Samir's job was corporate banking, but for the first nine months he was the project manager for setting up the bank—vice president of projects.

Abhay Was Thinking of
Switching to Farming

Almost all the members of the founding team came from the banking industry except for Vinod, who was a corporate executive. Abhay Aima had seen both the banking and the corporate worlds. He had worked with Citibank in treasury but had left, along with his boss Harjit Sawhney, to join Ravi Ruia of the diversified Essar Group, which was trying to forge a joint venture with Paine Webber & Co., an American stock brokerage and asset management company. But that did not take off and Paine was bought by UBS in 2000.

Abhay had been thinking of switching to farming and had taken a few months off work to explore the idea, but the plan did not work as he had problems acquiring land. And so he had to go back to his job.

But now he wanted to be an investment banker. He started negotiating with Shankar Dey, an ex-Citibanker who was with the Indian outfit Peregrine Investments Holdings Ltd. Shankar was happy to take him but Abhay needed to meet the company's CEO, Francis Bruce Pike. In 1994, Francis set up the first foreign-owned Indian investment bank, Peregrine India, where he became chairman in 1997.

Abhay took an instant dislike to Francis. A historian and journalist, Francis was related to Britain's royal family. His wife India Jane Birley was the half-sister of Jemima Khan, former wife of Pakistani cricketer-turned-politician Imran Khan, and the daughter of James Goldsmith. Francis did not have nice things to say about India and that made Abhay uncomfortable, though he found Shankar, who would be his proximate boss, brilliant.

So when Shailendra, who had been Abhay's boss for some time in Citibank treasury, checked with him, Abhay was happy to explore the opportunity of working with a start-up bank. By that time (November 1994), Aditya had already joined and the bank was operating out of Sandoz House.

The job profile was not well defined but Shailendra told Abhay that they would find a place for him in the team. Abhay knew Samir, Paresh and Aditya besides Shailendra and thought the comfort of working with people he already knew was critical. He had never worked with Aditya, but there had been chance meetings at Citibank when Aditya was the institutional head and Abhay was in treasury. Aditya told Shailendra that he didn't have a problem with having Abhay in the team.

The comfort factor apart, the strong parentage of the bank attracted Abhay. 'At that time, there were two big brands in India—HDFC and Bajaj [Auto Ltd]. As an equity guy, I thought they were the best brands in India. The Tatas also have their brand but I think the HDFC brand name has been utilized to the fullest,' he told me.

He was made the vice president of treasury, reporting to Shailendra, an executive director. His cabin was the coldest because it was carved out of the software storage area where the air-conditioning was very strong. By the time he joined, there was no room for creating a cabin elsewhere.

Before his banking days, Abhay had been a fighter pilot in the Indian Air Force. He had spent two years with the Air Force and three years with the National Defence Academy. He had once told Jerry Rao at Citibank that since he could handle a fighter jet on his own, he could also do banking.

'In the Air Force, you actually sign off for the aircraft and technically not even the chief of air staff can tell you what to do because you are in command. I went solo after flying for eleven hours and the Government of India entrusted me with a multimillion-dollar aircraft. So, after three months of training in banking, if you are not as conservative as them, you should be able to give me responsibility,' he told Jerry.

A graduate in international relations from Jawaharlal Nehru University in New Delhi, Abhay, at a well-built six feet and three inches, always sports an unkempt look with panache. He hates wearing a tie.

Abhay is the only one in the team who smokes cigars, at times, in office after blocking the smoke detectors in his cabin.

Abhay's colleague at the Essar Group and previously Citibank, Ashish Parthasarthy, also joined the bank. In fact, Ashish had prepared Abhay's resume as the bank's human resources department had wanted a resume and Abhay didn't have one ready. Twenty-six-year-old Ashish joined as head of money markets, basically in charge of the domestic part of the treasury. Ashish had worked with Shailendra and Luis at Citibank where he had dealt with local currency and treasury risk management, and Shailendra was instrumental in getting both Ashish and Abhay to HDFC Bank. When Ashish joined the bank at Sandoz House in November 1994, a huge board hung outside the treasury division with the word 'CASH' written in capital letters. Presumably this was the place where the cash counter of the previous occupant was located.

Ashish is the exact opposite of Abhay. At just a shade above five feet, he is the shortest of the group heads. Quietest of the lot, he drives a Nissan X-Trail.

The last of the founding team was G. Subramanian, who came from the RBI to head compliance at HDFC Bank. Hierarchically, it was not a top-end job but a very critical one as in HDFC Bank the head of compliance reported directly to the chairman and not to the managing director and CEO. This was an exception that exemplified the bank's strong focus on corporate governance—the tradition continues.

One day in November 1994, Subramanian, GS to his colleagues in the bank, got a call from his boss at the RBI, A. M. M. Sarma, chief general manager in the department of banking supervision. 'Are you looking for a challenging assignment?' he asked. Forty-seven-year-old GS, a deputy general manager, was only too willing. He went to Ramon House to meet Thakur who was looking for a bold and confident person who would be able to withstand the vagaries and temper the enthusiasm of 'foreign bankers'—a favourite terminology of the banking regulator in those days.

When GS called on Aditya, he was advised to meet the others first—Shailendra, Ram and Rajan—in that order. Aditya told him, 'I am fine with you joining us but I don't want your wife to accuse me later of being responsible for her husband's heart attack. There will be a lot of stress in a new bank. I suggest you spend a week with us and then decide.'

GS took his decision on the spot and didn't regret it till the first offsite of the bank at Lonavala in April 1995. At the offsite, all the group heads were to make presentations on their game plan for the next financial year. The presentation made by GS was on audit and compliance. One of the slides showed Sherlock Holmes with a magnifying glass in hand, bending forward to peer at something on the floor. Luis instantly said: 'GS you need to take care; the back side is unprotected and tempting.'

That rattled GS. It was a huge culture shock for a man who had spent twenty-three years at the formal and staid RBI. Aditya promptly came to his rescue. 'Luis, GS comes from a different background; let's respect it.' That put him at ease. 'The way Aditya intervened, I was convinced that I had made the right choice,' GS told me.

On his way to Delhi for the first audit of the Delhi branch, GS came across Deepak at the airport. When Deepak got to know why he was travelling to Delhi, he told GS that earlier whenever he used to get a call from Sarma, he would pick up the telephone quickly as he knew that it could be for his views on some banking issues, but now he thinks twice before picking up the telephone as he worries about whether Sarma is unhappy with the way the bank is being run.

Vinod, Bharat, Harish, Ram, Rajan, Shailendra, Paresh, Luis, Samir, Abhay, Ashish and Subramanian formed the dirty dozen—the 'A team'—that launched the bank. Two other gentlemen who played stellar roles in the making of the bank were Neeraj Swaroop and Sashi Jagdishan, but they weren't a part of the founding team.

And there were Kaizad Barucha and Jimmy Tata.

The Thought of Leading a
Team Excited Sashi

Sashi, the bank's second CFO, joined the bank in February 1996, after close to a three-year stint at Deutsche Bank AG, first as a trainee officer and later a senior officer in financial control.

When he was head-hunted by the human resources division of HDFC Bank, thirty-one-year-old Sashi had no clear idea about the bank's profile—whether it was a public or a private institution. He knew about HDFC but didn't know how much stake it held in the bank.

His wife Nagsri, who was working for Thomas Cook (India) Ltd, wondered, 'You are leaving an MNC bank to join HDFC?'

Sashi had an offer to join Deutsche Bank's investment banking division in Singapore.

'It wasn't money or the organization or the pride of working for a domestic firm but the thought of leading a team that was the most exciting part,' he told me. The bank needed someone to head financial control.

It was not the CFO's job—Vinod was doing that as an executive director. Sashi was made the manager of finance. By that time, the bank was 'listed' and getting ready to announce the earnings of its first full year.

'Don't Waste Time Neeraj, Join Me Now'

Neeraj remembers Aditya calling him during the Diwali of 1998. Apparently someone had strongly recommended him to Aditya at a Diwali party. They met over coffee at the Taj Mansingh in Delhi in December and without much ado, Aditya offered Neeraj a job to steer the bank's retail operations.

At Bank of America, Neeraj was looking after retail marketing, sales and distribution. Tony Singh was the head of retail and Neeraj was reporting to him. It was a critical juncture as around that time Bank of America had taken a decision to diversify its retail business in Asia following its takeover by NationsBank of the United States in 1998. The management assured the employees that nobody would be laid off but Neeraj had seen that his colleagues were either losing their jobs or being transferred to other parts of Asia. Bank of America wanted to sell the India business.

It wasn't an easy decision to leave a foreign bank as Indian banks weren't doing much in retail banking. State-run banks didn't have the products and private banks lacked a wide branch network, as did foreign banks. Bank of America had four branches at that time and HDFC Bank had forty. But the foreign banks were trying to overcome the handicap with product innovation, backed by technology. Besides, the previous retail head of HDFC Bank, Samit Ghosh, a former Citibanker, did not even last a year because of serious differences with Aditya on business philosophy.

This was Neeraj's first meeting with Aditya. The HDFC Bank boss was direct: 'Don't waste time Neeraj. Join me now and do whatever you want—strategy, planning, products.' After the one-hour meeting over coffee and cookies, Neeraj accepted the idea of joining HDFC Bank in principle.

Bharat carried the offer letter to him the next week.

'To be honest, I was excited. Partly because of Aditya. The money was not good—just about what I was getting at Bank of America, but there were also the stocks that later became valuable. The excitement was the job,' he told me.

Neeraj had a few ex-colleagues from Bank of America working with him at HDFC Bank. Ram was Neeraj's batchmate at IIM-A. Neeraj was aware of Aditya's reputation of being a quick and effective decision-maker. That was very different from what he had seen at Bank of America, which had a matrix organizational structure where a division head typically had a dotted relationship with the local CEO but reported to the global head of business in another geography.

The decision-making process was superior and faster in a single-country organization than in a matrix organization structure that came with its share of checks and balances.

With his two young children, Neeraj moved to Mumbai from Delhi. And predictably, Deepak stepped in to ensure that Neeraj's children got into Bombay Scottish.

At Sandoz House, Vinod asked Neeraj whether he could do without a cabin. So Neeraj operated from a closed meeting room that was fitted with a round table, a computer, a telephone and a shared secretary. It took almost a year for Neeraj to get his own cabin and a little less time to get a secretary. Neeraj joined as one of the group heads in retail. The other person was J. K. Basu, who was running branch banking. Vinod was cost-conscious and that was the culture of the bank.

Kaizad started his career at the Bank of Credit & Commerce International, registered in Luxembourg and founded by Agha Hasan Abedi, a Pakistani financier. When it was liquidated in the early 1990s for its involvement in massive money laundering and other serious financial irregularities, SBI took over its Indian operations and named it SBI Commercial & International (SBICI) Bank Ltd.

Kaizad, the squash champion of Bombay University for two successive years, and also part of the national team at the Asian Junior Squash Championships in Singapore and Malaysia in 1983, was in trade finance at SBICI Bank. He was about to join Standard Chartered when his wife and colleague Havovi asked him to explore whether there was any opportunity at HDFC Bank. Around the same time, a head-hunting company too called him.

He joined the bank in October 1995 as a senior relationship manager but after a couple of years he moved to the risk management unit.

Everybody in HDFC Bank talks about his significant contribution to risk management across wholesale and retail banking. His beige-coloured Skoda Laura is the last car to leave Bank House, the bank's headquarters at Lower Parel. Last year, in his annual performance appraisal form, Paresh, his boss, made leaving office early one of the goals for Kaizad. He did follow Paresh's advice, but only for a few days.

Ask him why he needs to sit late every day, his answer is, 'In credit risks, the devil is in the details; one needs to be very careful about every document and that takes time.'

He has no time to play squash anymore. Often, he is seen at Otter's Club, near Jogger's Park on Carter Road in Bandra—a Mecca for squash—not for squash but for a drink. No wonder, he is growing a paunch!

Jimmy was two years junior to Kaizad at Sydenham College in Mumbai, the first college of commerce in Asia. (Incidentally, Paresh too is from the same college.) Jimmy used to work for Apple Industries Ltd, a non-banking finance company that was into lease finance and term loans.

Jimmy joined the bank in December 1994 as a relationship manager in corporate banking. It was tough as Aditya, Harish, Samir and Paresh had all been relationship managers in the past and were demanding. 'If I could do it as an RM, why can't you?' was the refrain. But Jimmy proved his mettle with his meticulous scoping of business opportunities for every corporate relationship and driving his team to close deals. When Samir left the bank to join Barclays, the UK bank that wanted to get into retail business in a big way, Jimmy was made the corporate banking head.

The key to the success of HDFC Bank, according to Vinod, was cobbling together a strong founding team. In Aditya's absence, the first meeting of most of the executives was with Vinod. The meetings often were at the Bombay Gymkhana bar over *lassi* or coffee.

'The whole story was around Deepak. That made my life easier. I used to tell them, "We are planning to set up the first private sector bank in India, promoted by HDFC, and you know we are trying to get the best of professionals." The only carrot we were offering was stock options. But that was secondary. The real thing was the challenge and independence of setting up a new private bank in India. Not a single guy said "no",' Vinod told me.

Indeed, there were a few who said 'no'. Piyush Gupta, who in 2009 became the CEO of DBS Bank in Singapore, was one of them. He was with Citibank in Indonesia when HDFC Bank was being set up. The trio—Aditya (to whom Piyush reported in India in Citibank), Bharat and Piyush—spent a lot of time talking about starting the bank.

Aditya offered him a job before leaving Malaysia. But Piyush, one of the original partners for creating the new bank, chickened out. 'I had spent just two years overseas and wanted to hang around for a few more years and create some savings. I told Aditya to carry on.'

For investors, today, HDFC Bank is the most predictable among Indian banks when it comes to earnings, but in the early days many things happened that were unpredictable and unheard of in Indian banking history—rats chewing off computer wires, a baby crawling on the treasury floor, bottles of wine hidden in the drawers and whatnot.

Finance was laced with fun in the early days.

Chapter 4

'There's a Baby on the Trading Floor!'

Thakur, chairman of the bank, joined in January 1994, about eight months before HDFC got the regulator's approval in principle to set up the bank and a year before the licence came. For most of the year, the sixth floor of Ramon House, HDFC's headquarters, was the camp office for Aditya's army. While the commander was in Malaysia serving his notice period, Vinod held the fort. As CFO, Vinod signed appointment letters, looked after the logistics and oversaw everything that a new company needed, including drafting the so-called memorandum and articles of association, searching for a new office, and even bargaining to bring down the price of granite for the office floor.

Till about July 1994, only Thakur, Vinod and Ram were in the office. Vinod's secretary Goretti used to order lunch from the executive lunchroom of HDFC. They would be served soup, starters, a main course and dessert, followed by coffee. While this ritual was abandoned when the team grew to about a dozen, other rituals were adopted. Every Monday, the top brass of HDFC, led by Deepak, would invite all the bankers working on the sixth floor for lunch at the executive lunchroom on the fourth floor. Deepak Satwalekar, Keki Mistry, Nasser Munjee, Renu Sud Karnad and Deepak Parekh would discuss with them the economy, inflation and interest rates over a light yet full-course lunch that started with soup and ended with dessert (mostly cut fruits) and coffee.

For Deepak, the starter often was a discussion on the macro economy. He would invariably come to the main course—the banking opportunities and what the yet-to-be born bank should do. He was very gung-ho and justifiably so, as he had just managed to get NatWest as a strategic partner. He would goad Ram to go to London, see NatWest's modern systems and figure out how best those could be used in India.

Aditya was a man in a hurry. The day he joined, in September 1994, he asked Rajan and Samir to prepare a list of all the things a new organization would need, right down to clips, pins, paper pads and vouchers. In turn, Rajan and Samir asked each employee for a wish list.

Monday Morning Meetings

Later, after the bank began operations in 1995 at Sandoz House, Monday morning meetings became sacrosanct. Aditya would talk about his vision for the bank with the dirty dozen. These boardroom meetings and the discussions were not on looking back at what had happened but on looking forward at what could happen. Of course, any significant event that had taken place in the previous week would feature in the discussions, but it was often new ideas on business opportunities, tackling a particular issue or doing things differently that dominated the content.

Starting at half past nine in the morning, the meeting would go on for about an hour or longer on some days. Aditya didn't like to see the senior managers for the rest of the week if the business was running well; he didn't even feel the need to talk to them. Everyone was empowered. But Aditya was ruthless if anybody came late for the meeting. A five-minute delay without a valid reason would invite a rebuke. If someone was not carrying a notepad, he would remember Aditya's cold stare for the rest of his life.

People would operate independently, but at the same time there was a culture of coming together and sharing thoughts and views. The Monday morning meeting was the biggest platform for collective ideation. On other days, communication was mostly through chits and notes (e-mail had not become widespread then).

By October 1995, HDFC Bank had relocated its office to Sandoz House in Worli, making it the first bank to have its headquarters in midtown Mumbai. Until then, all the Mumbai-based banks had their corporate offices either in the business districts of Nariman Point or Cuffe Parade or in the vicinity of Fort where India's central bank, the RBI, has its headquarters.

The emergence of the Bandra Kurla Complex, in the western suburb of Mumbai, as an alternative business district years later prompted many banks to set up their corporate offices there as the cost of real estate was relatively lower. Many banks moved out of rented places and opted for their own spaces at the Bandra Kurla Complex. HDFC Bank chose to stay at Sandoz House as the rent there was almost half of what an office space in Fort or South Mumbai would have cost. The bank got three floors and the basement—a total of some 30,000 square feet—in the building, which had just been vacated by Sandoz subsidiaries. It was taken on a twenty-year lease.

The team moved in even before the interiors were done. The desks were rented from the previous occupier. Quite a few of the cabins had windows so small one could just about put a hand through, something a bank teller would have found useful. As there weren't too many chairs, the rule was 'first come, first served'. Anyone coming in late had to stand for the day.

So the latecomers would invariably huddle in the conference room—a large place with a long table and quite a few chairs—on the pretext of a meeting. More importantly, unlike in the rest of the office, the chairs in the conference room were not broken and the tables were not three-legged. The air-conditioners were rented and painting was considered a waste of money till the bank neared its inauguration date.

As D-day—16 January 1995—approached, the architect issued an ultimatum to Aditya to vacate the place if he wanted the work completed on time. The drilling and the hammering and the humongous amount of construction work had anyway made life difficult for most of the bankers at Sandoz House.

Ram remembers an incident before they moved to the new office. 'Aditya told me some guy would come and show me a place where we could set up a temporary office. I was dealing with all sorts of vendors then. So when I saw a new guy in the office I thought "here is the broker, let him wait." I took around fifteen minutes and this guy waited patiently. When I came out and started looking for my car, he said, "Come, let's go in my car." It was a Mercedes Benz. He was Ramesh Gowani, the owner of Kamala Mills.'

Samir was made the project manager. And Rajan would wear a helmet and supervise the work when Samir was out.

'Bank Bandh Ho Gaya'

Ramesh was developing an office space at Kamala Mills Ltd, an old textile mill that was still running. Over a weekend, everybody working at Sandoz House was told to report at Kamala Mills the following Monday. In those days, dozens of appointment letters were being couriered every week and in January, just before the formal launch, a large number of people were to join.

The existing team moved to the temporary office but did not realize that a bunch of new employees would be reporting at Sandoz House that Monday. When the new recruits turned up, the security guard told them, *Bank bandh ho gaya.*

At the makeshift office at Kamala Mills, Aditya's team was wondering why the newly hired employees had not turned up. When they realized what had happened, they began making calls to each of the new recruits, and put up a sign at the entrance of Sandoz House asking them to report at Kamala Mills.

Ashima Bhat, who would later head HDFC Bank's SME (small and medium enterprises) business, had joined the bank only the previous week. She had summered with Citibank during her MBA days, when Aditya was heading institutional banking there. When she got to know that Aditya would be heading the new bank, she wanted to join.

When Ashima walked into Sandoz House that Monday, she didn't find a soul. It was nine in the morning. Her mind was a whirlwind of panic: 'What have they done?' 'Have they changed their minds and shut the bank?' 'For half an hour, I was shell-shocked. I had left a good job at Ferguson to join them and there was no bank,' she recalls. Tears rolled down her eyes.

The bank had not advertised for candidates in the newspapers as the team was not sure how they would handle the applications. In any case, who would look for a job in a new bank? Besides, Aditya wanted people with experience. Through word of mouth, people got to know and started coming in for interviews. Typically, Rajan would interview a person for a position in operations for about twenty minutes before Harish would come in and ask for the only table available for job interviews.

Kamala Mills today is abuzz with activity—it houses banks, media outfits and outsourcing units. Hundreds of cars are parked in the compound and security guards check every vehicle that drives in. In late 1994, the textile mill was still in operation and there was hardly anyone else besides the mill workers.

Training Sessions Under a Tree

Since there was no meeting room at Ramesh's office at Kamala Mills, the bank held meetings under a Peepal tree like in the ancient gurukul system.

Luis remembers his first training session on foreign exchange under the tree and Samir remembers the session on corporate banking. When the mill siren wailed to announce lunch hour, workers would troop out in groups only to see a bunch of young bankers sitting round a Peepal tree. Curious, they would surround the bankers to ask them questions. They would not believe that a banking class was on as there was no blackboard or any other prop by the tree.

In the two-floor makeshift office, the bank set up the systems—connecting the computers with a server. It was done through coaxial cables like the ones used to connect a TV with the antenna. The unshielded twisted pair cables are more expensive and normally used in finished buildings. For the bank, the Kamala Mills office was a stopover. The coaxial cables were laid all across the floor and people were furiously testing the systems as training had to be given.

There was a lot of energy and a lot of drama. People would

scream, 'this is how we want to set this up'; 'savings account could go this way'; 'current account could go that way', 'letters of credit have to be done like this' and so on, as if they were *discovering* banking.

In some sense, this was true as India's public sector banks in those days worked manually. Their chiefs had just started getting computers but the machines were largely used as showpieces because they didn't know how to operate them. And the bosses' secretaries, who belonged to the unionized cadre, were not allowed to use computers. Trade unions resisted computerization in banks till the first decade of this millennium as they feared the machines would replace them and shrink employment opportunities.

The training sessions under a tree were fine for certain subjects but a proper place was needed for more complicated subjects. So a *gala*—or an industrial shed—was rented at the nearby Kewal Industrial Estate on Tulsi Pipe Road in Lower Parel.

Typically, SMEs operate in such *galas*, which are nothing more than an industrial floor where heavy-duty machinery works. This particular *gala*, measuring about 500 square feet, had four walls, a wide front door and a ceiling from where a dozen fans hung. It had just one toilet.

The bank began training its IT and back-office people at this industrial shed, with the help of internal and external experts. Often during the training the electricity would go off, but the training would continue by candlelight with the computers powered by an UPS.

The women employees—in the early days of the bank there were only a few of them—were not worried about the darkness in the mill area as, if they needed to go somewhere, a male colleague would always escort them. They were all working long hours and late into the day.

Aditya was firm that he would not get into the business without the systems and procedures in place. His mandate was that the systems had to be up and he would not have anybody doing anything manually. Rajan, head of operations, was also insistent that the bank needed to be run entirely on automated systems.

The wires that connected all the computers in the *gala* were stuck to the floor with tape, but even so once in a while someone would inadvertently trip on them and bring down the entire network. Women employees, particularly those wearing saris, had to be careful not to trip on the mess of wires.

Typically, such *galas* were infested with rats. There were times the rats chewed on the cables but no one could figure out why the systems weren't working because the wires were concealed. So while one person would shout out that he could not log in, those not working on the computers would find everything normal, until someone inspected the wires and they would come off as they'd been gnawed by a rat!

At Sandoz House, Ashima was selected to be the prototype woman customer for whom the teller counters were to be designed. The counters had to be of a comfortable height for the typical Indian woman, not requiring her to stretch herself or bend forward too much to submit her cheques or get her cash. The contractor made Ashima work for hours, asking her to stand straight or bend forward and backward or turn right and left so he could get the right measurements.

Baby's Day at the Bank

Luis used to bring his daughter Mihika, who had not yet turned one, to the office on Saturdays. He would pull two chairs together for her to sleep. If she was awake she'd crawl all over the dealing room. 'My wife was at home but I loved having my daughter with me in the office. That's me,' Luis told me.

She would crawl on the trading floor and try to stand holding on to the sides of the dealing tables, which had exhaust fans at the bottom. That raised a bit of a scare in the dealing room as Mihika would try to reach for the fan blades. Eventually, the office fixed wire mesh over the fans to keep her fingers from getting cut.

Once, Mihika refused to sleep and began bawling. Luis had to make an internal presentation that day. He made the presentation cradling his precious daughter in his arms.

Some of Luis' colleagues, too, would bring their children to the office, though not as frequently as he did.

It was an informal environment that allowed the bankers to bring along their babies. The children have grown but still share a bond. In August 2010, Paresh organized a get-together in his house at Lower Parel for those children, who, of course, had grown into their teens or early twenties. They exchanged stories about the peek-a-boos in the office and the Christmas parties at Madh Island where Luis used to play Santa Claus.

The initial days also meant hard work, long hours and chaos. The people being recruited were young—for some, it was their first job. The founding team was also relatively young, with many in their thirties and forties.

A bunch of mostly foreign bankers had left high-profile high-paying jobs, expensive cars and spacious houses in tony localities to drive Premier NE-118s, earn less money and live in smaller flats in the suburbs. Their children went to Bombay Scottish, though, thanks to Deepak.

Tequila Shots in the Evenings

Some of the executives would sneak in a drink in the office once in a while, mostly in the evenings after office hours to celebrate the little successes—the first deposit, the first loan. Luis had a mini bar in his room—mostly a few bottles of wine and beer in a small fridge, meant to be hidden, of course. Many remember the tequila shots they had late evenings to celebrate when the bank got its 1,000th customer or when it became a part of a consortium of lenders for the Birla Group.

Aditya is fond of his whisky but prefers to drink at home when he is with his family. Deepak loves Beck's and Heineken beer with his Sunday lunches. His evening preference is Johnnie Walker's Blue Label. He holds the glass but hardly drinks, only taking small sips every once in a while. A smart strategy, especially when he has to hop parties for networking.

Ram doesn't drink. For Paresh, even tea is poison. Rajan finds beer too strong and, given a chance, will dilute it. Vinod, the 'original Brit' as some of his colleagues dub him, is always measured in drinking, like his steps while walking.

They are all very different from one another; they have their whims, their fancies, their idiosyncrasies, but they have coexisted wonderfully well in professional harmony.

The ATM Swallowed HDFC
Managing Director's Card

All of them swore by the HDFC brand. Day in, day out Aditya reminded them that the bank's services had to be perfect and must not sully the parent brand. But there were the odd glitches, and one of these was quite embarrassing. Hardly a week had passed since Singh launched the bank when the bank's ATM swallowed the ATM card of Satwalekar, managing director of HDFC. Satwalekar was also a director on the bank's board.

But this was an accident. The bank was meticulous in its plans for integrating its ATMs with the overall architecture. It bought an ATM switch to ensure an online real-time interface connecting individual ATMs and the host system.

When a customer swipes a card at an ATM, there are two ways to verify the balance money in the account. One is the online real-time system that checks with the host on how much money is available in the customer's account. The other is the offline system in which details of a customer's account are fed to the host server only at the end of the day. That leaves a bank open to a potential credit risk. A customer can go to a bank branch, withdraw the last rupee from his or her account, then head to an ATM and withdraw money again as the main server wouldn't know until the end of the day that the customer had already withdrawn all the money from his or her account.

Now all banks follow the online real-time system, but in the 1990s even some new-generation private banks had opted for the offline system. They lived with that mainly because the then popular banking software, Bancs 2000 of Infosys Ltd, did not provide for a centralized service.

HDFC Bank opted for a centralized online real-time system both for its ATMs and for its Internet banking. This enabled managers to view a single statement for each customer across all channels, regardless of how the bank was accessed. In some sense, this was its first step towards riskless banking.

HDFC Bank short-listed ten vendors for the software, including Tata Consultancy Services Ltd and Infosys, the country's biggest software companies. It was left to Ram to make the call.

Ram went to London to study NatWest's system. He came back extremely disappointed. 'Those were very ancient mainframe-based systems. It would have been hugely cost-ineffective and inefficient for us to tie our fortunes with NatWest's IT department,' Ram told me.

Coming from the bureaucracy of Bank of America's IT department, Ram knew what he was talking about. 'It's a nightmare dealing with those people as each country has to make its own plan. You have to make presentations to various committees saying, "If you do this, I can assure you this much of revenue," and that's the basis on which they short-list you,' Ram explained. India was always way down in the list for Bank of America because Japan, Korea and even Indonesia were larger markets than India at the time.

Ram was in favour of cutting the cord with NatWest as far as technology was concerned. He was keen on getting a centralized system as it would have been impossible for a new bank to sustain separate systems at individual branches.

'Are you sure?' Aditya asked him. 'You are asking for so much money.'

Ram was sure. A centralized processing system would pull together data on all the accounts proposed to be opened in different parts of the country to one central place for verification. If the verifications were to be done by the many individual branches, the bank could not have ensured a standard application of its rules and regulations.

HDFC Bank was the first Indian bank to have a centralized system. As it opened more branches, the documents started pouring into the central data centre for verification, and many of the applications had to be turned down because the branches hadn't properly scrutinized the papers. The branches, in turn, would contact the customers for additional details or verification of data. The resultant delays in opening accounts frustrated many customers. 'We took a firm stand to bring down the percentage of wrong processing to an acceptable level. It was around 20%, we brought it down to 2%,' Rajan said.

A centralized system is expensive to set up as a bank needs to buy large servers upfront but, in the long run, it's cost-effective as it wouldn't need to add or expand these servers every time it opened a branch. In 1994, telecommunications in India was far from ideal and reliability was always a concern, but Ram's logic was simple: it had to improve; it could not get worse. So he asked the management to place its bets on a centralized system. He convinced them it was the most convenient way to roll out services, and the fastest because the bank wouldn't have to waste time setting up servers at each new branch. That ruled out Infosys' Bancs 2000 software.

Nandan Couldn't Sell the Infosys Software

Nandan Nilekani, then head of marketing and sales at Infosys, came to Vinod at Ramon House to market his product. Nandan and Vinod knew each other reasonably well. Both are from the same community—Chitrapur Saraswat, a community that originally hailed from Kashmir and moved south. There are only about 25,000 of them across the world.

Ram, Vinod and Thakur went to Bangalore at Nandan's invitation. Infosys had just built its campus at Electronic City in Bangalore, India's Silicon Valley. It was listed in 1993 and by 1994 its turnover was ₹30 crore. The company had some very interesting people, hired from the nation's largest lender SBI, to advise it on the features a bank would look for in software. Nandan demonstrated Bancs 2000 to the trio but it did not meet the requirements of HDFC Bank. Plus, it was not centralized.

Nandan eventually became chairman of the Unique Identification Authority of India, the government agency that is assigning digitized and centralized identification numbers to each Indian resident, similar to the social security numbers in the United States. Nandan was CEO and then co-chairman of Infosys before he took up this assignment.

'Infosys didn't get it. And we never got the Infosys account,' Vinod told me.

Ram considered some international systems instead, including Fidelity Information Services' mainframe-based Systematics, though he was clear that in India a company would need a UNIX-based system because support would always be a problem for the mainframes. Mainframe systems were reliable but expensive and the support cost was high as most of the people who were trained in mainframes preferred to go to America, Japan and Germany to work on the systems there. That's where they got their money. HDFC Bank would have had to pay handsomely to retain such people for support services. It would not have been worth it. Ram had first-hand experience of that at Bank of America.

The other issue was that International Business Machines Corporation, commonly called IBM, was the dominant main-frame vendor and it would have been tough for a start-up to deal with it. UNIX was less proprietary and had many vendors.

The bank knew exactly what it was looking for and how to go about it. There was consensus on two critical aspects: the system had to be centralized and had to be based on UNIX, even if that meant spending tonnes of money.

MicroBanker, a fully integrated online banking automation system, developed by Citicorp Information Technology Industries Ltd (Citil), a Citibank subsidiary, fit the bill, but Citil was not willing to deal with HDFC Bank. A small outfit, Citil thought, would not be able to afford the system. Citil was expanding operations in Africa and Europe and was not too keen to sell the software to a start-up Indian bank.

While Citil reluctantly made a presentation on the system, Citibank intervened before a deal could be signed, saying that selling MicroBanker to HDFC Bank could give the Indian bank more muscle as a competitor. Aditya had to call Rajesh Hukku, Citil head, to play ball and he relented. Citil later became i-Flex Solutions Ltd (now Oracle Financial Services Software Ltd).

MicroBanker was designed for corporate clients and had almost nothing for retail banking, except that if someone were to open an account with any branch, however remote, it would show up in real time in the central database. Ram's team had to build the interface for ATMs and Internet banking, and, of course, train colleagues at the industrial shed at Kewal Industrial Estate, often by candlelight.

A great business model, a bunch of talented people and high-end technology made for a cocktail of sure success, but even all these ingredients would not have yielded results had the bank not been cost-conscious.

Vinod drove costs like a miser. For most of his colleagues, especially those coming from multinational banks, it was a shock to be asked why they wanted to stay in a hotel till their flats were ready. He was stingy in allowing senior executives to buy furniture for their flats; he preferred they took furniture on rent. It would take months to get the CFO's nod for even buying curtains.

The same philosophy worked for the bank branches. The first branch was fancy, bejewelled with marble and granite. But the bank realized that customers did not want fancy branches: they expected to transact and get out, with the least hassle. The decorative granite was a sheer waste of money.

HDFC Bank did not really believe in offering customers a banking experience; it just wanted to ensure a fast and efficient transaction—nothing more, nothing less. When one is a start-up operating from rented offices with rented furniture, one can't splurge money, which is why HDFC Bank had its training centre in a *gala* though it had the cash for a better location. This became the bank's culture—'spend less, spend smart'.

'Even on leasing documents [for flats], people used to make fun of me. Cost control is extremely important and we executed it seriously. I used to do interiors of branches at ₹800 per square foot. The equivalent amount spent by Citibank and Grindlays would be at least ₹2,500,' Vinod told me. 'The bank doesn't say "don't spend" but it questions the reason behind every spending. If you need it, you will get it, but give me the cost benefit of doing it.'

'Coffee in Office? Bring Your Mugs'

'There used to be paper cups for tea and coffee. We banned them in 1997. We said each one will have to bring his or her own mug from home. We were probably spending about ₹50 lakh a year on the cups across India. If you don't do it at the initial stage, it will be difficult to curtail costs if you are a large bank with 2,000 branches,' said Sashi, the bank's second CFO.

People did ask why: 'Why are you doing this?' 'Is it such a big thing?' 'You have gone bonkers.' 'You are being penny-wise, pound-foolish.'

'If you do it now with 65,000 people, even if they take four to five cups a day, it is a staggering amount of wasteful expenditure. So we nipped it in the bud,' Sashi says.

There were many such decisions—hard and unpopular. For instance, traditionally, most banks in India offer lunches to all their employees at the end of every fiscal year on 31 March and at the end of every half-year on 31 September. HDFC Bank followed this ritual only for the first couple of years.

The lunches had become a tradition in the Indian banking industry where accounting was done manually and people had to put in extra hours for closing the accounts at the end of September and March. But the fully computerized HDFC Bank didn't require any great effort from its employees for closing the accounts.

Another tradition the bank shunned was presenting calendars, diaries and Christmas and Diwali cards to its customers—not to talk of corporate gifts. Well, not entirely true. Of its twenty-five million customers, a few hundred rich individuals get diaries, if the bank's management approves the budget for it. The bank also does not believe in retreats, annual strategy meets or partying.

Biscuits Banned from Meetings

HDFC Bank even stopped giving biscuits with tea at meetings. The only exception was for board meetings, where biscuits are still served. It also does not offer subsidized lunches at its canteen. Each employee has to pay for the food.

Even senior bankers cannot treat anybody to a round of beer without Aditya's permission. Every liquor bill from across India and across the hierarchy comes to Aditya for clearance. There is no prohibition on liquor but it is the bank's policy to keep a check on the money being spent. Aditya has the last word on any foreign travel too.

After Vinod retired, the person who drives the cost-control exercise is Sashi. In this role, Sashi often has professional skirmishes with Jaggia, head of the largest cost centre in the bank—information technology. After years of resistance, Sashi allowed the use of BlackBerrys in late 2008, provided employees bought the BlackBerry device at their own cost. The monthly usage charge for each employee, even for official use, is capped. Before the BlackBerry days, employees were all given a cheap Samsung mobile handset and the monthly charges were capped under a corporate plan.

A firm believer in practising what he preaches, Sashi is

most spartan with spending in his own department. One of his team members, Saurabh Jambhekar, had to celebrate a tenth birthday party for his calculator before Sashi yielded and permitted him to replace it.

On 14 January 2011, Saurabh sent this e-mail to some of his colleagues:

On this day, exactly 10 years ago, I was delivered the Thakral Casio, the calculator that cost some Rs 1000. Sashi's reaction then was nothing short of sensational for a newcomer. Purchase of calculators was banned by Fincon [read: financial control unit] from then on, for several years, and that's now part of Fincon folklore. Poor Mr [Deepak] Majithia had to bear with the PC-based adding software for several years, until he managed to pick up one on the sly from some unsuspecting team member's desk.

Over the years, my calculator has travelled to various offices before coming back to Bank House…I have never managed to lose it and it remains one of my prized artefacts…

Please join me in wishing my Thakral Casio a happy birthday.

Sashi seamlessly took over the CFO's role when Vinod retired and masterminded the transformation of Fincon into the bank's nerve centre and the vital driver of the bank's MIS-based performance monitoring system, MIS referring to the 'management information system'. The Fincon team works closely with each business group or support function and tracks hundreds of operational and financial parameters. Business managers know that, through Sashi and his team, Aditya would have as much if not more insight into the nitty-gritty of their businesses as they themselves do.

Samir narrated one incident to illustrate Aditya's policy on spending the bank's money. In 1996, when the bank was hardly a year old, Sealand Services Inc., a shipping company, invited it to Dubai for a meeting to bid for managing its cash. HDFC Bank was among those on the short list.

Cash management is nothing but collecting the cheques that a company's customers give the company, drawn on various locations. A bank needs to find ways to clear the cheques without delays.

Aditya decided to go to Dubai for the meeting and asked Goretti to book economy class tickets for the team—Aditya, Samir and Rajan. HDFC Bank tied up with the Mangalore-based Corporation Bank for the cash management service, which was then driven by a general manager, M. Narendra, who went on to become the chairman of Indian Overseas Bank.

On the plane, a passenger, a blue-collar Keralite employed in Dubai and seated in front of Aditya, kept pushing his seat back while Aditya was trying to have his in-flight meal. Samir called the steward and asked him to tell the person in front to be a little cooperative as a fellow passenger was being inconvenienced. The steward said such things happened during flights and asked Aditya to try the airline's business class the next time he was flying.

'Even though we've been called, I don't think we are going to get the deal. There's no point in wasting money,' Aditya told Samir. 'We are a start-up, let's behave like a start-up.' For the record, HDFC Bank did not get the deal.

Anand Dusane, a senior vice president at HDFC Bank and its regional head of wholesale banking in Pune, has another story. When the bank began its currency chest operations, it ordered chairs without handles! Its logic? When a person counts notes, he or she would have both hands on the table. When one doesn't need something, why buy it?

For the employees of HDFC Bank, the culture of cost-consciousness begins in the bank and percolates down to their families. A young owner of a ten-acre mango orchard once applied for a job with the bank. He didn't get the job but got an order for 200 dozen Alfonso mangoes from the bank's Pune branch.

The employees paid half of what they would have paid in the market because of the economics of bulk buying. Employees of the Pune branch still apply the practice when buying apples, pomegranates and even rice so they can cut costs by exercising their collective bargaining power.

Chapter 5

Business Before the Shop Opens

HDFC Bank's first corporate customer was the German electronics company Siemens. The bank landed the borrower even before it received its licence. Siemens issued a letter to HDFC Bank committing to induct it in its consortium of lenders. Siemens' CFO Mahesh Priolkar knew Aditya's team well, particularly Harish. The company had banking relationships with both Bank of America and Citibank, the two foreign banks from where the start-up bank got most of its employees. Harish, in fact, showed the Siemens letter to Samir to impress him about the bank while trying to hire him.

Getting a customer before a bank is set up is no joke. The news got around and prompted quite a few other customers to approach the bank. Pudumjee Pulp & Paper Mills Ltd was one of them. The company wanted money. The bank grabbed the opportunity even before it formally opened its doors to customers. It could not give a loan without a banking licence;

so it gave money to Pudumjee Pulp in the form of an inter-corporate deposit—a smart way of using the initial capital that was lying idle.

The entity was then registered as a company under the Companies Act and was not governed by the Banking Regulation Act. So an inter-corporate deposit was legitimate. It placed such a deposit of ₹2 crore with Pudumjee Pulp, a small sum now but not in those days.

Deepak began exploring ways to get deposits for the bank. He started tapping the wealthy Indian diaspora in Singapore, Malaysia and China. Satpal Khattar, who later became the chairman of Khattar Holding Pte Ltd in Singapore, was one of them. Deepak's classmate Deepak Vaidya, who was then heading Schroders Capital Partners Ltd in India, knew Satpal well from his days with Schroders in Singapore. Vaidya arranged a meeting between Deepak and Satpal in Mumbai. At the meeting, Deepak unfolded his vision for the bank, and Satpal laid out his business plan and an interesting past.

When Partition happened, Satpal and his sister, born in the small town of Behra in Pakistan, found their way out of the country in a cargo plane to Ambala in Haryana, where their uncle stayed. Satpal's father and grandmother walked across the border and boarded a train to Ambala. Satpal did not even know whether his father had survived the traumatic Partition. Soon after the grand union of three generations, in February 1949, his father moved to Singapore to start a business.

Khattar Holding is a family investment holding company that has operations in the United Kingdom and investments in India, Europe, Vietnam and Indonesia. Satpal is a lawyer by profession and had founded Khattar Wong & Partners, a law firm in Singapore.

Satpal gave HDFC Bank a $20 million deposit for three years.

Deepak also offered him shares of the bank worth $4 million. A part of the public issue, around 5%, was kept for NRI investors.

'I sounded out a few banks for a loan which I could use to keep the deposits but no one was willing as HDFC Bank was not known in Singapore. I put my own money both for the equity and the loan,' Satpal told me over the telephone from Singapore.

Singh, then finance minister, conveyed a message to Satpal—that his investment would be approved only if it was made from Singapore and not via Mauritius. Satpal agreed. He retained his shares in a Singapore holding company right through even though opportunities did crop up later to reduce tax by transferring the money to Mauritius. He also invested in Centurion Bank of Punjab (Centurion BoP), which incidentally later merged with HDFC Bank.

And Quiet Flowed the Money

After the first branch was opened, many companies came to HDFC Bank to keep their monies in bulk. Thakur recollects that one company wanted to keep with it a deposit of ₹33 crore. But the bank would not take the deposit as the officials of the company, which Thakur declined to name, wanted a commission.

On another occasion, a broker approached Thakur with an offer to deposit ₹20 crore from a clutch of companies. This time too the bank would not accept the deposit as it entailed giving a commission and paying commission for deposits is not permissible by the banking regulator. 'If you pay commission, the average cost of money goes up and the interest margin shrinks. If you want to maintain the margin, then you can't lend to triple-A-rated companies,' Thakur said.

Besides, there was an accounting issue. How would a bank show the commissions in its books?

There are ways to skirt such hurdles. One way is for a bank to take, say, ₹10 crore from one depositor and have a back-to-back arrangement with a borrower who will take the money as credit at a relatively lower interest rate, and pay a commission to the depositor. It's not an unusual practice in the Indian banking industry but it affects a bank's interest income as the borrower, who passes on the commission to the depositor on behalf of the bank, pays a smaller interest.

The only benefit a bank will get from this is that such a deal will prop up its business and build its balance sheet. The industry's obsession in those days was not profitability but a big balance sheet. For some banks, it's true even now. Towards the end of every financial year, in March, typically, a bank may get money from a company in the form of deposits and the money may, in no time, travel to the company's group firms as credit. Nobody can catch a bank for this circular trading as money is fungible. How does one prove the same fund is used for giving loans? After all, the colour of money is the same. Besides, entities at both ends may not necessarily be the same firm—they could be two separate firms from the same group.

In the first year of its operations, HDFC Bank, which was actually a mere two and a half months old, recorded a deposit base of ₹642 crore, advances of ₹98 crore, investments of ₹221 crore and a profit of ₹80.20 lakh, after paying tax of ₹40.60 lakh. There was not much business to talk about and hence its first annual report spoke about the four core values the bank stood for—operational excellence, customer focus, product leadership and professional people. The report tried to tell shareholders and investors what the bank stood for rather than what it had done, as very little had been achieved so far.

Many employees of HDFC Bank came from foreign banks. For them, the first general meeting at Birla Matoshree Sabhagriha in Mumbai was quite an experience. Shareholders asked for good tea–coffee and bonus shares.

Leave Money on the Table

HDFC Bank was the first of the private lenders to go public— even before it completed a full year. 'It was a mistake,' Deepak told me. The RBI required the new banks to go public within a year but all other lenders went back to the regulator and got extensions. 'We didn't ask for it. We were too naïve,' Deepak said. 'Everybody took time as they wanted to get a premium. We sold at par, ₹10. But I have no regrets.'

Deepak pushed for a par issue as the bank had nothing to show.

And the disaster of parent HDFC's listing was still haunting him, though that had happened a decade and a half ago. In 1978, India's capital market was in a different shape and mortgage was a new product, not understood by many. HDFC put the photograph of its first borrower on the cover of its balance sheet, a D. B. Remedios from Thane, who took a loan of ₹35,000 to build his house.

The public issue of HDFC bombed. In an initial public offering (IPO) of ₹10 crore, the face value of one share was ₹100. ICICI, IFC (Washington) and the Aga Khan Fund took 5% stakes each in the mortgage lender and the balance 85% equity was offered to the public, but there were few takers. The stock quoted at a steep discount on listing.

For the bank, Deepak did not want to take any chance. So portions of the issue were reserved for the shareholders and employees of HDFC as well as the bank's employees. HDFC decided to own close to a 26% stake in the bank and NatWest 20%. Satpal was offered about 5% and the public 25%. The size of the public issue was ₹50 crore.

'We didn't know whether it would succeed. Our experience with HDFC had been a disaster,' Deepak said.

But Deepak had grossly underestimated investors' appetite for the new bank. The issue, which opened on 14 March 1995, was subscribed a record fifty-five times. The stock was listed on the Bombay Stock Exchange (now known as BSE Ltd) on 26 May that year at ₹39.95, almost at a 300% premium. The listing process was long and arduous in those days.

Any HDFC shareholder owning between one and ten shares was offered a hundred shares of the bank. Those holding between eleven and twenty shares were offered 200 shares in the bank. A maximum of 500 HDFC Bank shares were offered to those owning forty-one or more shares in the mortgage lender. This was to benefit small shareholders.

Investors in those days used to hold shares in a physical format and not in the dematerialized form that depositories hold now on behalf of the shareholders. And the shares were held in folios. One shareholder from Ahmedabad had split his seven shares into seven folios and applied for 700 shares under seven different names. He was caught just before the share certificates were issued.

This shareholder became a regular at every annual general meeting of the bank and HDFC after that, demanding the removal of Aditya and Deepak. HDFC filed a criminal case against him some years ago.

The track record concept didn't exist then. And there was no road show. A public issue was more about distribution of application forms. The bank heavily focused on its strategic partner NatWest's technology, customer relationships and international reach to sell the issue.

'A lot of us asked why we weren't pricing it at a premium. We could have got a premium but Deepak said, "leave money on the table for investors. They will appreciate this in the long term." Today, when we have arguments with our promoters, one of the big lessons I learnt from our float is to price an IPO cheap,' Luis said.

'Should we really scalp the shareholders? This is a

start-up company. On what basis are we putting valuations? Today they will put a valuation even on a start-up idea,' Satwalekar was blunt in his assessment.

Abhay, who heads wealth management and private banking in HDFC Bank, has a slightly different take on the IPO. 'People had said ₹20, ₹30, even a ₹40 premium was fine. I asked Deepak, "Shouldn't you quote at least ₹20 when the grey market is offering ₹30?" In those days and even today, I think our bank stock enjoys the highest multiple in Asia. By and large, everything has gone our way: 20% by default and 80% by design.'

By the end of its first full year of operations, in the fiscal year 1996, the bank had 203 employees on its rolls and branches in Chennai, Delhi, Kolkata (then Calcutta), Bangalore and Pune, besides Mumbai. It had 50 corporate clients, at least 19,000 deposit accounts, and was adding 2,500 accounts every month.

Liquidity Crisis

The growth could not have been faster as the Indian banking system was struggling with a severe liquidity crisis. There was no money in the system; companies kept knocking on banks' doors but their vaults were empty, and interest rates had skyrocketed. C. Rangarajan, then RBI governor, and S. S. Tarapore, deputy governor, jacked up the interest rates and raised the reserve requirement for banks to fight a persistently high inflation. For instance, CRR, or the portion of deposits that commercial banks need to keep with the RBI, was 15% in 1995 and SLR, or the banks' compulsory investment in government bonds, was 38%. So, the banks were left with very little money to give loans to companies (retail loans almost didn't exist then). Many blamed the RBI's tight money policy for the slowing economic growth that followed and the piling of bad assets at banks as many companies lost their ability to pay back. Large-scale loan restructuring followed in steel and a few other sectors by the end of the century.

Samir Arora of Helios Capital Management Pte Ltd, who was then heading Alliance Capital Asset Management (India) Pvt. Ltd, owns HDFC Bank stock from day one. It has all along been his No. 1 holding.

His investment theory was simple. In any business where the public sector competes with the private sector, the private sector will win. State-owned banks had the strength of distribution but not service; multinational banks had service but they were not allowed to open branches. So, a private company that used the working model of a foreign bank but was free of the constraints of public sector banks in terms of unionized employees and government interference would succeed, he reasoned.

HDFC Bank is a prime example of this thesis.

Alliance Capital began its India operations in February 1995, just a month before HDFC Bank's IPO. Arora used the asset management company's capital to buy HDFC Bank shares, which he was not supposed to do. When he was told that, he decided to buy back the shares himself. He even made a rule that the company's capital will not be put in stocks and will not compete with other funds run by the asset management company.

He was running a fund of ₹80 crore and put around ₹10 crore in the HDFC Bank IPO. Because of the oversubscription, he got much less though. 'Till now we are holding the stock and have continuously been adding . . .' he says. Personally, he owns a few thousand shares since 1995.

Hemendra Kothari, one of the famed three Ks of Indian investment banking—the other two being (Nimesh) Kampani and (Uday) Kotak—said investors were convinced of HDFC Bank's business plan.

'Aditya is credible. He performs what he promises. He even over-performs many a time. In difficult times, he knows how to manage the risks by staying away from risks,' Hemendra said. He is liberal in his praise even though he doesn't like Aditya's hard bargaining with investment bankers to cut down their fees.

DSP Financial Consultants Ltd of Hemendra-bhai, as he is addressed in the investment banking circles, and Ind Global Financial Trust Ltd were the lead managers for the float. They earned a fee of 0.5% of the issue. The overall expense for the lead managers, registrar, brokers and listing fees was ₹4.25 crore.

Hemendra was also present at the New York Stock Exchange (NYSE) in July 2001 when HDFC Bank's American depositary shares (ADS) were listed. He remembers Aditya making road shows from morning till night, covering more than a couple of cities a day, catching flights and meeting people and telling them the bank's story with a lot of passion.

By that time, the new private banks in India were six years old and had captured at least 5% of the market share, in terms of assets and deposit liabilities, but still less than the foreign banks' market share and even that of old private banks. The state-run banking industry's share dropped—close to 78% of the assets and 79% of the deposits.

On 20 July 2001, HDFC Bank made its $150 million global offering, the second Indian bank to do so after the country's largest private lender ICICI Bank in March 2000. The bank opted for ADS to reach a wider investor base for comparatively inexpensive capital. Each ADS, representing three underlying shares, was priced at $13.83, the average trading price of HDFC Bank's underlying shares in India in the previous ten days. On the day of the ADS listing, the bank's Indian shares closed at ₹225 apiece on the BSE.

We Need Capital for Growth

Sashi, who rose to be HDFC Bank's CFO, remembers every detail of the six-month-long process that began in January 2001 with Aditya meeting a battery of lawyers. 'We were growing very fast. So we needed capital. The markets were buoyant and investment bankers told us there were lots of investors in other markets who would love to buy our stock. We also wanted to diversify our shareholding,' he said.

To comply with the strict regulations of the US Securities and Exchange Commission, the core group of Sashi, Vinod,

Paresh and a few others had to work long hours every day with the lawyers, accountants and investment bankers. An essential prerequisite for an ADS is compliance with the generally accepted accounting principles in the United States (US GAAP).

'We were all scared. "Will our profits be lower in the US GAAP than in the Indian GAAP?" That was kind of a conservatism that we had. In reality, however, our profits in the US GAAP were higher than those in the Indian GAAP,' Sashi recollects.

In the Indian accounting system, when a borrower is unable to pay interest or principal for three months, the account is deemed to have turned bad and the bank needs to set aside money to provide for it. Was HDFC Bank making adequate provisions? In the US GAAP, one needs to know a company's forecast on its expected cash flow, collateral and the present value of that. Net of that is what a bank has to provide for. There is a science behind provisioning. But the Indian norms are a bit different.

'We realized that we were slightly more conservative in the Indian accounting framework. We had to sort of write-back some of the provisions in the US framework. Our profits were slightly more in the US GAAP,' Sashi said.

The US Securities and Exchange Commission is a tough regulator. It goes through every document with a fine-tooth comb. Every claim in an offer document has to have supporting evidence and one cannot make a forward-looking statement. If one does, the Commission will ask a company to explain why.

This rules out loose claims such as 'we are the best Indian

bank'. One needs to explain why one is the best. Also, one has to be precise when one talks about the numbers—whether for ATMs, branches or customers. An NYSE listing teaches a company to be precise and moderate in the use of language. It cannot be pompous and make aggressive, forward-looking statements without substantiating them.

HDFC Bank's ADS issue was subscribed many times over and everybody who put in money couldn't get as many shares as they wanted. Book building of an overseas issue in those days was primarily the decision of the book runners. But Aditya didn't allow Merrill Lynch and Co. and Morgan Stanley, the book runners for ADS, to decide who will get the shares and who won't. For him, public issues were not about getting money alone but about acquiring long-term loyal investors; however, unlike local shares, ADS don't give voting rights to the holders.

'I want to make it very clear. The people who supported us should be given fair amounts. I don't want you to come with your list,' he told the book runners.

'There was a firmness in his tone. It's the first time I saw him outside the office. He didn't mince words,' Sashi recalls. The team went through the list, name by name, and ensured adequate allocation for those who had been supporting the bank.

Along with Hemendra, Nimesh, Deepak, Aditya, Paresh, Sashi and a few others, Anil Ahuja was also present on the NYSE trading floor. He was on the bank's board representing Chase Capital Partners, a private equity company that had bought a 15% stake in HDFC Bank from NatWest when the UK bank got out.

'All of us in the room were saying, "show us the book. Who gave the order? Somebody must give us the book so that we can do proper distribution to everybody. We are already a listed company. We already have shareholders, long-term holders of the stock." We didn't want hedge funds coming in. We needed some quality investors but the lead managers were interested in their own global relationships,' Anil recalls.

An ex-Citibanker, Anil had worked with Aditya, Paresh, Samir, Shailendra and Abhay. He had left Citibank to join Chase Capital in early 1997.

At around two in the morning, Morgan Stanley and Merrill Lynch executives told Aditya and his team to go to sleep and that they would finalize the list. Aditya left reluctantly but not before giving them Anil's mobile phone number (Aditya didn't carry a mobile phone and still refuses to have one). 'Whenever you are ready with the list, you call us; we will come back. We will do the allotment,' Aditya told the book runners.

'They were very keen to give it to whoever they wanted to rather than to the bank's key relationships, but Aditya didn't let that happen,' Anil told me.

Anil and Paresh oversaw the allocation process. The pricing was already done but they wanted to close the exercise as early as possible as news started trickling down on the Central Bureau of Investigation raids at the residence of P. S. Subramanyam, former chairman of India's largest mutual fund UTI, and a few other top officials of the fund, for alleged corruption in private placement of funds.

Anything Can Happen over Golf

In 1997, there was a golf tournament organized by ABN AMRO at the Bombay Presidency Golf Club Ltd in Chembur, a central suburb of Mumbai. Aditya and Anil were playing. Anil did not find Aditya his usual self. Something was bothering him.

That was when NatWest wanted to get out of HDFC Bank after the three-year lock-in period. Aditya was worried that NatWest's 20% block could effectively get dumped into the market and push the stock price down.

Over golf, he shared his concerns with Anil. The private equity investor's reaction was atypical: Here's an opportunity to partner with one of the finest banks in the country. 'Fine, why don't we do something?'

With Aditya's nod, Anil started negotiating with Christopher Fitzgerald, general counsel for NatWest, based in London—sort of the chief operating officer, pretty much the top guy, but not the business head. Christopher was looking after legal and regulatory issues.

It was almost a year before the deal was struck. When the discussions started, the trigger for an open offer in India was 10%, but by the time the negotiations got closer to completion, India's capital market regulator had raised it to 15%. (The trigger was subsequently raised to 25% in 2012.) Chase Capital could buy close to 15%. Had it opted to buy more, an open offer would have been necessary.

By 2005, when Chase Capital completely exited HDFC Bank through three block deals over the previous years, the bank's market capitalization was about $3.9 billion. When Chase Capital entered, it was about $250 million. Anil had made his killing.

'As a private equity investor, I do well if the people I partner with do very well. It's a question of alignment of interest. How do you retain somebody like Aditya Puri? After many years even when I resigned from the board his salary was ₹21 lakh; his bonus would never get approved as the RBI had some limits about how much bonus a bank's CEO could get. How would you retain people?' Anil asked.

Anil was on the bank's board for six years, between 1999 and 2005. He was the chairman of the risk management committee of the board and a member as well as chairman of the compensation and the audit and compliance committees in rotation.

'A team of less than half a dozen people can change the culture of the whole organization and drive the business strategy. What's important is that the core team is retained and aligned to make sure that shareholder value is created,' says Anil, who went on to head the Asia operations of the London-based 3i Group.

As a shareholder, Anil's objective was to grow the bank's share price ten times so his investors could make money. All that mattered was how many dollars one put in and how many one took out. He knew the bank could only do well if the top team was retained and motivated.

Policies and stock options that were implemented in HDFC Bank, Anil believed, were by far the best in the market. 'Look at the stock options that were granted. Mind-boggling numbers . . . This is not easy to pass through the board as a number of members come from government and quasi-government bodies.'

'If you lose Aditya Puri, you lose a big chunk of the market cap of the bank in one day. Today Aditya has crossed the age of sixty; at that time he was fifty and there were too many takers for him.'

Anil was thirty-six years old when he got on the board.

Chapter 6

Doing Ordinary Things in Extraordinary Ways

A ditya wanted a free hand to run the bank. The others were allowed to express their views but he was clear there could be only one boss and that was he. He made that clear to Deepak as well. A gentleman to the core, Deepak kept his word. He was always there for advice and guidance, if sought, but never interfered.

Once the team was in place, Aditya explained to his colleagues how they would create a bank to match the best of global parameters. 'If we can put together the products and services of foreign banks and the relationships, funding and distribution of the nationalized banks, nothing should be able to stop us,' he told them.

Each member of the core team was given the freedom to hire his own staff. They would sit down as a team and define the vision—the target market, technology and products. The initial focus was not on retail but on corporate banking because the cost of setting it up was lower and any loss they might incur would be smaller.

The bank decided to deal first only with triple-A-rated companies. The team had the contacts. They could develop products and services specific to companies, on the basis of their experiences at HSBC, Bank of America and Citibank. Efforts were focused on making these better than what was available in the market, across transaction banking, foreign exchange, bill discounting and supply chain management through multiple delivery channels. But funding, at least initially, had to come from retail.

So the bank needed to open branches and then go full-fledged into retail to reflect the composition of the Indian economy—consumption, investment and government expenditure. Domestic consumption, which plays a major role in the Indian economy, was around 55% at the time. One could not afford to ignore the consumer.

As the plan was to start with the triple-A-rated companies, the bank needed to cater to their finance and cash management needs, and manage their business dealings and foreign exchange. The target companies were the so-called blue chips that were highly profitable with a good volume of business and not companies with high market capitalization, as value in the market can always be drummed up even if a company is not fundamentally strong.

HDFC Bank could meet their needs as it had the right technology—an open system that had the flexibility to introduce products faster in alignment with cheaper, centralized processing and distributed servicing.

The architecture had multiple delivery channels, such as the telephone, ATMs and the Internet, besides the branches, to ensure the efficiency of the operating systems. Credit and risk were to be handled separately.

This was the broad vision Aditya had sketched in Malaysia. All members of the core team contributed their expertise and experience to flesh out the main idea. 'Our aim was to focus on consumer satisfaction and have a professional, transparent and fair organization to work in and be associated with, whether one was a shareholder, investor or an employee,' Aditya says.

After economic liberalization, competition just started in certain segments with the ring of protection being slowly withdrawn. Companies would take loans from Indian banks but seek letters of credit and guarantees, cash management, treasury products and foreign exchange from foreign banks. That was the mix of business for most corporate treasurers.

HDFC Bank was positioned right in the middle. It was an Indian bank—it understood the environment, was adequately capitalized and, over a period, had enough rupee funding capability. At the same time, in terms of product range, technology, quality of people and turnaround times, it could offer most of the things that a foreign bank could offer in the Indian market. And at a lower cost too.

The CFOs of large companies could always get money by making just one phone call to banks. 'What will you give me that others don't?' they would typically ask.

So it was important for HDFC Bank, which was crawling then, to convince the CFOs that the baby in the woods too could provide them what the existing banks offered, and more efficiently, quickly and at competitive prices.

A good brand, relationships, technology and smart marketing can open doors but after that the business has to be sustained by delivery. Many companies had their doubts about HDFC Bank's capability on that front. They liked the product roll-out, competitive pricing and advanced technology, but worried if it could deliver. Paresh remembers how a multinational engineering company in South India shooed him out. 'You have highs and lows after every call. Many a time we waited long to be told politely to come back another day. This was one occasion when it wasn't graciously done,' Paresh says.

Siemens was the first corporate client. Slowly, the Ambanis (the group was undivided then), the Tatas, the Birlas, TVS and other industrial houses came forward. Given the pedigree of the team and its vision, they all promised to help the bank in its teething stages.

The bank was also choosy in picking customers. There was pressure on it as other banks not only were growing faster, as they chased relatively smaller firms who could give high rates, but also were less demanding. Aditya worked hard on marketing. When he approached B. M. Munjal, the patriarch of the Hero Group, the consortium of banks associated with the group protested. But Munjal remembered how Aditya, while at Citibank, had been the only banker to lend to him when he launched Hero Honda. He wanted to return the favour.

'They all backed me up and told me that I would not have to return empty-handed. I was assured of a place in the consortium within a couple of years,' Aditya said.

The team's contacts in the corporate world were extensive. Aditya, Harish, Samir, Paresh and Rajan managed to push through quite a few deals. In their presentations, they emphasized that they did not want any privileges based on pure relationship. They would offer products better than what the companies already had. Only then should the companies sign on the bank.

Initially, they made several cold calls, informing potential customers of the birth of the bank and how they planned to proceed with its road map. After the second call, they went with a product line.

One such product was broker financing. The bank, the broker and the stock exchanges created their own closed group to deal online.

Similarly, the bank suggested to Asian Paints Ltd and ADB Ltd that they could have their vendors online with the bank and it would offer them loans at a relatively cheaper rate. For Tata Motors Ltd, it drew up a complete supply chain. Each of these solutions helped HDFC Bank grow.

Ishaat Hussain, a director on the board of Tata Capital Ltd, said that big industrial houses like the Tatas and the Birlas do not face any difficulty in accessing bank finance, but their customers and suppliers find it difficult. HDFC Bank grabbed that important niche. It became a pioneer in vendor and dealer financing.

'Tata Capital used to consider this its preserve. Being a Tata company, it felt that it should be the natural owner of this market—financing the vendors of Tata Motors, Tata Steel, Titan Industries and Tata Chemicals. But HDFC Bank got a larger share through aggression and innovation,' Ishaat told me.

Conglomerates such as the Tatas look for two things from their bankers: One, the transaction should be smooth and fast; and, two, the bank should respond to their monetary requirements quickly. 'There should a bond between a banker and a borrower. I want a bank on which I can rely upon and which should be ready to help and give money in times of difficulty,' Ishaat said.

So if the Tata Group were to get a banking licence, would HDFC Bank be its role model?

'Yes, most definitely. You cannot be a copycat. But certainly, it would be my model,' Ishaat said.

HDFC Bank figured out the needs of the customer in the existing inefficient payment system: a good transactional banking facility—collection, payment—and an MIS. Citibank was offering such products but HDFC Bank wanted to upgrade the quality. In his Citibank days, Aditya had sub-contracted certain products to Corporation Bank, a smart public sector bank that was ahead of its peers in many niche areas, but HDFC Bank intended to design a better system in terms of reach, MIS and cost.

It developed a suite of products for companies to cover their receivables, products for financing vendors, advice on treasury and multi-channel banking. A meticulous product plan, the pull of the HDFC brand and aggressive marketing did the trick. Every day the bankers would call on ten customers. If any company asked them to call a day later, the team would do it yesterday.

Aditya would call; Harish would call; Paresh would call; Samir would call. They would be in Mumbai in the morning,

Pune in the afternoon and Chennai the next morning. Clients always wanted to deal with one of the top executives personally. A senior banker would take the local representative with him to meet the customers. After that, the local recruit could handle the delivery.

A Peaceful Night's Sleep

Harish had a reputation of delivering what he promised. Almost every customer he had worked with while at Bank of America came to HDFC Bank. As a corporate banker, Harish's philosophy is quite simple—to sleep peacefully at night. 'We went for top-end corporates. We didn't get a good price but the portfolio was top-notch. The spread was low and profit marginal, but that was a defined policy. We didn't want to lose sleep over bad assets.'

'Don't bullshit your customers. They will figure it out soon. Tell them what you can do and also what you cannot. So they do not have false expectations,' Harish says.

'Everybody has pain. Advise them on how to alleviate pain. We didn't charge extra for that. It's free advisory. Just to convince them that we aren't taking advantage of their weakness,' Harish used to tell his team.

After settling in Mumbai, the bank headed to Chennai. Harish had worked in the southern city for ten months at Bank of America. He knew almost every industrialist in Chennai, Hyderabad and Bangalore—A. C. Muthiah and the bosses of

Ashok Leyland Ltd, TVS Group and TI Group.

The next stop was Delhi. Aditya had worked there and knew a host of potential top customers. In Kolkata, Samudra Sen, a young IIM-A graduate, hired from Arthur Andersen LLP, quickly built relationships with ITC Ltd, Coal India Ltd and other local companies.

Partha S. Bhattacharyya, who later became the chairman of Coal India and took it to the market, was a junior officer then. Harish called him and sought a meeting to introduce the bank. Coal India was at the time banking with SBI. Partha, then assistant manager for finance, told Harish that SBI could perhaps give ₹10 crore of its share to HDFC Bank out of a total exposure of ₹500 crore.

Quick research revealed that Coal India had an accumulated loss of ₹4,000 crore. Paresh, who was heading risk management, was against doing business with a loss-making company. But Harish's argument was that the Union Government owned the company, which was also a core sector operator, and so it would not allow it to fail. It took enormous effort, including a joint meeting with the company top brass by Paresh and Harish, to convince Paresh and Aditya. HDFC Bank's exposure to Coal India was ₹700 crore at its peak.

D. D. Rathi, director of Grasim Industries Ltd and Ultratech Cement Ltd, Aditya Birla Group companies, likes the speed with which HDFC Bank operates. 'I needed an extra limit of ₹150 crore. It was an overnight affair and I wanted complete secrecy. I called Harish in the evening after banking hours and asked for the money. It was done the next day,' Rathi recalls.

Rathi's office was in the same building—Sakher Bhavan at

Nariman Point, Mumbai—that Aditya, wearing a half-sleeved shirt and a tie, used to operate from while at Citibank for many days.

'Those were tough days for a new bank as the big brothers wouldn't allow anyone to enter the consortium. One day, fifteen years ago, [Aditya] Puri called me and asked for a ₹2.5-crore limit in my company. I agreed,' Rathi recalls. After that, Aditya would quietly go to Industry House, then the headquarters of the Aditya Birla Group, have lunch with the executives and get a ₹2.5-crore limit from every group company. In those days, HDFC Bank was in the bottom twenty in the consortium for Grasim Industries; today, it's in the top tier.

HDFC Bank also opened an extension counter at the Aditya Birla Centre in Worli, the group's headquarters now where at least 400 employees work.

Transactional Banking Is No Great Science

The bank started its capital market infrastructure business a few years after it was set up. The period was seeing a determined shift in behaviour from savings to investments and the opening up of huge potential in the investment banking and mutual fund businesses. 'Since we were getting the banking business on the ground, we figured that rather than getting into businesses that will dissipate our energy and take time to build expertise and scale, there was a need for somebody to provide very reliable, efficient and low-cost banking and transactional services to all these participants in the growing capital market space,' Paresh said.

What kinds of businesses were required? Collection of money and applications for IPOs and new fund offers by mutual funds. Whenever money is invested, there is an array of businesses—the entire application process, refunds, custody (as shares and bonds have to be managed), and the clearing and settlement business.

'We identified some of the clear inefficiencies and risks in the way these things were being done. We developed a structure and backed it with appropriate technology which substantially mitigated those risks because of the collapse of time and better information flow,' Paresh says.

There is very rapid flow of a large amount of money in the clearing and settlement business. It could be just for a day, but over time a continuous flow creates a steady stream of free money.

The transactional banking business, such as cash management and clearing and settlement in stock exchanges, is no great science. Corporation Bank was Citibank's correspondent bank for cash management. There were a few others who had launched cash management. New private banks, particularly HDFC Bank, could offer cash management because the basic configuration was centralized processing and distributed servicing, and all its branches were linked online in real time. They had supplemented the movement of money with MIS and integrated this with the customers' systems.

Cash management is all about managing the cash flow between a company and its suppliers.

For example, a Mumbai-based company selling its products

across India gets a payment as a cheque drawn on some bank's branch in Ludhiana, Punjab. When the Mumbai company deposits the cheque in its account, the cheque goes back to Ludhiana for clearing and the money could take up to a week to be credited.

In a cash management system, the company deposits the cheque with the bank's branch or a partner bank in Ludhiana and gets the money almost immediately. The bank either charges a commission or gets to keep the money for a day or two.

Today, HDFC Bank is the market leader in transactional banking services. A lot of transactional banking services involve movement of money and this is probably why it has the cheapest rate of funding among all banks. Clearing, cash managements, payment of dividends, tax collections and anything that involves processing high-volume transactions is transactional business. It was not a new business, but what HDFC Bank did was recognize transactional banking as a huge opportunity, give it the right focus and scale it across products and geographies.

Plain vanilla cash management was developed into value-added supply chain management solutions. Wherever there were inefficiencies in the system, the bank tried to address them through its products.

Of NIM and CASA

The raw material for a banking business is the money savers keep with a bank in the form of deposits. The challenge before all banks is to keep the cost of deposits low and the net interest margin (NIM) high.

NIM and spread are the two key parameters that give an indication of a bank's operational efficiency. As a concept, NIM and spread are similar, but there is a subtle difference between the two. While NIM is arrived at by dividing a bank's net interest income by its average interest-earning assets, spread is the margin between the yield on assets and the cost of liabilities, or the difference between interest income and interest expense as a percentage of assets. NIM can be higher or lower than the net interest spread.

When a bank cuts its loan rate, its interest income declines, and if it is not able to cut its deposit rates by an identical margin, its NIM gets affected.

Normally, when interest rates rise, banks hurry to raise their loan rates but are slow in offering higher interest to depositors. Conversely, when the rates fall, banks are quick to cut their deposit rates but take time in passing on the benefit to borrowers.

There is a reason behind this. The impact of any hike or cut in loan rates is felt immediately as a bank's entire loan book is re-priced, but that's not the case with deposits as the new rates are applicable only when the existing deposits mature or new deposits flow in.

CASA plays an important role in lowering the cost of

deposits. The 'CA' of CASA stands for 'current account', primarily meant for companies, public enterprises and entrepreneurs who perform numerous banking transactions daily. Such accounts are cheque-operated and a customer can deposit or withdraw any amount of money any number of times. Banks generally insist on a higher minimum balance to be maintained in a current account. As the balances maintained in the account are often very volatile, banks generally levy a certain service charge for operating a current account. The money kept in such accounts comes free to a bank as no interest is paid on current accounts.

A savings account, or the 'SA' of CASA, is the most common operating account for individuals and others for non-commercial transactions. Banks generally limit the number of withdrawals an account holder can make, and also specify a minimum average balance. Till 2011, the interest on savings accounts was regulated. Even after deregulation, most banks, including HDFC Bank, are offering 4%, which was the last rate in the regulated regime. Every bank wants to increase its CASA, as a higher portion of CASA in the overall deposit liability brings down its cost of money.

Among private lenders, HDFC Bank, ICICI Bank and Axis Bank have high CASA ratios. Among public sector banks, the CASA ratios of SBI and Punjab National Bank (PNB) are high.

The credit for coining the acronym CASA—which every analyst now swears by—can possibly be attributed to HDFC Bank. Every internal presentation of HDFC Bank made since 1995 talks about CASA. But this is only one contributing factor to low-cost money. Even in non-CASA term deposits, one should have a higher proportion of retail than the high-cost certificate of deposits and bulk deposits. Small deposits are granular, stable and less price-sensitive.

A high NIM alone cannot make a bank profitable as operating expenses and credit costs, including provisions for bad assets and write-offs, can erode a substantial portion of NIM. Banks also need to cut their operating costs and increase efficiency. They can remain profitable even when NIM shrinks, provided they start generating more fee income.

Transactional banking was the key to HDFC Bank's business model initially because a bank typically does not get current and savings accounts on the basis of price but on the basis of other aspects that differentiate one lender from the other. This could be the strength of the brand or the distribution network or customer service or even product range.

A smart bank tries to ensure that a customer chooses the bank for his or her primary savings account. Many customers in urban India hold more than one savings account, though about half of India's adult population doesn't have any access to banking services. This often happens as people change jobs, and thus their salary accounts, or residences (in a city like Mumbai, a typical 'leave and licence' agreement is for eleven months; a tenant needs to move out after that time frame if the landlord is not willing to extend the agreement by another eleven months).

A smart bank also tries to make a customer have only one account for salary, dividends, making utility payments and so on. A customer will do so with a bank that offers an entire suite of products, including credit cards, car loans and home loans.

Cross-selling of products has been possible at HDFC Bank because of the establishment of a data warehouse—one of the first Indian banks to do so in 2002. The warehouse keeps a tab on all transactions irrespective of the channel that a customer is using (branch banking, telephone banking or net banking). The data can be used to develop a credit scoring model and a marketing analytics. This helps reduce the turnaround time. So a loan that used to take seven days now can be disbursed in a day or an account that used to take three days to open now can be done in a few hours. Cross-selling of products using data warehousing brings down the cost-to-income ratio.

The cost-to-income ratio is a key financial measure, particularly important in valuing banks. It shows a company's costs in relation to its income. To get the ratio, one needs to divide the operating costs (administrative and fixed costs, such as salaries and property expenses, but not bad debts that have been written off) by the operating income. The ratio gives investors a clear view of how efficiently the company is being run—the lower it is, the more profitable the company will be. HDFC Bank's cost-to-income ratio was 49% for the fiscal year 2012; it has been coming down by half a percentage point every year. When it was a predominantly corporate bank, its cost-to-income ratio was much lower at 38%. A bank's cost goes up for retail loans because of higher customer acquisition and servicing cost.

Micro Marketing

Banks acquire customers by cross-selling products, using them as hooks to take the relationship forward. When a bank sells a car loan to a mortgage client, the borrower not only pays interest but also comes closer to the bank in the basic relationship. Such customers tend to keep their account better funded, to pay for the car loan instalments. Later, they may start paying their income tax or children's school fees from this account. The average balance swells.

Shirish Apte, co-chairman of Asia-Pacific banking at Citigroup Inc., prefers to call the HDFC Bank approach 'micro marketing'. 'What this involves is picking one relationship and capturing relationships with everybody who is associated with that one relationship,' he says.

'Think about it—they've got a large company which has got suppliers who have other suppliers. So you keep going down the chain, knowing fully well where the risk element automatically comes in. Then, you get people who work for those companies. Micro marketing really helps you expand business both horizontally and vertically. From what I hear from people, that's what HDFC Bank does extremely well,' Shirish told me.

The Big Bang Settlement Business

In the mid-1990s, there were no guaranteed settlements and both the Bombay Stock Exchange (BSE Ltd) and the National Stock Exchange (NSE Ltd) had one clearing bank each—Bank of India and Canara Bank, respectively.

There was always an element of uncertainty about whether a settlement would go through. In those days, a settlement was done once a week and so meant carrying the risk of an entire week, accumulating pay-ins and pay-outs.

HDFC Bank came up with a solution. With the exchanges sitting in the bank offices, it offered to build a closed user group—of exchanges, pay-in brokers and pay-out brokers and the bank—by allocating specific clearing and settlement accounts. So before running a settlement file if an exchange ran a test, it would be able to find shortfalls in a broker's account, if any, and could ask the broker to pay up. This meant when the actual settlement was run, it would be a smooth process.

It was not about transferring the risk from the exchanges to the bank. By putting in place online real-time settlement and ensuring better information flow, the bank was essentially eliminating a system risk. Also, a broker's ability to get money from one exchange and then transfer from his bank in terms of managing his own liquidity became more efficient. A broker would have a pay-in from one exchange and a pay-out in another exchange, as most brokers were members of both exchanges.

NSE used to run a settlement fund to take care of any default. As it had no idea about a broker's balance with banks, it started to consolidate brokers' accounts at Canara Bank's capital market branch at Fort. A floppy from the NSE system with the data of the dues from various brokers would be taken to the bank branch, which would run the disk to check whether the brokers had enough funds. The findings would then go back to NSE. This was an everyday affair.

'We studied the whole process and said, "why don't we have them open accounts with us?" We could give them visibility on their screen. They could log into my system and find out which of the brokers didn't have funds. We created 24×7 access. We told the brokers to bank with us—"we are a networked company and your money will be credited instantly",' Ram said.

HDFC Bank and NSE are of the same age and both were excited about the potential for the securities market. One day, in 1997, Aditya invited NSE's then deputy managing director Ravi Narain to talk at the bank's retreat at Madh Island in Mumbai.

There were about thirty senior employees and Ravi told them the whole arena of securities transactions would explode one day, provided there was a technology-aided initiative. He envisaged a massive opportunity in the area.

Aditya grabbed the mike and told his people, 'You wouldn't believe me but Ravi and I have not spoken about this at all. Clearly, this is a reconfirmation of what I have been telling you guys all along.'

'I didn't know him [Aditya] at all,' Ravi told me. 'We tied up with a group of banks as clearing banks and HDFC Bank was one of them. From day one, they were very certain in their mind of the potential of business and their ability to manage the risks.'

If a broker defaults to the exchange, it's the clearing

corporation's problem. If there is default in terms of lines of credit, then banks have a problem. In manufacturing or any other business, one doesn't see daily volatility but bad assets can hit a bank suddenly.

Being appointed as a clearing bank for NSE was only the entry point. This could have been leveraged to do many other businesses and the bank was shrewd enough to capture them.

The bank marketed this service to all exchange members. The service implies that any exchange member who chooses to operate through HDFC Bank has to open a clearing and settlement account with the bank. When a file goes by a certain stipulated hour, HDFC Bank has to bring in the pay-in money on behalf of all those brokers to the exchange. Back to back, they have to figure out their arrangements to collect the pay-in money.

Similarly, after a few hours, a clearing corporation calculates the pay-out and a reverse flow occurs for a completely different or not-so-different group of brokers and back to back for the investors.

This cycle is repeated every single day for cash equity and derivatives and all other asset classes.

What kind of risk does the bank run?

The biggest risk for a bank is the processing risk. When NSE started, it ran very tight cycles. Typically, the gap between a pay-in and a pay-out would be a couple of hours. In the early days, it didn't matter much as the volumes were small but as the volumes grew and the banks started dealing with brokers all over the country, one can imagine what can happen if they cannot meet the cycle at some point and the exchange slams the gate.

The pay-in and pay-out cycle time is sacrosanct. If there's an interruption in processing and, in turn, the flow of money, the brokers will vent their ire on the bank. This is one part of the business. The second and bigger part is the opportunity that Aditya and his team sensed—that brokers need lines of credit, working capital and other banking services. It's entirely possible that a broker would enter into a pre-arranged understanding that he would put in 70% of the fund and the bank would have to cover the rest. That's a line of credit. This is the big opportunity and the bedrock on which all other businesses get built.

The bank gets a float and there could be fees for lines of credit. The bank may not charge for actual processing of inflows and outflows, but certainly they would charge for credit lines. If it's a daily occurrence, brokers keep balances and that becomes the float.

For all this, a bank needs to have the ability to handle very tight processing cycles every single day. It also entails understanding the credit risk of brokers and brokerages as the bank takes exposure on them. This is the hard part, given all the volatility and cycles of the market and of individual broking companies.

'It is the question of marshalling your resources—what we used to call in the early days a Germanic obsession for very tight processes with no tolerance for error and processing risk, and they [HDFC Bank] have built that in the way they operate. It was very clear very early on,' Ravi said.

Bankers Flew in at Midnight for Stress Testing of Brokers

Ravi recalls one incident of a very sharp market movement when many brokerages were in stress. With a market share of around 75% then it was inevitable that HDFC Bank had a tough time. Late at night and in wee hours of the day, the bank flew executives in various directions across India, sat with the brokerages, figured out their stress points and ensured that no accident would take place the next morning as the market is relentless.

It needn't be a default; it could just be a stress point. If not addressed, it could lead to a default. A bank that does not support its clients can cause serious financial problems. Risk magnifies for any transaction where a brokerage is involved, simply because of the nature of the business.

Just as a normal corporate entity or an individual account can become a bad asset, the brokers can also add to the bad assets if they take money but cannot pay back. The difference is that in any other business, one doesn't see the daily volatility of the capital markets and bad assets can hit one out of nowhere. If one is unprepared or has not built a risk scenario, one can be caught.

Clearing bankers scarcely know what's in store for them on a given day. Typically, the day begins with assisting the brokers to pool in their funds into their respective settlement accounts by the deadline stipulated by the exchange/clearing corporation, say by half past ten in the morning. Often it's routine, but when one is dealing with the settlement system of a dynamically volatile phenomenon like a stock exchange, there's always a very large element of risk.

18 May 2006: Markets Crashed

Chetan Shah, head of capital and commodity markets group, who had been with HDFC Bank since 2005, recalls 18 May 2006, which was not exactly a calm morning. There were some apprehensions of the trouble that was brewing but no one was prepared for what actually happened on that day. The Sensex, BSE's bellwether equity index, tanked 826 points. The margin calls started mounting; brokers started making frantic calls to move their funds lying in various accounts in the bank.

A *Bloomberg* report ('India's Sensex Tumbles Most in Two Years: World's Biggest Mover') by Pooja Thakur in Mumbai that day said:

India's Sensitive index posted its biggest drop in two years, the steepest move among markets included in global benchmarks.

Reliance Industries Ltd. led [stock] declines with a 6.8 percent drop, its biggest loss, as faster-than-expected U.S. inflation fanned concern [that] rising interest rates in the U.S. may lure money out of emerging markets. Hindalco Industries Ltd. and Oil & Natural Gas Corp. led commodity stocks lower after prices of metals and oil dropped.

'Higher interest rate expectations are fueling concerns of a slowdown of flows into emerging markets,' said A. Balasubramaniam, who oversees about $3.8 billion of Indian stocks and bonds as chief investment officer at Birla Sun Life Asset Management Co. in Mumbai. 'Falling commodity prices are aggravating the decline.'

The Bombay Stock Exchange's Sensitive index plunged 826.38, or 6.8 percent, to 11,391.43 at the 3:30 p.m. local time close. That's its biggest drop since May 17, 2004. The index has lost 9.7 percent since it reached a record 12,612.38 on May 10.

The S&P/CNX Nifty Index on the National Stock Exchange lost 246.20, or 6.8 percent to 3388.90.

The rupee, the second-worst performing currency in the Asia-Pacific region, dropped after overseas investors sold almost $550 million of equities in the four days through May 16. That compares with a daily average purchase of $118.6 million earlier this month. [...]

'Weak Trend'

U.S. stocks fell the most since January after consumer prices, excluding food and energy, rose 0.3 percent in April, Labor Department figures showed. Economists had forecast a 0.2 percent increase.

The Fed said it would monitor incoming data to set future policy after raising the benchmark lending rate a 16th straight time last week, to 5 percent. Higher borrowing costs may leave consumers in Asia's largest export market with less to spend on goods and services.

'We are mirroring the weak trend in global markets,'

said Nilesh Shah, who manages about $4.42 billion in assets as chief investment officer at Prudential ICICI Asset Management Co. in Mumbai.

Finance Minister Palaniappan Chidambaram refused to comment on the stock market's tumble, saying he doesn't speak on daily market movements, when questioned by reporters in New Delhi.

Another *Bloomberg* report ('Asian Stocks Fall Most in a Year on U.S. Inflation') by Malcolm Scott and Stuart Kelly, datelined Singapore, said:

Asian stocks fell the most in a year as faster-than-expected U.S. inflation fanned concern [that] rising interest rates will slow demand in the region's biggest export market. Sony Corp. and Samsung Electronics Co. dropped.

'Some of the falls are eye-watering,' said Donald Williams, whose fund at Platypus Asset Management in Sydney was the best performer over three years among open-end Australian equity growth funds tracked by Bloomberg. 'Sentiment has been turning against stocks lately, and the inflation report last night really pulled the trigger.'

Japan's Nikkei 225 Stock Average slipped 1.4 percent to 16,087.18. South Korea's Kospi fell 2.6 percent, wiping out this year's gains. Benchmarks in regional emerging markets such as India, Indonesia and the Philippines declined the most.

The relationship managers of HDFC Bank, who were the first to get calls, immediately swung into action, getting the balances in the various accounts of their respective relationships as well as keeping tabs on their overdraft limits. Senior managers also started looking at the broker-wise data provided to analyse the magnitude of requirement for money vis-à-vis the expected fund flows of the brokers.

On that morning, P. V. Ananthakrishnan, then boss of the capital market division at HDFC Bank, was on a vacation in a different time zone and Harish, group head, whom the capital market division used to report to, was on an official trip abroad.

Chetan, assistant vice president and seven months old in the bank, was managing the floor. His two mobile phones, one direct line and the intercom were ringing nonstop. The case was the same for other relationship managers and regional heads R. Balasubramanian from Delhi, Sandeep Jhavar from Kolkata, Deven Pandit from Gujarat and C. K. Venkatesh from the south.

Aditya's office started getting calls from the regulators, exchanges and broker members.

On the shop floor, Chetan was fighting the fire to manage the pay-in of the exchanges, submit margins to exchanges and send reports to Aditya's office.

Kaizad, head of credit and market risk management, with his team of Deepak Maheshwari and Benjamin Frank, had taken charge of the shop floor.

By noon, the bank completed the pay-in of funds. The real-time gross settlement of the RBI was still not in place then and the cut-off time for banks for clearances of high-value cheques to the RBI was half past two in the afternoon. Normally, the pay-out from the exchange would have been completed by that time. But this was no ordinary day—the pay-in of the exchange was delayed and therefore the pay-out of funds was also delayed.

This was a catch-22 situation. If the pay-out of funds of the exchange didn't take place, brokers who had sold shares wouldn't receive their money. The total pay-out and high-value cheques added up to thousands of crores. The high-value cheque clearance timeline was to be met. There was no option but to let the cheques bounce, and this would have created havoc.

The brokers were requesting money from the bank against the expected pay-out of the exchange. But it was impossible for anyone in the bank to take the call. It could not give thousands of crores or the go-ahead for clearing the high-value cheques. On the other side, the pay-out from the exchange was getting delayed.

Chetan came up with a solution. He walked into wholesale banking head Bhavesh's cabin. 'Can we request the RBI to delay the high-value cheque clearing?' he asked.

Bhavesh called the RBI. The regulator agreed to make an exception in that hour of crisis. The delay gave HDFC Bank time to clear the pay-outs. The customers' accounts got the money to honour the cheques.

For every stock that ended higher on the BSE, eight ended in the red. The thirty stocks that constitute the Sensex all ended in the red, and twenty-four of them lost 5% or higher. Erosion in investors' wealth on that day was ₹2.25 trillion.

18 May 2006 was also the day Lakshmi N. Mittal launched his bid for Arcelor S. A.

The Lowest Touch Point

Brokers' requirements change with time. There were days in 2000 when they wanted loans against securities and bank guarantees. Now brokers want cash management service as they have branches across the country. They want Internet banking.

The bank tries to go to the lowest touch point of a broker—his customers, family members—and all are captured in one loop. To manage risks, knowing a broker's balance sheet is important, but more critical than that is knowing a broker personally—his family, from where he comes and with whom he deals. Knowing these aspects comes in handy when looking for funds in times of crisis.

'In the last ten years, the maximum money we have lost is ₹3 crore. There wasn't a single instance of forced selling of a share in the 2006 crisis,' Chetan said. This makes it abundantly clear that there is a distinction between real risk and perceived risk. While many banks stay away from broker financing presuming it is risky, HDFC Bank's experience is different.

According to Chetan, the brokers tell him, 'your MD [Aditya] is a Panju [Punjabi] but his mind-set is Gujju [Gujarati]. If he asks for a ₹20-crore fixed deposit, and I give it, he would offer me 9.5% while the market rate is 9.8%.' (The popular perception is that Punjabis are large-hearted whereas

Gujaratis count every penny.)

This is a bank that does not know anything beyond business. Chetan told me, 'When we make presentations to our MD, he says, *"Teri unchi English mere ko samajh me nahi aati hai; mere ko ye bata ki ladoo kidhar hai."*' Everybody in HDFC Bank understands what *ladoo* (a ball-shaped sweetmeat) stands for.

The presentations don't last more than four to five slides. Aditya loves talking to the point. *'Paisa kidhar hai woh dikha, mujhe aur kuch nahi samajhta hai, seedha baat pe aa. Mujhe tu global gyan mat de.'*

Chapter 7

The Change in Course

HDFC Bank wanted to be a corporate bank. Its business plan submitted to the banking regulator said so. The plan was to be a wholesale lender and a retail fund mobilizer as the cost of money borrowed from individuals is always less than what a bank pays to companies that keep money with it. For a new bank, it was a struggle for survival on capital and very little borrowings. Most foreign banks were cynical and even their junior employees would fire a volley of questions at HDFC Bank's managers about the bank's credibility. Bank of America was a friend but not Citibank from where Aditya came.

Within the first couple of years, it was pretty clear that the business plan needed to be tweaked as public sector banks have more resources: They have a vast branch network and hence can lend to companies at a lower price. So, if HDFC Bank was serious about business, it had to be on both sides— retail borrowing and retail lending. Three years after it was born, HDFC Bank decided to go the whole hog in retail, and started to look beyond the universe of triple-A-rated companies to double-A-rated ones.

It had started as a corporate bank for three reasons.

First, till it built a branch network it could not go for retail banking. In fact, any bank that starts with a limited branch network has very little choice but corporate banking because retail customers cannot be acquired without a distribution infrastructure.

One can always argue that there are Internet banks without physical distribution but this is a phenomenon restricted to sophisticated and developed markets. Although the banks in India have indeed gone beyond branches and are using other channels to service customers, they have a long way to go before they can use the Internet to mobilize deposits.

Second, most of HDFC Bank's senior employees, including Aditya, came from a background of wholesale and corporate business in foreign banks. By definition, most foreign banks are corporate banks. Some of them such as Citibank have large retail businesses, but the HDFC Bank recruits had worked in the wholesale side of the bank business.

Third, corporate business, in comparison with retail business, requires much less investment in physical infrastructure in terms of technology, branches and people. As a start-up, HDFC Bank had to earn its way before it could invest in all of those requirements.

This was the most logical way to go in the first stage because corporate business was the sort of business they understood and where they had relationships. And even if they had the expertise (which they did not) and wanted to get into retail from day one, they could not have done so because of cost factors.

The market opportunity was clear. At that point, if one were a corporate treasurer, one would be dealing with two sets of banks. Public sector banks had a large distribution network and plenty of rupee liquidity, but in the mind of a corporate treasurer they didn't have great recall in terms of service and products. The foreign banks, on the other hand, didn't have rupee-funding capability and so couldn't lend much. But they had technology and service capability.

Retail Is No Half-Way Affair

'Once we started growing, we realized that we couldn't be a big bank dealing with only triple-A clients. Also, if we wanted to enjoy economies of scale, we would have to fast track our retail banking franchise,' Aditya says.

Now, the retail business isn't really a difficult thing but many banks—both local and foreign—have failed simply because they take half-way measures. In retail, there can't be any half-way affair. If one puts one's money behind something, one has to see it through right till the end and be convinced about one's strategy.

For instance, if a lender gets into car and two-wheeler loans, it can make money only if it has the scale. It is not just the suite of products that matters because the lender may not want to venture into all products at the same time but the scale has to be there.

Retail banking is a volume game. A bank needs wide distribution, a lot of branches, a plethora of products and a completely different mind-set. One needs to have many products to straddle the economy of the country.

On the other hand, it is risky to embrace scale at the cost of asset quality. British bank Barclays PLC and Germany's Deutsche Bank AG, among others, had made half-hearted attempts to get into the Indian retail lending market. Both saw a huge opportunity in the burgeoning Indian middle class and its rising disposable income.

As the economy grew at an average of 9.5% for three successive years between fiscal years 2005 and 2007, millions of individuals rushed to borrow money to buy homes and cars. Money was cheap and inflation, relatively low. There was a surge in personal loans and issue of credit cards—both in the category of unsecured loans.

But every bank wasn't successful in seizing the opportunity. Barclays had to pull out of the retail business and Deutsche Bank couldn't make much progress even though it was its second coming in this space in India after an unsuccessful entry earlier. Citibank, too, could not handle its retail business with care. Its non-banking finance arm, CitiFinancial Consumer Finance India Ltd, crumbled under the burden of rising bad assets, with many branches downing shutters and people retrenched. Even ICICI Bank, India's largest private sector lender and undisputedly a pioneer in retail banking, had to apply the brakes as bad assets grew.

The unsecured part of the retail business is particularly vulnerable. Overtly aggressive banks sold credit cards and personal loans as if there was no tomorrow. In most cases, they were sold not by the banks' staff but by the so-called direct sales agents who did not care much about the quality of the borrowers and their ability to repay. Their focus is always on the numbers as the commission comes from the number of customers and not the volume of business.

With many such customers the banks did not have any other relationship. When customers started defaulting in a slowing economy after the 2008 collapse of US investment bank Lehman Brothers Holdings Inc. and an unprecedented global credit crunch that followed as banks stopped trusting each other and stopped lending in the inter-bank market, many banks were left holding the can.

There were instances when banks' collection agents were beaten up or legal suits filed against them for alleged coercive recovery practices. Many banks abandoned the space and others slowed the business considerably. HDFC Bank quietly stepped up its presence, using the wisdom of others who had burnt their fingers in retail business.

But that's a more recent story. In 1998, when HDFC Bank wanted to start retail, it felt it must extend its reach beyond the metros. 'We wanted to go into the interiors, though then this only meant adding about a hundred more branches to our existing fifty,' Aditya said. As of 2012, it is looking at 2,500 branches.

In the first year, it got just twelve branch licences. By the third year when it decided to start the retail business, Vinod was made responsible for branch expansion. He was involved in setting up at least 500 branches. For every branch, he would select a location after a survey by the marketing people. He also drafted a four-page template on why a particular location in a particular city or town was selected. 'I had to justify [the location] as the licences were scarce,' Vinod said. This system is still in vogue when the bank is getting 300 licences every year.

Indeed, the scale was different in the late 1990s but one thing was very clear—the liability side of the bank's balance sheet should be partly retail and partly wholesale. This is simply because a bank cannot totally depend on wholesale funding. Good deposits will come only if a complete range is offered to the customers. Otherwise, customers will come but not stick around. Products and a distribution network are essential ingredients for success.

Losses Are Natural in the First Few Years

Again, in retail banking, losses are natural in the first three or four years. But the way HDFC Bank's shares were quoted at that time, the market was not willing to give it any concession. So, it had to grow the profitability of corporate business more than the market expectation to cover up the retail losses.

'It's not entirely wrong to say that by three years of age, when we were a toddler, we had actually become an adult in our field. We had the systems, the products, the brand. Now more success depended on the efficiency of our execution skills and God's grace,' Aditya said.

Till it started the retail business, the boss did not know the 'R' of retail. Aditya was an out-and-out corporate banker. Some say Aditya's retail vision was influenced by that of Jerry Rao, Aditya's colleague in Citibank, who had been heading consumer banking when Aditya was heading corporate banking. He was convinced that retail gives sticky income and investors like retail. Which came first is anybody's guess.

Globally, investors give much better multiple for retail earnings than for wholesale earnings because wholesale earnings are considered risky, volatile and uncertain, while retail earnings are sticky and long term.

Maximizing the Valuation

Whether or not he would admit it, at one stage, Aditya did want to maximize the valuation of HDFC Bank and he knew the retail business would do the trick. Unlike in corporate lending, the risks are well spread out in retail and a bank can never sink because of one or two bad borrowers.

At an internal meeting, Aditya, by then a complete retail convert, made this statement: 'I want to make money on every transaction, every payment that happens in this country. If I am an efficient provider of transactional services of both retail and corporate side[s of the business], I can make money on every card swipe and every fund transfer. I want that.'

An offshoot of transactional banking is the financial institutional group, formed in 2002–03, under Harish. The target was the government business. Harish kicked off the business by signing an agreement with Life Insurance Corporation of India for handling its cash management. Then he set his eyes on collection of income tax, a business done by only state-run banks till then.

Harish went to Delhi and met Ravi Kant, then chairman of the Central Board of Direct Taxes (CBDT), and asked for a slice of the pie. Kant liked his presentation but left the decision to his accounts department—the controller general of accounts (CGA), the accounting authority for all departments of the CBDT.

Harish repeated the same presentation to the CGA, and was asked to make yet another presentation after three months by when CGA's new conference room would be ready.

At that time, they used to get money from nationalized banks after fifteen days. 'Can your bank give us the money in five days?' the CGA asked Harish. Without batting an eyelid, Harish said yes. He was very keen to get the government business.

The CGA asked him to cut it to four days. Harish agreed.

Amazed, the CGA then made the point that if HDFC Bank failed to deliver, it would be penalized. Harish agreed. 'That's our USP.'

By the time the CBDT agreed to issue the letter, Kant had retired. The RBI opposed the plan and it became a sort of turf war between the regulator and the tax authorities.

'Who's the CGA to take a call on which bank will collect tax?'

'Who's the RBI to tell us what to do?'

Finally, the CGA issued the letter but asked the bank to get an authorization from the RBI.

Today, HDFC Bank is the second-largest collector of direct tax after the SBI. In the fiscal year 2012, it collected ₹1.5 trillion. The bank earns a minuscule commission but gets one-day free money, called a float.

People such as Neeraj, who later headed the retail business, must have played a role in influencing Aditya, but a big contributing factor to his belief in retail was definitely the fact that, from investors' perspective, retail could create maximum value.

Technology is critical for retail banking. HDFC Bank opted for the i-Flex product, which was then used by Citibank globally. The whole shift of the system, from corporate banking to retail banking, Vinod says, was done over a weekend, after Saturday closure of the bank.

Samit, a close friend of Aditya and a former Citibanker, was hired as an executive director to run the retail business, but he did not last long. The first thing Samit did was to change the logo of the bank. The original logo was black–red–white, similar to that of HDFC. Samit changed it to blue–red–white. Everybody loved the new logo, but Samit could not do much beyond that as he had serious differences in terms of business strategy with his friend-turned-boss, Aditya. After a brief turbulent time Vinod asked Samit to leave.

Samit and Aditya had been trainees together in Citibank and Samit's wife too was a Citibanker. He had left Citibank (where he was heading retail) and was working with Standard

Chartered in the Middle East when he approached Aditya for a job as he wanted to come back to India.

'I told him "we have been friends for so long and I'm not sure how it will work, I being your boss." I was not very keen,' Aditya explained. So why did they part ways? 'He had different ideas of the way the bank should grow and I had different ideas. It was better that we parted and remained friends. The differences were on cost, on the target market segment and even on how the bank should look. He was bringing Citi[bank] here and I was setting up HDFC Bank.'

Samit, who heads a Bangalore-based micro-finance firm Ujjivan Financial Services Pvt. Ltd as its founder and managing director, has a slightly different story to tell. 'The new logo was not my only contribution to the bank. In fact, Aditya chose the colour of the logo. I set up the ATM network, telephone banking and the basic infrastructure for retail banking. We were targeting savings bank accounts aggressively to get low-cost money,' he said.

Samit claims that he was doing well in Dubai as the regional head of South Asia and the Middle East for retail banking in Standard Chartered but as a Citibanker and an outsider, he faced a lot of opposition within the bank and that frustrated him. In HDFC Bank, he was the only executive director who was operating out of Bangalore where he was building his house. Besides, his three children were studying at the Kodaikanal International School in Tamil Nadu, some 300 kilometres from Bangalore but closer than the distance from Mumbai.

'Retail is a high-profile business . . . You're always in public glare. Many of my colleagues didn't like that and I became a victim of politics. That was the worst time in my career. I left an overseas job to set up the retail business in the bank but I had to leave within two years. It was shocking,' he told me.

Samit joined Bank Muscat as India CEO and remained there for six years till the bank merged with Centurion BoP and the merged entity was eventually gobbled up by HDFC Bank.

Samit and Aditya are still friends, though the old warmth may be lacking. HDFC Bank is one of the principal bankers for Ujjivan. 'Aditya is the best corporate banker I have come across in my career,' Samit says.

The Real Push

Neeraj gave the real push. Before Neeraj joined, J. K. Basu—an ex-Grindlays person—was heading branch banking. Neeraj joined as the head of marketing, products and retail business in 1999. He came from Bank of America where he was part of a team, setting up the retail business in India. Like many retail bankers, Neeraj too had a background in the fast-moving consumer goods (FMCG) industry. He had worked with Ponds (India) Ltd, which later merged with Hindustan Unilever, for nine years. At IIM-A, he had turned down offers from banks as he found banking boring then.

'Aditya gave me a lot of space. I enjoyed setting up business after business. We started recruiting the team, giving retail loans, loans against shares, loans for cars, two-wheelers, commercial vehicles and credit cards,' Neeraj recollects.

The only business in the retail space where the bank could not enter was home loans as its promoter HDFC, India's oldest mortgage company, had reservations about the bank competing with its parent, though HDFC Bank investors were keen to see it have this product in its retail portfolio, a product that its peers ICICI Bank and SBI were selling aggressively. They worked out a formula to solve the issue. The bank started sourcing housing loans for HDFC with the right to buy-back up to 70% of such loans. (More on this in Chapter 13.)

Selling Underwear from Bank Branches

After settling down, Neeraj wanted to set up a sales company. At that time, all foreign banks used direct sales agents for new customer acquisition. Neeraj wanted a subsidiary, a sales company that would source retail loans for the bank exclusively.

His logic for having an exclusive sales outfit ran like this: The direct sales agent outfit would never jack up the acquisition cost as, being a subsidiary, it would not get offers from competing banks. So, the bank wouldn't have the risk of distribution going out to somebody else. But creating a legal vehicle wasn't easy—it involved hiring people, managing the governance and running it.

There was stiff opposition from others. 'We are a respected bank, not an FMCG company. Tomorrow, will we sell underwear from our branches?' Vinod remarked. Even the RBI was not particularly enamoured of the idea. But Aditya backed it, overruling all opposition.

This way, HBL Global Pvt. Ltd was set up, the first by any bank in India. Aditya pushed Neeraj hard to open more HBL branches than what Neeraj was able to. At one point, the outfit had almost 30,000 people. They are 'feet on the street', not sourcing customers in the branches but going out and selling credit cards, auto loans and so on. It still exists but all its employees who were selling deposit accounts have been shifted to the bank, pushing the bank's head count up by 10,000 people.

The sales company transformed the pace of growth of the retail business. 'Once he is convinced that someone has got a good idea, he always wants to go faster and faster. He can also withdraw very quickly if he feels you're failing,' Neeraj says of Aditya.

After JK left and Times Bank merged with HDFC Bank, Neeraj was made the head of retail. Uma Krishnan, head of retail at Times Bank, was given JK's portfolio—branch banking. But Uma, also from Grindlays like JK, quit and Neeraj became the boss of the entire retail business.

In some sense, HDFC Securities Ltd was also part of the larger retail business. Aseem Dhru built the securities outfit. Today, the securities company has a lot of synergies with the bank as it focuses on retail business and does institutional broking to a limited extent. The bank's retail team leverages HDFC Securities' partnership, cross-sells products and offers three-in-one accounts (savings, demat and online broking— all in one) just like ICICI Bank does.

HDFC Bank is either the leader or a close second in whatever retail products it offers. Its retail balance sheet is bigger than that of any other bank, including ICICI Bank, which had started the retail business ahead of all others. About 50% of HDFC Bank's assets are retail assets and no other bank has that. As a business philosophy, it exits any business that fails to capture any of the top three slots in a few years. Small ticket personal loan is one such business. HDFC Bank dropped it as it could not make much progress. Similarly, in 1996–97, it started investment banking but abandoned the business as it did not progress well, only to revive it much later in 2010–11.

Banking Made Simple

If one looks at HDFC Bank, one will notice that it does not do any complicated banking. What it does is simple transactional banking. Take, for instance, the savings bank account. Common sense says people keep more money in a savings account, which is also a conduit for dividend warrants, transactions, bill payments and so on. The bank did not do any sweep to fixed deposits—something that ICICI Bank used to offer its customers—because that would have raised costs.

'Why should we do that? And shoot ourselves in the foot?' Neeraj asked. The sweep facility ensures that when the money kept in a savings account crosses a certain level, say ₹5,000, the excess amount automatically flows into a fixed deposit and earns higher interest.

It's not a returns account but a transactional account, which makes transactions easy but doesn't offer higher interest rate. That's the underlying philosophy.

HDFC Bank also demonstrated technology as a differentiator. So, it would advertise only those products that are technologically superior. HDFC Bank was the first to launch mobile banking in 2000 even when it was not fully launched in the West. It was not a great offering but the bank went ahead and launched it first to demonstrate what technology could do.

Even on the corporate side, there's nothing exotic that the bank does. Every product is common and simple but executed well and serves the purpose.

The Risk–Reward Trade-Off

The most critical element of the bank's philosophy was never to look at growth as absolute—growth has to be seen in the context of certain margins as rewards and risks one has taken to achieve the growth.

The bank wanted to grow from day one but kept saying it would grow the balance sheet, volume and market share but the growth should not been seen as an absolute. This is as relevant in 2012 as it was ten years ago.

If one is growing faster either by taking higher risks or by accepting lower margins—as pricing can be dropped—it is better to run a hundred-metre race. But the team was building an institution, a franchise that needed a strong foundation. It was hard to achieve, but it was the right thing to do.

The bank has done that over a period of time. In doing so, there is probably no customer segment that it has not touched—from a customer who is part of a self-help group (SHG) and borrows ₹10,000–15,000 for a small self-employment opportunity to regular retail customers, small businesses, emerging corporations, large companies, institutions and government.

When one gauges a bank, there are a lot of things to look at—profitability, growth, solidity. There is also a critical component of trust. One associates the concept of a bank with something one can trust—'you can bank on somebody!'

Globally, banks have never failed because of lack of technology or great products or people. One can live with that. What the failed banks really missed is risk management—they did not manage the risks well. Herein comes the understanding of the risk–reward trade-off or balancing of business growth with risk taken in delivering that. When one talks about large companies, one may give up little in margin but one takes fewer risks. That lower margin can be made good by selling letters of credit, guarantees, cash management and so on. The less received from interest income can be made up by getting the rest of the business and still retaining the advantage of lower credit costs and lower bad assets because one is managing the risks better.

It may sound a bit didactic but in banking, sometimes, it is not only what one has done but what one has not done that can make a difference between failure and success.

The 'Eat Well, Sleep Well' Dilemma

Indeed, there are risks in every business. In fact, banks typically make money by taking risks. It's the classic 'eat well, sleep well' dilemma. If one collects deposits and puts them in government bonds, one has no risks but one also doesn't have much return. On the other hand, if one puts in one's last penny in high-risk debt or equity, one may earn handsome returns (and thus get to 'eat well') but one certainly won't be able to sleep well (with the worry of the risks).

HDFC Bank did two things. When it took risks, it didn't bet the bank on anything—something, say, that Ramesh Gelli did at Global Trust Bank. He played the money in the market and lost it.

HDFC Bank normally takes moderate risks and runs a highly diversified book. It takes risks only after it sees the dimension of each risk, appreciates how much it can price that risk, and ways to mitigate it.

At one point, a major issue was HDFC Bank having gone in for broker exposure, something that could be a major risk. In more recent times, most banks vacated the credit card and personal loan business but HDFC Bank hung in there. When everybody else got scared, this bank got careful and moderated the growth rate but did not withdraw from the business. 'As long as we can manage the risks in a particular manner, it's a worthwhile thing to do,' says Paresh.

It's not true that they hate taking risks; they do take risks, but in a measured manner, and manage the risks. Paresh says, 'If we are risk averse, we shouldn't be doing credit cards or personal loans. Even in the past couple of years when the banking systems put down their shutters, we were doing it.'

In any business, a bank would have certain portfolios in some segments and geographies where it has high delinquencies. It needs to recognize that and react to that by changing policies. One can always make mistakes, but blunders can be avoided if one is aware of what one is doing and has constant checks and controls of a diversified book with exposure to multiple segments.

The bank's risk management system is strong because the organizational structure provides complete independence to the risk function, with the reporting line convergence at the CEO level. Kaizad, group head of credit and market risk management, reports to Paresh who in turn reports to Aditya. In many banks, the credit or risk management head for certain businesses reports to the concerned business head. The independent reporting line ensures that both business and risk functions can interact on an even footing with equal emphasis on growth and asset quality. Besides, the business managers in the bank share ownership for the asset quality of their businesses along with volume and profit.

K. V. Kamath, non-executive chairman of ICICI Bank, does not want to comment on the differences between the two banks but admits ICICI Bank's strategy is entirely different from that of HDFC Bank. 'You can't compare strategies in reasonable short term, particularly when there will be volatility, momentum and a whole lot of other things happening in our own country as well as the globe. The growth designs that both banks have chosen are very different: one is significantly entrepreneurial and the other is focused on steady progress. The entrepreneurial path will create turbulences as well as opportunities which can be called path-breaking. I don't think it's right to judge either strategy because each might be more relevant at different points in time. Nothing prevents any players, anyway, from changing their direction and path,' Kamath, the guru of Indian retail banking, says.

ICICI Bank, according to Kamath, has always set an agenda in everything that it has done and has followed that religiously: 'We believed what we did was right and it is for time to see whether or not our strategy has been successful. If I had to set up a bank tomorrow, I would probably do what ICICI Bank is doing. I've always been a very entrepreneurial guy and understand the spirit of enterprise.'

Entrepreneurship Is the Ability to Sniff Opportunity

For Kamath, entrepreneurship is the ability to sniff opportunity. An entrepreneur has the ability to recognize a lucrative area before anything substantial happens there, tries to seize it and deliver on it, and corrects course, if necessary, but is always keen to look for a path that allows the entrepreneur to grow faster than the system.

ICICI, the parent of ICICI Bank that merged with it, was a project finance institution. The bank needed to do something different to grow as the days of long-term cheap resources were over. So, it decided to get into retail. It saw the next opportunity in going global. After that, it started looking at rural opportunities.

This, according to Kamath, is the entrepreneurial way—a path-breaking approach; looking for opportunities and taking chances that others may or may not be willing to take.

'I go back to 2000, when there were less than a hundred ATMs in the whole country and we said we wanted to set up a thousand ATMs. People laughed at us. In 1996, when we were a project finance company, we said we wanted to be a universal bank. Again, people laughed at us. A universal bank is exactly what we are doing today. Largely speaking, we have achieved what we had envisioned in 1996, in an entrepreneurial way.

'But by emphasizing the entrepreneurial way, I don't mean that the path taken by HDFC Bank is an incorrect path at all. I think taking a well-measured path and executing on it is a good way to go.

'Interestingly, the parent HDFC is an entrepreneurial company. Its founder H. T. Parekh is probably one of the most entrepreneurial people I've ever met . . . I got to know Mr [H. T.] Parekh when I started my career. He always had an idea a day. And at one stage, he singled out the idea of housing finance companies and promoted that. So at the parent level they chose to be entrepreneurial, but at the bank level they chose to remain steady, growth-wise. In our case, everything was rolled into one. I think that is the key difference between the two banks,' says Kamath.

According to Kamath, HDFC Bank does take risks in the areas it does business and sticks to those risks; it does not stray. 'You may question whether they have taken risks in that or not—that's a question that time and the success of their business can answer. They are growing by about 25% every year, have carved a niche in retail for themselves, and are doing what they have immense expertise in.

'That makes them neither boring nor risk averse. It's not a question of having made any mistakes or not; it's a conscious choice of strategy that they have made. As a competitor, I have tremendous respect and admiration for them,' says Kamath.

Same DNA for HDFC Bank and ICICI Bank

Kamath also says that the root culture for both the banks is the same: 'We get our cultural genes from Mr H. T. Parekh because, for almost fifteen to twenty years, he provided us leadership. I think those genes go down to Chanda's [Kochhar, ICICI Bank's fourth managing director and CEO] level because she has seen the way ICICI functions even though she may not have worked directly under H. T. Parekh. The dominant gene for both banks comes from H. T. Parekh. If you look at ICICI Bank, the predominant genes we inherited were those of Mr H. T. Parekh and Mr [S. S.] Nadkarni. In HDFC Bank's case, it is H. T Parekh and Deepak Parekh.'

H. T. Parekh joined ICICI in 1956, a year after it was formed, and was its third chairman and managing director between 1972 and 1977 till he founded HDFC. Nadkarni was its sixth chairman and managing director, appointed in

1983–84. Nadkarni also headed another project finance institution, the erstwhile ICICI's younger peer, IDBI.

Chapter 8

The Entire Pyramid

The shift of focus or rather expansion of credit activities from corporate to retail banking was not sudden for HDFC Bank. It was a meticulously planned move that went step by step. After dealing with the top 200 companies, the bank targeted the suppliers and dealers of those companies to grab the supply chain management business.

The next opportunity it sniffed was in financing this sector—the smaller companies involved in supply chain management who already had a credit history with the bank. 'Why not give them funding on a standalone basis?' Aditya asked. That was the genesis of the transition in 2000 from, in the bank's parlance, 'SCM' to 'SME'—supply chain management to small and medium enterprises.

'The initial focus was on the travel portals and auto ancillary firms,' says Ashima, who built the emerging corporates group for the bank. Gradually, hospitals and academic institutions crept into the list as exposure to them was considered safe: students' fees and patients' charges can always be securitized.

By 2006, the bank decided to go one notch lower, to companies with a turnover of up to ₹150 crore. This was christened the business banking division. In late 2008, the bank started looking at small firms too. Its emerging enterprise group covers firms in this bracket, with a turnover of ₹5 crore. These three divisions complete the ₹40,000-crore SME division of HDFC Bank, spanning around 15,000 companies. It is almost as big as its corporate business.

The earning from this group is pretty good as, typically, smaller firms pay higher interest than the triple-A-rated companies and, if properly managed, delinquency is not high. In 2008, in the wake of the collapse of Lehman Brothers and the credit crunch that followed, HDFC Bank stepped back; it reviewed and reduced loans to such firms. It also got rid of some of the loans that it had obtained through the acquisition of Centurion BoP as these loans did not meet the bank's norms.

Companies hate a bank that shuts the tap when they need money the most. So a few borrowers withdrew from HDFC Bank, but the bank seems to have no regrets. 'We took hard decisions which many other banks didn't. If we had a loan outstanding to any company that we considered unviable or where we were uncomfortable with management integrity or transparency of information, we asked it to pay back first before giving fresh money,' Ashima says.

She finds promoters of small firms extremely sharp. 'The kind of wealth you see in these companies is unbelievable. They would teach us a couple of things on how to invest. Unlike professional managers, they deal with their own money. Their strategies are very different,' she says.

Credit Filters

HDFC Bank's ratios of bad assets to good ones have always been lower than the industry average, both gross as well as net, after setting aside money. One of the reasons why the market gave a thumbs down to its acquisition of Centurion BoP was Centurion's relatively high non-performing assets (NPAs), but the impact was not severe as the size of the acquisition was relatively small.

Maheshwari, head of corporate credit risk management, explains why the bank doesn't have too many bad assets: 'Our credit filters are high. We also deal with companies that have the ability to face a business downturn. We limit our exposure per account.' The bank also always tries to have a diversified portfolio.

Going by its internal norms, theoretically, not more than 12% of advances should be given to one industry but, in practice, the threshold is much lower—between 6% and 8%.

The bank has very limited exposure to airlines, power, real estate and non-banking finance companies, the troubled pockets in the Indian economy in 2012. There are sectors on the caution list but that is confidential and nobody discusses it. What they officially say is that they have very limited appetite for certain segments such as greenfield projects from new promoters, film financing, hotel and real-estate construction businesses. They are not banned as such but loans to these sectors are given with extreme caution and after approval from the highest level.

It has exposure to liquor baron Vijay Mallya's breweries but not to Kingfisher Airlines Ltd, which ended the fiscal year 2012 with a negative net worth of ₹5,082 crore and a debt of ₹8,023 crore. Many banks that had lent to Kingfisher Airlines had to restructure their exposure by converting part of their debt into equity.

'We pick up early signals. The moment we know a company is heading towards trouble we review our exposure strategy and collaterals. We may decide to hold, cut the loan exposure or even completely exit. We give the company time to find another bank as our replacement,' Maheshwari says.

A company may take three or six months or even a year to find a replacement but it obliges. It is a smart strategy, as if HDFC Bank were to formally announce its exit the company would find it difficult to get another lender. Maheshwari recalls one incident where the bank made an exit but the same account came back to it through Centurion BoP.

The Exit List

The exit list is not very long. At any given time, there are thirty to forty companies on the bank's watch list, not even 1% of its universe of borrowers in terms of numbers, and roughly a third are on the exit list. Both lists are dynamic. The companies keep shifting from one to the other and some borrowers even bounce back into the healthy category, rarely though.

Maheshwari has handled very few bad accounts—those in three digits. One of them at just over ₹100 crore was the combined exposure of HDFC Bank and Centurion BoP to Subhiksha Trading Services Ltd. The banking industry sank about ₹750 crore and private equity investors, including ICICI Venture Funds Management Co. Ltd, the private equity arm of ICICI Bank, and PremjiInvest, the private equity arm of billionaire Azim Premji of Wipro Ltd, had to write off a hefty amount.

Trouble for Subhiksha began in late 2008 when the company ran out of cash, bringing its operations to a standstill. The cash shortage eventually resulted in Subhiksha closing its nationwide network of 1,600 supermarket stores and defaulting on loans, vendor payments and staff salaries. Premji dubbed Subhiksha as the retail industry's Satyam—the infotech company whose promoter B. Ramalinga Raju confessed to the largest fraud in India's corporate history. Media reports suggested that Subhiksha filed a ₹500-crore defamation claim against Premji.

From India to Bharat

The bank's increasing focus on retail was driven by its aim to diversify its assets and raise valuation. Its failure to meet priority sector lending norms forced the bank to look closer at rural India. For the financial year that ended in March 2010, HDFC Bank miserably failed to meet the sub-target of the so-called priority sector lending norms. Banks are required to give 40% of their loans to farmers, small-scale industries and economically backward classes. Within the overall 40% limit, 18% should go to agriculture; within this sub-target of agriculture, 13.5% should be given directly to farmers and the rest 4.5% can be disbursed through intermediaries such as micro finance institutions (MFIs). Banks that fail to meet these targets are punished. For instance, if a bank does not give 13.5% credit directly to farmers, it needs to put the shortfall in the Rural Infrastructure Development Fund of the National Bank for Agriculture and Rural Development (Nabard). The interest earned on this forced lending is much less than what a bank can earn from other loans.

In 2009–10, HDFC Bank's direct agricultural lending dropped to around 6% and it had to place ₹2,000 crore with Nabard, earning half of what it would have otherwise made. Aditya blew his top. When things did not change even in the first half of the next financial year that ended in September, at an emergency meeting of all group heads, in October 2010, he asked how many of them had travelled to Bihar, Jammu & Kashmir and the north-eastern states. Not too many hands were raised. 'Lift your warm little arse and go there. We'll talk after you visit these places,' he told them. The bank's officers were reluctant to go deep into rural India, since retail lending in urban India was thriving, with more and more people buying homes and cars. On the liability side, they could always get more companies for their employees' salary accounts.

After Aditya cracked the whip, a group was formed and it was decided that the heads of every business group—corporate, retail, products, branch banking and so on—be personally responsible for any shortfall in meeting the priority loan targets. It was made an essential ingredient for their performance appraisal.

Apart from commercial vehicle and tractor loans, gold loans and two-wheeler loans are the two planks on which the rural thrust was built. Then there are loans given to shopkeepers and small entrepreneurs. The bank found that the best—and most cost-efficient—way to make its presence felt and reach out to the rural population was through loan *mahotsavs* or festivals where its officers sanctioned loans on the spot to credit-worthy borrowers. Till March 2012, about 300 loan *mahotsavs* have been held across India.

'At Pimpalgaon, once a villager came and asked me how much loan the bank can give against gold. He wanted ₹5 crore. Can you imagine how much gold there is in rural India? We can monetize that,' Aditya says.

Pimpalgaon is a village in Ahmednagar district of Maharashtra. For loans against gold ornaments, a bank keeps a 20–25% margin and considers only 75% of the weight of ornaments as pure gold to allow for the copper and silver that is alloyed with the gold to make the ornaments strong. The next day, the villager turned up at the bank branch with a few kilogrammes of gold ornaments in a gunny bag as he had to offer about ₹10 crore worth of ornaments to get the loan of ₹5 crore!

By one estimate, the value of gold with Indian households could be as much as ₹28 trillion, 50% of fixed deposits in the Indian banking system in June 2012.

Checking whether the ornament is made of gold is relatively easy, with the right equipment. The 'acid test' is done at the branches, using a small tablet of black stone, called touchstone. The ornament is rubbed on the touchstone to create a gold mark, and a drop of nitric acid is put on the gold mark with a sort of glass cocktail stirrer. Then a drop of salt water is dropped on the mark. If nothing happens, the gold is of good quality; if it turns green it is of low purity; if the mark disappears, the gold is spurious.

The next question is about the degree of purity: is it 24 carat, 22 carat or 18 carat? That again is not a big issue and can be sorted out with help from professional valuers. The gold business has low credit risk as the value of gold is always more than the loan amount, but there are operational risks: every bank branch needs a special vault and a valuer's expertise.

Sashi says that even in Mumbai there is huge demand for gold loans. In May 2010, the business took off with a corpus of ₹25 crore. In June 2012, it rose to ₹3,000 crore, about 3% of the bank's total retail loans.

Apart from forcing the bank executives to change their mind-set, the other big challenge was to decentralize the operations and servicing—which was centralized—for faster decision making on credit proposals. So HDFC Bank linked up all its branches across 1,400 small towns and villages in India with a broadband network of 512 Kbps.

The managers could now zip across scanned copies of loan applications to regional credit hubs as couriers would take days. Also, more and more branches were opened in rural and semi-urban India. Of the branches opened since 2009, at least 60% are in these pockets. RBI norms stipulate that 25% of a bank's branches should be in rural and semi-urban centres. HDFC Bank has 46% of its branches in rural and semi-urban centres—1,154 branches of a network of 2,564.

The portions of gold loans given to small and marginal farmers are priority loans. The bank's direct lending to agriculture, which was 6% in 2009, has risen to 11% as of 2012, still short of the regulatory requirement of 13.5%.

Learning the Hard Way

Reaching out to the unbanked people, a business model that HDFC Bank calls 'sustainable livelihood banking', is something that the bank learnt the hard way. The bank started a business division for this purpose in 2003. The ambition was to directly reach out to people who do not have access to banking facilities. But this was not possible earlier as the bank did not have enough branches at that time.

To understand the business model, it was imperative to go through the MFIs that are in the business of giving tiny loans to poor people. They knew how to reach out and had a sustainable business model till the industry faced a crisis in 2010. But that's a different story. Some of the MFIs wanted to work for poverty alleviation, others rushed in with growth motivation and yet others, profit motivation. That led to distortions in the rules of the game: multiple loans were given to many borrowers who took money from different MFIs but were not in a position to repay. So, pressure mounted on them to repay loans and there were stray incidents of excesses done by a few MFIs for collection of loan instalments.

In October 2010, Andhra Pradesh, which accounts for at least a quarter of the micro lending industry, promulgated a law to control micro lenders after a spate of reported suicides following alleged coercive recovery practices adopted by some of the MFIs. The law restricts MFIs from collecting money from borrowers on a weekly basis and makes government approval mandatory for borrowers taking more than one loan. Subsequently, an RBI panel capped the loan rate by MFIs at 26% and the margin at 12%.

About 9.2 million borrowers in the southern state— India's fourth largest by area and fifth largest by population— defaulted in repaying money borrowed from MFIs, the largest number of defaulters in any location in the world. As Andhra Pradesh has a population of 84.6 million, theoretically one in every eleven Andhraites is a defaulter. This, however, is not the actual case as many such borrowers have more than one account. By industry estimates, around four million people of the southern state—almost all women—have turned defaulters. As the female population in Andhra Pradesh is

42.1 million, one in every ten women in this state has borrowed from MFIs but not repaid.

With borrowers not paying back their money, MFIs defaulted in paying bank loans. Typically, banks give money to MFIs—who in turn give tiny loans to poor people in rural India—to fulfil their quota of priority loans to weaker sections.

To come back to the HDFC Bank story, in 2003, it had about ₹75 crore worth of exposure to about twenty-five MFIs for many of whom this was one of the first banks to give money. By 2005–06, the bank had given close to ₹600 crore to around seventy-five MFIs. That was 90% of its viable finance business and the rest 10% was direct loans, handled by business correspondents. These people are the retail agents of the banks who deliver banking services in rural India for a commission. Retired bank employees, retired teachers, retired government employees and ex-servicemen, chemists' shops, fair price shops, telephone booth operators, owners of grocery stores, among others, can be business correspondents.

HDFC Bank at that time was operating in thirteen states with 60% of business coming from the four southern states. There were at least 200 business correspondents and six lakh clients spread over 35,000 SHGs. The bank's ambition was to reverse the ratio to 10:90—10% through MFIs and 90% through direct lending, which could not be done at that point because of the lack of an extensive branch network.

By 2010 when the MFI industry was hit by the crisis, HDFC Bank's exposure to the sector rose to around ₹1,350 crore and the overall size of the viable finance unit was ₹1,500 crore. It shrank dramatically after the sector nearly collapsed but because the loans were mostly short term, for twelve to eighteen months, and monitoring was tight, the impact on the bank's balance sheet was not severe. It has since reduced its exposure to the MFI sector to a fourth of what it was in 2010 but the direct exposure to the so-called bottom-of-the-pyramid borrowers is rising.

The intermediation through business correspondents, mostly the non-government organizations (NGOs), also did not work well as the NGOs put their own interests first. 'They did what we wanted them to but also did some irregularities,' says Rajender Sehgal, country head of the financial institutions group. 'Suppose there are 300 groups one NGO caters to and only a hundred are eligible for loans, they will not disburse the full amount to the eligible groups. Instead, they will cut their money and distribute it among others who are not eligible for loans. We found out such irregularities.'

The NGOs started pretending to be the loan givers to influence the SHGs, and in certain pockets there were problems of misappropriation of money too. They took the money from the borrowers when they were repaying but did not give it to the bank. It happened in Odisha, Himachal Pradesh and Maharashtra. 'There are a dozen-odd cases but as a bank we don't want even one such case,' Rajender says.

K. Manohara Raj, business head of sustainable livelihood banking, insists that it was a part of the learning process and the bank always believed in directly reaching out to these people.

It's possible now as the bank has more rural and semi-urban branches in 2012 than it did in 2003—about 700 against 50—

and the technology is ready to create the so-called last-mile connectivity. Eliminating the MFIs and in some cases even the intermediation of NGOs, the bank is directly dealing with borrowers through its field agents and forming joint liability groups (JLGs), which are slightly different from SHGs. Here, loans are given to individual households but the liability is collective when it comes to repayment.

A bank's business model is very different from that of the MFIs, who can give loans but are not allowed by the RBI to take deposits and sell other financial products such as mutual funds and insurance. But a bank can do so; it can go beyond giving loans and meet the multiple financial needs of the poor. HDFC Bank wants to step in with a suite of products, with minimum intermediation for delivery and collection of money under strict monitoring.

So, business correspondents who play a useful role will continue to do so but instead of directly collecting cash, now they use a handheld device, called a point-of-sale terminal, in which the borrowers swipe a card and the data gets transferred to the bank instantly, depending on the bandwidth of the telecom connectivity in that location.

This gives the bank some control over collections. Along with this, the bank also directly calls on the customers once a month. Its field officers do so in close coordination with the business correspondents. The bank hands over money only at the branches. 'This is critical as, for a borrower, the person who is physically giving the money is the loan giver. They think of the business correspondents as their lenders. It's important to tell them it's the bank's money,' Rajender says.

The loan origination is also done by the bank directly. A field officer keys in the data on his laptop and the bank's credit team takes the call on who to give the loan to and who to deny the loan. 'To intensify the drive, a bank-on-wheels, a sort of mobile ATM, is moving around a branch at Coimbatore, covering two dozen villages at a specific time on certain days, every week. If the pilot project succeeds, there will be more such vans,' Rajender says.

As of 2012, the direct banking approach is being practised at 219 locations across nineteen states and lending through MFIs and dependence on banking correspondents has drastically come down. The bank is dealing with the SHGs directly as well as through creation of JLGs.

Unlike the JLGs, being formed by the bank, the SHGs are entities that are already in existence; they have a track record and the members of such groups do not keep money in the form of deposits with the bank. The SHGs keep their members' savings and play the role of an intermediary between the members and the bank.

The bank is giving money to four lakh households through SHGs and JLGs, as of 2012. The overall exposure is still small, about ₹300 crore. It's a tiny fraction as MFIs have covered around thirty million households and SHGs, traditionally used by all banks, another fifty million.

Rajender sees a disbursement of ₹1,000 crore and ten million households being covered in the next five years. At least half of the adult population of the world's largest democracy and one of the fastest growing major economies does not yet have access to banking services. The possibilities are enormous.

Profiles of some of the beneficiaries illustrate this:

- Chinnamoppanpatti village in Virudhunagar District of Tamil Nadu has 150 families. Most of them belong to the Kattunayakan community, a primitive tribal group in South India whose livelihood is soothsaying and palmistry.

  HDFC Bank has given loans to five SHGs, formed by sixty-one members of the Kattunayakan community in Chinnamoppanpatti. They were motivated to take up alternative livelihoods for improving their socio-economic status and entering the mainstream. The bank started by training them on how to make phenyl, a household cleaner. While doing that the bank officials got to know that these people are highly skilled in making bead jewellery.

  The bank is planning to train the tribal group in making fashion jewellery and to lend marketing support.

- Sashi Kumar, a forty-year-old widow with two daughters, lives in Dehradun in Uttarakhand, the setting for most stories by famed author Ruskin Bond. To earn a living, she cooks and delivers food to students and salaried employees for whom Dehradun is not the hometown.

  When she learnt that HDFC Bank was offering loans for livelihood support, she formed a group and sought a loan of ₹10,000. With the money, she bought a gas stove and utensils.

At the centre, she got to know that the bank also offered training in capacity building and helped create market linkages. She approached the bank for help with identifying more customers and added seventeen to her list of customers. She now earns about ₹9,000 a month, 50% more than what she was earning a year ago.

- Sharda from Chomu village in Rajasthan took ₹10,000 to invest in her tailoring business. Earlier, she was stitching only clothes. With this money, she started buying saris from the wholesale merchants and selling them at her tailoring shop, keeping a margin. She also started a beauty parlour at her home.

  As income grew from multiple activities, she started saving money. Every month, she keeps ₹1,000 in her recurring deposit. She could never save earlier as there were sources of taking loan but no avenues to save. When a saving avenue is created along with a loan facility, the entire model of financing people like Sharda gets changed; it becomes sustainable.

VINOD YENNEMADI: *The first employee on HDFC Bank's payroll.*

PARESH SUKTHANKAR: *His offer letter came on an A4 sheet of paper, with the words 'HDFC Bank (proposed)' neatly typed on the top*

HARISH ENGINEER: *Harish-bhai, as he is popularly known in the bank, was an early catch*

CN RAM: *His role in IT was to see how HDFC Bank could make a difference to its customers*

The Dirty Dozen

SAMIR BHATIA: *A company flat on Warden Road and extensive travel to Africa and Eastern Europe – all gone in minutes*

G SUBRAMANIAN: *As head of compliance, he reports directly to the chairman*

A RAJAN: *Taking a leap of faith, he decided to join the bank*

LUIS MIRANDA: *Thinking not so much about the salary, as about the prospect of working for an Indian company*

BHARAT SHAH: *He was still serving his notice period with UBS when he got drawn into the HDFC Bank project*

ABHAY AIMA: *Abhay had been a fighter pilot in the Indian Air Force before turning banker*

SHAILENDRA BHANDARI: *Staying with Citibank vs. going ahead with HDFC Bank – it was like tossing a coin where both sides seemed equal*

ASHISH PARTHASARTHY: *He had prepared Abhay Aima's resume for the human resource department of HDFC Bank*

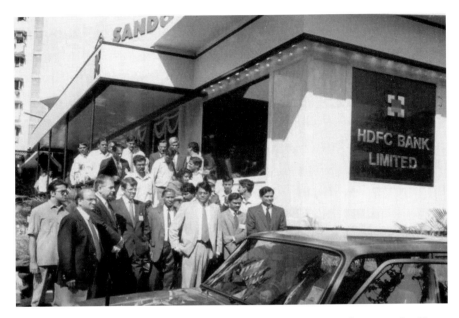

WELCOME TO NEW BANK: HDFC Bank's corporate office at Sandoz House, the old logo and the ubiquitous NE-118 given to the bank's chairman and managing director.

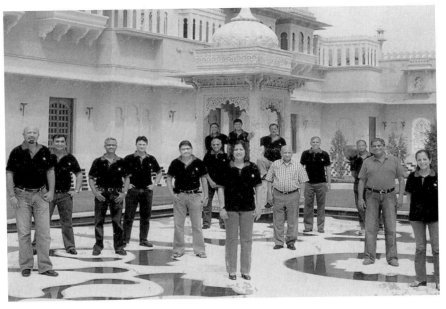

WORK AND PLAY: *Aditya's A team at an off-site meet at Jaipur, Rajasthan*

NEW BEGINNING: *Prime Minister Manmohan Singh (then finance minister), with Aditya Puri and Deepak Parekh, at the bank's launch in Mumbai*

MONEY TALK: *Former RBI governor C Rangarajan, along with Prime Minister Manmohan Singh (then finance minister), Paresh Sukthankar and Deepak Parekh at the opening ceremony*

SPREADING WINGS: *HDFC Bank's ADS listing at New York Stock Exchange in July 2001*

Top of the Pyramid

While the experiments to reach out to the vast masses of unbanked population and create a meaningful business proposition are on, the art of getting at the top of the pyramid and even snatching customers from competition is something this bank does with élan.

The cabin of private banking head Abhay in the bank's headquarters has lots of plants and resembles more of a tropical forest littered with books than the office of a wealth manager unless, of course, he follows a simple principle that money grows on trees! Possibly it does. If one listens to Gayatri Krishna Rao, who oversees a cluster of branches in the western suburb of Mumbai, getting top-end customers does not seem to be a big deal if one is taught the right way.

Asim Ghosh, former managing director and CEO of Vodafone Essar Ltd, is one such customer. Gayatri managed to get his relationship moved from HSBC to HDFC Bank. When HDFC executives were going to Asim's NCPA Apartment at Nariman Point to deliver the sanction letter for his home loan, Gayatri joined them. She managed to convince Asim to open an account with HDFC Bank.

That was the first step. Later, when Asim was changing his status from that of a resident Indian to that of an NRI with an overseas citizenship of India (OCI) card, he wanted to know some rules from the RBI. (An NRI with an OCI card is ensured visa-free travel to India even if he or she has acquired citizenship of another country.)

HDFC Bank got him the information in a jiffy while the

other bank faltered. He shifted his account from HSBC to HDFC Bank without batting an eye-lid.

Another high-net-worth customer was cheated by his personal assistant. Gayatri and her colleague went to his office at midnight and in his presence dug out demand drafts and physical share certificates kept by his personal assistant without his knowledge. The personal assistant was arrested by the police for defrauding him, and Gayatri even became the prime witness in the case. The customer, former chairman and managing director of Shipping Corporation of India Ltd P. K. Srivastava, wrote a lovely letter to Aditya, saying he has seen many bright and young officers in his long career but these two young officers were among the very best. Aditya's people bought his lifelong loyalty.

Chapter 9

Merger, Merger on the Wall

Akira Kurosawa's 1950 crime drama film *Rashomon* opens on a woodcutter and a priest sitting beneath the Rashomon gate at the southern end of Suzaku Avenue between the ancient Japanese cities of Heijo-kyo (Nara) and Heian-kyo (Kyoto) to stay dry in a downpour. When a commoner joins them, they begin recounting to him a disturbing story that they had witnessed.

The woodcutter claims to have found the body of a murdered samurai three days ago while looking for wood in the forest. The priest says he saw the samurai and a woman travelling the same day the murder happened. Both men are then summoned to testify in court, where they meet a captured bandit, who claims responsibility for the rape and murder.

The film narrates the bandit's story, the wife's story and the samurai's story—told through a medium. Every story lends a fresh perspective to what had happened, adding new layers of truth and dimensions to complete the picture.

The *dramatis personae* involved in Times Bank's merger with HDFC Bank in 2000 also tell us different stories. Or different pieces of the same story. They are no less dramatic than Kurosawa's *Rashomon*. Collectively, they present the big picture of the most fascinating merger in Indian banking history, complete with the minutest details.

Let's hear their stories.

Deepak's Story

'Ashok Jain [then chairman of Bennett, Coleman and Co. Ltd, the promoter of Times Bank] was known to me. We used to play bridge regularly at [former petroleum minister] Murli Deora's house on Breach Candy and later Peddar Road. Jain would come every Saturday and Sunday if he was in Bombay. He always felt that his group didn't know how to run financial companies and told me to take his bank.

'I was ready to pay cash and take it but he would never sell it for cash. He wanted shares. We kept talking about this occasionally on the bridge table. When he fell ill and was admitted at AIIMS [All India Institute of Medical Sciences] in Delhi, I got a message that he wanted to see me. I took a flight and went there. Samir [Jain], Vineet [Jain] and Amit [Judge] were standing beside his bed. [Samir and Vineet are Jain's sons and Amit is his son-in-law.]

'He said that he had told all three to get out of the bank and sell it to me, but only for shares. I heard him; subsequently, I spoke to Aditya about it. Both of us felt the time was right for such a deal . . .'

Amit's Story

'Chase Capital, headed by my friend Anil Ahuja, owned about 15% of HDFC Bank at that time. Anil called me one day and said he wanted to discuss something. He was on the HDFC Bank board. I didn't know Aditya at all but knew his wife Smiley through Satsang. [Satsang is a philanthropic organization founded by Shree Shree Thakur Anukulchandra. It has hundreds of centres in the form of *mandirs* and *viharas* spread all over India and Bangladesh.]

'Anil suggested a merger. He did not actually use the word merger but said something on those lines. The next day, I hosted a lunch at my house on Malabar Hill [in Mumbai]. By that time, Nimesh Kampani had done all the numbers because we were sort of getting into an equity agreement with the Old Mutual Group of South Africa and Nimesh was our investment banker. I had with me all the numbers.

'We discussed the merger over lunch. Aditya knew his numbers and proposed a ratio. I calculated my own ratio. There was a small difference. I remember after we finished lunch and were washing our fingers, Aditya said, "Look, what should we do?" I said, "Let's go half–half." He said, "Fine." I told him it would be difficult to do a formal due diligence because everybody would come to know. Aditya said, "I trust you."

'On a Sunday, we drew up the agreement, just a two-pager. The next week we merged.'

Anil's Story

'One day Amit and I were playing golf at the US Club in Colaba, just the two of us. While playing, we did discuss the bank and the opportunity for Times Bank to merge with HDFC Bank. One person who figured out something was happening while two of us were playing was Rana Kapoor [of Yes Bank Ltd]. He, in fact, actually commented: "You guys are cooking something."

'It was a complicated process. I remember having meetings with Nani Javeri, the CEO of Times Bank, and there was a lot of discussion on how the board would react to such a merger. Obviously, the key issue was valuation.

'The defining meeting was held at Amit's house on Malabar Hill. We went to wash our fingers after our meal and that's when Amit and Aditya said this was something that they should definitely try and do.

'I still remember there was a final phone call that I made—I was speaking to Deepak Parekh on one side and Amit Judge on the other, and trying to get them to agree to the merger ratio because there was a range of valuations that were floating around. No merchant banker was involved in the deal.'

RBI Deputy Governor S. P. Talwar's Story

'After Times Bank was set up, the RBI observed that there were certain regulatory issues pertaining to its promoters. We were not very comfortable with them. It was informally discussed with the chairman of the bank who volunteered to step down from the board of directors. In course of time, the bank was persuaded to voluntarily merge with some other bank.'

~

These are different parts of the same story. Let's see how the merger actually happened. But before that, a word about Times Bank. Bennett, Coleman and Co. Ltd, which runs India's largest media house, was the promoter of the bank. The RBI approved the bank in principle in December 1993; the company was incorporated in July 1994; it got a banking licence in April 1995, and opened its first branch on D. N. Road, Mumbai, on 8 June 1995.

For the fiscal year that ended March 1999, it had a deposit base of ₹3,012 crore, advances of ₹1,312 crore and investments of ₹1,043 crore. Its net profit for the year was ₹27.06 crore.

For the same year, HDFC Bank had deposits of ₹2,915 crore, advances of ₹1,401 crore and investments of ₹1,904 crore. Its net profit for the year was ₹82.40 crore.

Times Bank's net NPA, a key ratio to gauge a bank's health, added up to 3.01% of advances. For HDFC Bank, it was 1.25%.

Times Bank had 541 employees in March 1999, 35 branches and 34 ATMs, whereas HDFC Bank had 827 employees, 57 branches and 77 ATMs.

HDFC Bank had its IPO in March 1995, within two months of opening shop. Times Bank made the public offering on 30 June 1999—four years after it opened the first branch. Its ₹35-crore IPO, at par, was subscribed six times. It was listed on 20 September 1999 at a hefty premium of ₹14.70.

Merger Reconstructed

It seems that Times Bank did sound out HDFC Bank and there were preliminary discussions ahead of its IPO but they did not lead anywhere. HDFC Bank had, in fact, done due diligence when Old Mutual was talking to Times Bank for a possible equity stake.

When the issue resurfaced again, HDFC Bank's chief risk manager Paresh led a small team for another round of due diligence, quietly and informally. Usually, deals are done with an understanding that they will be subject to due diligence. But, in this case, due diligence—however informal—was done before the deal was closed.

So far, the RBI had brokered all bank mergers in India, mainly to protect the interests of depositors. In the case of HDFC Bank and Times Bank, the RBI did not play the matchmaker. So nobody knew how the RBI would react to such a friendly merger.

Paresh's team had Kaizad, GS, Samir and Luis.

Five of them would travel together in a car and get off somewhere near the Bombay Municipal Corporation (now known as the Brihanmumbai Municipal Corporation or the Municipal Corporation of Greater Mumbai) headquarters, and then walk down to the Times Bank office at the Times of India building, opposite Victoria Terminus on D. N. Road. After getting off the car, they would walk down separately, pretending not to know each other. Anyway, it was hardly a couple of minutes' walk and no one would be dressed like a banker, in striped shirts and grey suits. Even the driver didn't know where they were heading.

They were coordinating with Arun Arora, then CEO of Times Music and *The Economic Times*, and president and executive director of India's largest media conglomerate with interests in newspapers, magazines, radio, television, Internet, music, multimedia and home entertainment.

Sitting in a conference room close to Arun's cabin, they would ask for all sorts of details, and Times Bank's executive director Pradip Pain would bring the documents in sealed envelopes. There were apprehensions about the quality of assets as Times Bank had a slightly different business model, heavy on retail and SMEs.

'What Are You Doing Here?'

Paresh once ran into a lady who had till recently been working with HDFC Bank before shifting to Times Bank. 'Oh! Hello! What are you doing here?' she asked when Paresh was about to enter the building. He mumbled something and almost ran to come back after half an hour. Nobody got a whiff of the merger till the day both the banks gave notices to the exchanges saying they were meeting to consider a potential merger—26 November 1999.

The positive factor was Times Bank's insistence on a share swap deal. 'We were very clear that if there were things we didn't know that the seller didn't want us to know, he wouldn't have asked for a share swap. He would have gone for cash. They were interested in continuing to be part of the bank, but didn't want to manage the bank as owners,' Paresh told me.

On 25 November, a day before both the banks gave notices to the exchanges for the board meeting on the proposed merger, Times Bank's share price closed at ₹18.30 apiece and that of HDFC Bank at ₹90 apiece. Both banks' shares had a face value of ₹10 each. Since there was a price discovery in the market, both banks felt it should be fair to go by that. That's how the swap ratio was worked out—twenty-three shares of Times Bank for five shares of HDFC Bank—with a very small control premium.

Tamal Bandyopadhyay

'Is Paresh Okay?'

Those seven days when they were checking the books, tension and stress were palpable on Paresh's face. He was not eating or talking to anybody. His wife, Sangeeta, felt something was terribly wrong with Paresh. She called up Aditya and asked, 'Is there something troubling Paresh at work?' Aditya, in his usual way, told her to relax.

The books were checked at three places—the Times of India building, a lawyer's office and an empty HDFC Bank flat on Napean Sea Road. 'We spent almost two weeks in the small flat, calling for all relevant files from the bank. Had we have sat in their office for long, people would have figured out,' Samir told me.

Relatively new in the organization, Sashi found the secrecy of it all quite amazing. On a Sunday, at a colleague's wedding, he got a call from his boss Vinod asking him to rush to a lawyer's place. For the next three days, no one in the bank knew where he was.

Sashi, Vinod and company secretary and head of legal affairs Sanjay Dongre, along with Paresh and Samir, did the desktop due diligence at the office of Wadia Ghandy & Co., at Fort, opposite the University of Mumbai. They were trying to figure out how the balance sheet would look after the merger.

There weren't any nasty surprises. And, on day one, this was an accretive merger for the bank. In other words, there was no dilution in return on equity and earnings per share for HDFC Bank after it offered a stake to the Times Bank promoters. It was beneficial for the shareholders. The Jains got a stake of around 7.7% in HDFC Bank, which they sold in stages, making pots of money.

'Even after knocking off whatever extra provisions we made on some of the loans that we felt may not be good, we came out well. It was day-zero accretive for the merged entity,' Sashi says. The combined entity had higher earnings per share—something rare in the history of mergers and acquisitions in India.

No wonder then that the markets gave a thumbs up to the merger. The HDFC Bank stock started hitting the circuit breaker almost every day after the announcement. Between 26 November 1999 and 26 February 2000, when the merger took effect, the stock rose, from ₹98.90 to ₹227.50.

'We Weren't as Bad as Projected'

Maheshwari, who was vice president in charge of credit and risk management at Times Bank in 1999, and went on to head corporate credit risk management at HDFC Bank, said the popular perception that Times Bank's loan portfolio was not as good as that of HDFC Bank was true only to some extent. The NPA ratio of HDFC Bank was better simply because it used to set aside money to provide for 80–90% of bad assets, something that Times Bank did not do. But gross NPAs of both the banks were in the same range.

He also pointed out that Times Bank had long-dated government bonds in its investment portfolio, bought when interest rates peaked. By the time the merger was happening, interest rates started coming down and the bond value started appreciating. That was a huge plus for HDFC Bank.

The biggest gain was Times Bank's thirty-nine branches, about two-thirds of HDFC Bank's own branch network then. It was adding about twenty branches a year at that time. At one stroke, the merger took the bank forward by two years. H. N. Sinor, then managing director of rival ICICI Bank (it was still a subsidary of the project finance institution ICICI), had told me when I reported the merger that they also looked at Times Bank and did not find it attractive, but they missed its branch network. This is very critical when the regulator is not liberal in giving branch licences.

Maheshwari was reporting directly to Nani, managing director of Times Bank. He recalls being summoned by Nani one day and being told that the promoters were trying to sell some of their stakes in the bank and HDFC was buying a 20% stake. 'I knew that the 20% figure was not correct. If they were to buy the bank, they would buy entirely. The MD asked me why I was looking so nervous. In my heart, I knew that the bank was being sold,' Maheshwari said.

Maheshwari was not the only person at Times Bank who did not know what was happening. Sudhir Joshi, head of treasury, couldn't in his wildest dream think this could happen. Just a month ago he had accompanied Nani on a three-week road show overseas. They were looking for ways to increase lines of credit from foreign banks.

After listing, Times Bank also took up a fancy office at Kamala Mills.

'There had been talks, but my sense was that had fizzled out. The African group also came to buy a stake but it didn't work out,' Sudhir told me. After (Ashok) Jain passed away, Nani officially told some of his senior colleagues that Jain's younger son was being groomed to eventually take interest in the bank.

An SBI Den

Times Bank was a den of bankers poached from SBI. N. G. Pillai, its first managing director, came from SBI. So did Pradip and Sudhir and quite a few other senior executives. Nani, though, was a former Grindlays hand.

There were people from other banks as well, but the culture was predominantly that of SBI. Suranjan Ghosh and Ujwal Thakar came from Standard Chartered. Suranjan was to head corporate banking but later was shifted to administration, whereas Ujwal was heading the retail business. Ujwal left before the merger to join BNP Paribas N. V. and Suranjan within three months of the merger. Pradip took six months to resign.

Nani was the first to leave, as one bank cannot have two heads. He was followed by Rama Sridhar, the head of direct banking.

But not all senior employees left the bank. Quite a few stayed back with larger responsibilities. Uma was one of them. Relatively new at Times Bank—she had come from Standard

Chartered as a replacement for Ujwal—Uma was made the head of retail branch banking at HDFC Bank till she decided to move to Chennai. As head of credit cards, she launched the credit card business at HDFC Bank. Mandeep Maitra, head of human resources at Times Bank, was another senior executive. Maheshwari came on board to head corporate credit. Sudhir was initially made the head of financial institutions and government groups but a few months later when Luis moved on, Sudhir got into his shoes. Anil Nath, regional head of corporate banking at Times Bank, went on to head business banking at HDFC Bank. Suresh Prabhu, head of money markets at Times Bank, continued in the same role at HDFC Bank.

This is what Luis told me: 'When the merger was announced, I went straight to the dealing room of Times Bank and I told the guys—I knew the treasurer Sudhir Joshi, and had worked with him in an RBI committee—I didn't want any of them to leave. I required people. They didn't believe me.

'I told them, "Just because HDFC Bank is taking over your bank it doesn't mean that you guys will have to report to the HDFC Bank people. I'm going to be very clear that whoever is best suited for that job will be running it." But a lot of Times Bank people didn't believe me. There were quite a few whom I wanted to retain but they left. Almost as a tribute, when I left, Sudhir took over from me. That's reflective of the fact that we wanted to build a culture of meritocracy—just because someone came from the conqueror's side doesn't mean that he will always remain on top.'

Maheshwari said that the HDFC Bank employees were equally apprehensive: 'An army of people from another bank—

and many of who were better paid and more qualified—were entering their bank. This would hurt their prospects too. The feeling was mutual on both sides; even HDFC Bank's staffers were under some stress.'

It took a few years for normalcy to return. But Aditya was on the job from day one. The first meeting on integration took place at the Times Bank boardroom at Kamala Mills. The boardroom was very impressive, equipped with the latest gadgets. The HDFC Bank boardroom wouldn't have accommodated so many people. It's another story that the bank quickly got rid of this office as it was too expensive. HDFC Bank had its office in the same compound at half the rental.

Sudhir attended the meeting, and recounts, 'Aditya gave a very positive spin to the whole thing. Till the merger, HDFC Bank was primarily a corporate bank and Times Bank was evolving more as a retail bank. He explained the synergies and the first people he took on board were from the retail segment. He told us how HDFC Bank looked at business and its strategy. I do remember telling him that we also have a lot to contribute and not all our strategies are wrong.' At the meeting, Aditya unveiled the business strategy for the combined bank.

William M. Mercer Ltd (now Mercer LLC), a human resource and related financial services consulting company, oversaw the human resource aspects of the integration process. It was done systematically, branch by branch, employee by employee amid redeployment, relocation of branches and large-scale resignations. The smartest move was making Mandeep the chief of human resources in the merged entity.

Typically, in any merger integration of people is as important as integration of business, if not more. By making Mandeep the head of human resources, HDFC Bank sent a strong signal that it believed in a fair process of evaluating people.

'Marriage of Your Vision and My Provision'

When they were discussing the merger, Amit told Aditya, 'You are a bank with a vision and I am a bank with a provision. My provision with your vision will get on well.' He used to look after the non-banking finance company of the group, Times Guaranty Financials Ltd, before coming on the board of the bank. A commerce graduate from St Xavier's College in Kolkata, Amit, a serial entrepreneur, is in the business of buying and selling companies.

There were professional managers for Times Guaranty but Amit was looking after it on behalf of the shareholders. He himself did not believe in the non-banking finance company model though—'an unnecessary appendage into the financial system, something that should have never even existed,' says Amit.

He also found banking very boring. Times Bank was not going anywhere because there wasn't enough capital and competent employees. Amit, who many believed came to the board with a mandate to sell the bank, scrapped the plan to sell a 20% stake in the bank to the South African group when they came very close to signing the deal. 'Mere equity partnerships were not the answer . . . Mr [Ashok] Jain had enough money to put in. That wasn't the issue. It was to get intellectual bandwidth as well as commercial capital and relationships. I put my foot down,' he told me.

Incidentally, Times Bank was not Bennett, Coleman and Co. Ltd's first foray into banking. The company's first Indian owner, Ramakrishna Dalmia, had a controlling stake in PNB. He sold the publishing house to his son-in-law—and business partner—Sahu Shanti Prasad Jain in 1948. Until 1969, when fourteen major Indian private banks with a deposit base of at least ₹50 crore were nationalized, Shanti Prasad and his nephew, Sahu Shital Prasad Jain, had a controlling interest in PNB. Shanti Prasad served as PNB's chairman and managing director between 1954 and 1959 and his nephew was a director on the PNB board. The Jains exited the business in 1969.

Amit joined the board of the merged entity but quit after a year as he found the board meetings 'absolutely boring'. Before every board meeting, a courier would come with so many papers and he didn't even read them. Ashok Jain's son Vineet joined the board in his place. 'Vineet never interfered,' Deepak said.

The merger of Times Bank with HDFC Bank was a landmark deal in the Indian banking industry in many ways. It was the first friendly merger in the banking space and the first done through the share swap route. It catapulted HDFC Bank into the big league in terms of business as well as market valuation.

That's one way of looking at it. The merger also tells us that the banking regulator often did not pick the right candidates for banking licences. The RBI withdrew the in-principle nod it had given to CRB Capital Markets Ltd for the eleventh new bank when it came to light that its promoter Chain Roop Bansali had defrauded at least 200,000 investors and the SBI of ₹1,200 crore. But this alertness was missing when it picked up the first ten candidates to issue the licences.

In fact, the Parliamentary Standing Committee on Finance, headed by former Odisha chief minister Biju Patnaik, was not happy with the RBI policy of giving licences to some banks. The committee wanted to know why the RBI had given a licence to Times Bank. Apparently, the promoter of the bank had a sick company Rohtas Industries Ltd in the group. (The report of the committee is not in public domain but an RBI official told me this.)

~

In retrospect, three banks floated by financial institutions— HDFC Bank, ICICI Bank and Axis Bank (UTI Bank renamed)—have done well. The fourth one, IDBI Bank, with which its promoter project finance company IDBI merged, hasn't done too badly either. IndusInd Bank was a laggard till a new management put it on a growth path. Among the rest, Ramesh Gelli's Global Trust Bank crumbled under bad assets after getting too bold in stock market play and was forced to merge with public sector Oriental Bank of Commerce. Bank of Punjab couldn't get its act together and offered to merge with Centurion Bank. And Centurion Bank, renamed Centurion Bank of Punjab after that deal, merged with HDFC Bank. That story is no less dramatic than the Times Bank merger story.

Chapter 10

Anatomy of a Big Bang Merger

The 1999 merger was an appetizer for HDFC Bank. It had to wait for eight years for the meal. In February 2008, the boards of HDFC Bank and Centurion BoP agreed to the biggest merger in Indian banking history, valued at ₹9,510 crore.

Centurion Bank, promoted as a joint venture between 20th Century Finance Corporation Ltd and its associates and Keppel Group of Singapore, was set up around the time that HDFC Bank opened shop, but it floundered till a group of investors led by Rana Talwar's Sabre Capital Worldwide Inc. took over the reins in 2003.

Rana, a former CEO at Standard Chartered, is a growth junkie and a strong believer in aggressive acquisitions, something that cost him the job at Standard Chartered. For Centurion Bank, he pushed through three acquisitions in a row, taking over the Indian operations of Bank Muscat in 2003, acquiring the Bank of Punjab in 2005 (becoming Centurion BoP) and Lord Krishna Bank Ltd in 2007. The latter two banks, a new one and the other an old private bank, were strong in the northern state of Punjab and the southern state of Kerala, respectively.

After the merger announcement, Aditya told the media the integration would be smooth as there was no overlap. He also said that with a 40% growth rate, there would be no lay-offs. 'It should take us about the same time as we needed to integrate Times Bank. Times Bank, as a percentage of our balance sheet, was much larger; we were smaller then. It was 35–40% of our size,' Aditya said. Centurion BoP added just about 20% to the balance sheet.

The market did not believe him. The stock tanked as investors rushed to sell on concerns that HDFC Bank had paid too much for Centurion BoP.

That is a summary of media reports. Now, the real story.

There were tough negotiations for this deal and quite a few breaking points—even at the board meeting that gave the nod to the merger. The meeting at Ramon House lasted for eleven hours, till almost midnight. Aditya wanted the board to take an independent view on whether or not the acquisition was required. There was intense discussion on valuation and certain tax liabilities of Centurion BoP.

PriceWaterhouseCoopers Pvt Ltd and Deloitte Corporate Finance Services India Pvt Ltd, representing both the banks, made long presentations to convince the board.

Deepak got to know Rana when he was working with Citibank in India.

Rana Gurvirendra Singh Talwar, son of a bureaucrat and son-in-law of K. P. Singh of DLF Ltd, India's largest real-estate company, began his career in the Mumbai branch of Citibank. He became head of Citibank's consumer business in the Asia-Pacific region and the Middle East before he left for Standard Chartered where he was group CEO till a bitter boardroom battle led to his ouster in 2001. In his consumer banking days, Rana used to pick up tips from Deepak on mortgage business. 'We weren't friends. I knew him as a banker and we used to meet at some parties,' Deepak said.

One fine morning, out of the blue, Rana called Deepak and offered to merge. The discussion didn't move much. Months later, Rana called again. This time, there was urgency in his voice. He wanted to do something very soon.

Deepak called him over for lunch at his house on a Sunday. Over Heineken beer and lunch, Centurion BoP's managing director Shailendra, Rana, Aditya and Deepak discussed a possible merger and swore to keep it confidential. 'They were in a hurry and for some reasons Rana was saying that either we do it today or he will go across the road,' Deepak told me. He possibly meant that if Deepak was not interested, he would approach another bank.

Too many retail loans were going bad and they had to set aside a fat sum to take care of bad loans. This would have affected Centurion BoP's earnings and stock price. Rana wanted to seal the deal to cover up the March earnings.

A few days later when they finally shook hands, Deepak called Venu (Yaga Venugopal Reddy, then RBI governor). Not too many in the Indian financial sector address Reddy as Venu and that shows Deepak's relationship with him, which goes back to the early 1990s when Reddy was with the Finance Ministry.

'I want to see you.'

'What for?'

'Something very urgent and important . . . We had a talk with Rana. We want to take over Centurion Bank of Punjab.'

'No need to see me. We are happy. Leeladhar [deputy governor V. Leeladhar] will call you.'

It was around six in the evening and Leeladhar had just left his office on Mint Road in Mumbai and was on his way home. Once he heard from his boss, Leeladhar called Deepak and returned to his office. He was heading the critical department of banking operations and development at the RBI.

Other deputy governors called Deepak and said he had solved their problem.

Reddy's reaction was instant not because he knew Deepak well but because it fitted well into the RBI's consolidation strategy in Indian banking sector. Centurion BoP was one of the relatively small and weak banks that the RBI was closely monitoring. The RBI was not hunting for any suitor but when Deepak appeared on the scene with the proposal, Reddy felt hugely relieved.

The Original Suitor

HDFC Bank was not the original suitor. Rana had first spoken to Deepak about merging his bank with Infrastructure Development Finance Co. Ltd (IDFC), of which Deepak was chairman. IDFC's managing director Rajeev Lall had always felt the need for a banking licence to get access to the cheap funds desperately needed for infrastructure financing, but could not take the idea forward because the then finance minister P. Chidambaram, I am told, was not inclined to say 'yes' to it. Creation of IDFC was Chidambaram's idea to address the infrastructure financing concerns in a growing economy. It was part of his 1997 dream budget.

'How about merging with HDFC Bank?' Deepak suggested. At this stage, Aditya got involved. Till then, V. S. Rangan, then financial controller of HDFC, was the other person in the know of things.

Shailendra remembers the lunch and beer at Deepak's home. 'Deepak suggested a swap ratio to which Rana said "no". He wanted to improve it,' he told me.

Rana wanted one share of HDFC Bank for every twenty-three shares of Centurion BoP. He was basically trying to squeeze the last drop and Deepak was not playing ball; they walked away from the meeting. After months of negotiations the deal was struck—but at a different ratio.

Rana insisted that HDFC Bank must agree to absorb all the people from Centurion BoP. Aditya agreed.

'Leave Offsite; I Want You in Mumbai'

Paresh was not in Mumbai. He was attending an offsite on credit at Jaipur when he got Aditya's call: 'Can you come back? There's work for you here.'

'I am required in Mumbai; something has come up. You guys continue with the rest of the agenda,' Paresh told his colleagues and took the next flight to Mumbai. It was a long drive to the airport.

Aditya wasn't in Mumbai either. He was on an all-India tour to review performance of all local offices of the bank. His colleagues call this the '*Bharat yatra*'. Aditya was in Hyderabad. After talking to Paresh, he called Sashi and asked him to look at all information on Centurion BoP available in the public domain.

Sashi picked up his laptop and headed straight to the conference room on the sixth floor at the bank's headquarters with his colleague Deepak Majithia. The security locked the conference room from outside. By midnight, a two-page fact sheet on Centurion BoP was ready.

Paresh was back in office the next day. Both Paresh and Sashi had apprehensions about the quality of Centurion BoP's assets. They were also concerned about the price at which the bank's stock was trading. Its price-to-book ratio was '4', equivalent to that of HDFC Bank. The bank was not cheap by any means.

Price-to-book is a ratio that compares a stock's market value with its book value. It's calculated by dividing the current closing price of a stock by the latest quarter's book value per share. A lower price-to-book ratio could mean the stock is undervalued. It could also mean that something is fundamentally wrong with the company. On the other hand, a higher ratio doesn't necessarily mean it's a great stock; it could simply mean investors are paying too much.

Aditya wasn't yet back in Mumbai. Over the telephone, he told Paresh and Sashi to meet Keki, HDFC's vice chairman and managing director then. Keki, Deepak's trusted lieutenant, was also on the board of HDFC Bank. On a Saturday, at Ramon House, they told Keki, 'It's not attractive and it doesn't make any economic sense to take over this bank at this point.' After the meeting, Paresh went to the Hanuman temple near St Xavier's High School at Dhobi Talao, his Saturday afternoon ritual in Mumbai.

Aditya returned over the weekend and joined Shailendra and Rana at Deepak's house for the Sunday lunch. Neither he nor Deepak was fully convinced but said, 'Let's try and explore.'

They were given just three days to do due diligence. A team of a dozen officers with heads of audit, credit, legal and operations trooped into the Centurion BoP headquarters at Mahalaxmi in Mumbai to check facts and figures. They also roped in Deloitte to scan the tax liabilities.

On the other side, Anil Jaggia, chief operating officer of Centurion BoP, and Amit Khanna, head of strategic planning, were assisting Shailendra.

HDFC Bank's core team had two members—Paresh and Sashi. The duo met Sanjay Sakhuja, CEO of Ambit Corporate Finance Pvt. Ltd, and Ashok Wadhwa, the boss of the investment bank, at Ambit House, literally next door to the bank's headquarters at Lower Parel. Even then they were cautious. Neither Paresh nor Sashi would give their names at the reception desk at Ambit.

For Times Bank, most checks were done at the lawyer's office because onsite due diligence had been done earlier. In this case, they needed to check every minute detail in seventy-two hours. So, twelve of them would pretend to go on calls. They would be in separate cars; land at the same place but at different times in the evening after office hours when most people had left. Each day the exercise would last till four in the morning.

50:50

The findings were 50:50. The numbers weren't great but Centurion BoP's network of 404 branches across India was a big positive. 'If I were to superimpose Centurion Bank of Punjab on HDFC Bank after cleaning it up, would the earnings per share in three years be more than what we would have done in organic basis? The answer was "yes". It made sense,' Sashi said.

Paresh had a certain level of comfort with Shailendra being a former colleague from Citibank and HDFC Bank, but nonetheless he decided to go through the entire exercise meticulously. When negotiations reached almost the last stage, he switched off for a few hours. 'I am willing to drop it,' Paresh told Aditya as he felt they were asking for a little too much.

There was hard bargaining. Ashok of Ambit was at his persuasive best. Centurion BoP, according to him, was a right fit for HDFC Bank. Rana's objective was not only to maximize the profit but also to make sure that the bank's employees had a career. But Paresh was a hard nut to crack.

Both banks being listed entities, there was price discovery in the market but Paresh still insisted on a discount to the market price. Only when everybody accepted that—one share of HDFC Bank for every twenty-nine shares of Centurion BoP—was the stock market announcement made.

Paresh's reasoning is quite simple: In a stock swap, had there been something drastically wrong, the other side would also suffer as they would hold HDFC Bank's shares. It's the same philosophy that clinched the Times Bank deal.

There were a few nasty surprises, minor though. The holes in the credit portfolio weren't deep but there were business-related issues. 'Our impression was that they hadn't run the shop tightly. It's more related to processes and integrity at lower levels. Some branch managers were taking deposits but not putting the money into the system,' Paresh said. Centurion BoP had done three acquisitions in quick succession but hadn't integrated all the portions fully. The issues surfaced from lack of control and loose supervision.

Four-Banks-in-One

The integration process this time was not as smooth as it was in the case of the merger with Times Bank as the size of the merger was larger. And Centurion BoP was four-banks-in-one. On day zero, HDFC Bank ensured that all incremental underwriting of credits was being done in accordance with its established norms.

Then came the integration of people. It wasn't easy as there were 7,500 employees, about a third of the number of employees of HDFC Bank. The solution, they thought, was to create new positions for both teams. No one would know whether he or she has gone down or up the ladder. Every belly button of Centurion BoP and HDFC Bank was evaluated as to who was doing what and the actual work involved. Again, Mercer was appointed as a consultant for the integration of human resources.

'I was given the offer to join the board as an executive director. I told Aditya I would think it over. I was there till they formally did the merger. Frankly, after having left once, to come back again and do the same thing didn't make sense for me. My role was to get the thing done, not the subsequent thing which can go on for years—the closure,' Shailendra told me. Formally, the merger happened in May. Shailendra left in August.

Jaggia got the head-of-technology post at HDFC Bank after Ram left in March 2008. Insiders say Jaggia's package, including stock options, was so hefty at Centurion BoP that at least for a year his salary was frozen and HDFC Bank had to be liberal in giving options to its senior executives to maintain parity. Centurion BoP treasurer Tarini Vaidya stayed back but left later for personal reasons. She didn't want to continue with a full-time job. Vivek Vig, head of retail, left as there was no defined role for him in the merged entity. Neeraj Dhawan, head of retail risk management, was made head of collections.

It took about a year to integrate wholesale banking, treasury and retail systems and many employees of Centurion BoP left. Integration of two banks is very different from integration of two manufacturing outfits. Here, beyond business models and employees, millions of customers have to be integrated. Cheques, debit and credit cards, ATM cards, demand drafts— every single instrument needs to be uniform. If one messes up, one will lose customers. Centurion BoP had 2.5 million customers.

Technology was indeed an issue but there was no disruption as many might have feared. Both banks had centralized processing but with different vendors—Finacle for Centurion BoP and i-Flex for HDFC Bank. Finacle was superior to i-Flex's retail solution but HDFC Bank stuck to its vendor. At the end of the day, apart from purely technical aspects such decisions are driven by facts such as how many people need to be trained, how many branches need to be converted and how much cost is involved. HDFC Bank has almost double the branch network and three times the people.

The Markets Give the Thumbs Down

On the day the share swap ratio was announced, Centurion BoP shares, which had run up in anticipation of the merger, fell by 14.5% to ₹48.25. HDFC Bank shares fell by 3.5% to close at ₹1,422.70 a share.

Investors felt HDFC Bank had paid too much for the branches. 'You've to realize that people were paying that for Centurion BoP as it existed. Its share price was reflective of the market perception about its business potential, branch network and the overall franchise as it existed. We paid less than what the market was paying. It might have still been high but we knew that when we would push it to our level of profitability, huge value would be created,' Paresh said.

Times Bank was quoting at 1 or 1.2 times the book and HDFC Bank was quoting 3 or 4 times the book in 1999. So, just the arithmetic of the deal created value. In this case, underlying valuations weren't very different though the underlying franchises were of different quality. HDFC Bank's defence for the high price was that it wasn't paying for what was only there; it was looking at the merger from the point of view of what it could make of the deal. Centurion BoP was about 20% of HDFC Bank's size in terms of the balance sheet (₹1.31 trillion versus ₹25,404 crore as of the third quarter of 2007–08) and even less than 20% in terms of profits, but was 55% in terms of branches.

Region-wise, Centurion BoP had about 170 branches in the north and around 140 branches in the south. Most of these branches were located in Punjab, Haryana, upper Rajasthan,

Maharashtra, Goa, Kerala and Tamil Nadu where economic growth is higher than in other Indian states. After the merger, HDFC Bank became No. 2 in Mumbai and Delhi in terms of branch presence, second to India's largest lender, SBI.

All for Branches

At an internal meeting, Aditya told his colleagues, 'Don't go by the fact that they have low businesses. They have only two products, savings and insurance. We have all the products. With our product range and execution, we can build the business. You're getting the infrastructure.'

Deepak admits they paid on the higher side but defends it saying it was for the branches: 'To get a branch licence from the RBI takes time and here we were getting readymade branches.'

On day one, on almost every parameter, including the three most critical ones, Centurion BoP was inferior to HDFC Bank.

HDFC Bank's CASA was about 47% of overall deposits, whereas Centurion BoP's CASA was 26%. For the merged entity, it came down to 43%.

HDFC Bank's cost-to-earnings ratio was 48–49% before the merger against Centurion BoP's 69%. On merger, it became 55%.

HDFC Bank's gross NPAs were about 1.3% of advances against a little over 3% at Centurion BoP.

The challenge before HDFC Bank was to get back to

where it was on all these parameters and create value after the integration was completed. It set a deadline of thirty to thirty-six months for the completion but managed to get it done in twenty-four months. In two years, HDFC Bank got back to the pre-merger CASA and cost-to-earnings ratio level, and in three years, it covered the ground on bad assets.

This was done in a very difficult environment. Four months after the merger, US investment bank Lehman Brothers collapsed, leading to an unprecedented credit crunch across the globe. Economic growth in India halted while the outside world plunged in a recession even as the government and the banking regulator joined hands for fiscal stimulus and liquidity to pump prime the economy.

For HDFC Bank, it was difficult but doable as it's a stronger brand, has a wider product range and has systems in control. As business flowed into the under-leveraged, under-utilized distribution network of Centurion BoP, the gap across segments was bridged.

The big difference between the Times Bank merger and the Centurion BoP merger was that the former was an accretive merger from day zero but the latter took three years to become an accretive merger. The stock market initially gave it a cold shoulder but that's the risk Deepak and Aditya took consciously—the biggest gamble that the normally risk-averse bank has ever taken.

There are critics of the merger even within the bank. Abhay is one of them. He personally thinks it was a very expensive branch acquisition. 'What have you got from the bank? The clients were a question mark, the quality of the portfolio was

not the best, not more than 10% of the talent stayed back...
What does it boil down to? I didn't celebrate the merger.
People gave me dirty looks,' says Abhay. He admits that the
merger hasn't panned out as badly as he had thought but he
still doesn't approve of it.

After the collapse of Lehman Brothers in September 2008,
one of Aditya's colleagues apparently said they could have
bought Lehman Brothers for $1 instead of paying so much
for Centurion BoP. In hindsight, it was possibly a risk worth
taking, to close up with ICICI Bank, the largest private lender,
and power the retail business. As of 2012, HDFC Bank has
the biggest retail portfolio in India, though ICICI Bank had
spotted the opportunity ahead of it and went headlong into
the field.

Chapter 11

Warts and All

We are recognizing our obligation for accounting purposes; however, it is clear that the company should never have been put in a position like this as we relied on Bankers Trust to advise us on these transactions. We have taken measures to ensure this will not happen again.

These are the words of Benjamin J. Sottile, chairman, president and CEO of Cincinnati, Ohio-based Gibson Greetings Inc., the third-largest greetings card manufacturer in the United States. Benjamin's comment came in 1994, in a filing with the US Securities and Exchange Commission, after his company discovered that it had made $20 million losses for the quarter that ended in March 1994 on interest rate derivatives transactions with Bankers Trust.

William L. Flaherty, Gibson's CFO, clarified that the loss being recognized for accounting purposes was the current market value of the derivatives transactions, as determined by a Bankers Trust valuation model, based on the projected value of the transactions at maturity.

Hundreds of companies in India—mostly small and medium and a few large—faced a similar situation in late 2007 and early 2008. With the greenback depreciating fast against some global currencies such as the euro and the Japanese yen, their losses mounted every day. Many moved court against banks. There have been a few out-of-court settlements and a few cases are still on.

In April 2011, the RBI penalized nineteen banks for their role in the so-called derivatives scam. HDFC Bank was one of them.

The banks were penalized for their failure to carry out due diligence with regard to the suitability of the products they had offered their customers. The regulator said the banks sold derivatives to companies that did not have risk management policies. The banks explained their positions but the RBI was not happy with their explanations. The regulator was convinced that, indeed, the norms had been violated—and hence the penalty.

Before we start dissecting the derivatives saga, let's look at the global perspective. Gibson announced the loss on an interest rate swap with Bankers Trust in April 1994. Under the arrangement, which covered a notional amount of $30 million, if the interest rates dropped Gibson would benefit, but if the interest rates rose Bankers Trust would make large profits and Gibson large losses.

Gibson made profits initially but was saddled with losses later. For financial sector observers in the United States, this did not come as a shock. As early as in January 1992, Edward Gerald Corrigan, then president of the Federal Reserve Bank of New York and also chairman of the Basel Committee on Banking Supervision, had warned of the danger of derivatives transactions. He did this in a speech delivered at the New York State Bankers Association.

Susan Philips, another member of the Federal Reserve Board, too, had warned the US Congress of the risks from over-the-counter derivatives. But not too many people paid attention to such warnings till Gibson announced its derivatives loss.

Procter and Gamble Co. followed Gibson and announced huge losses before filing a complaint against Bankers Trust, claiming a loss of more than $100 million due to alleged fraud. The government of Orange County, California, declared bankruptcy after losing $2 billion in speculative transactions. It had invested its entire tax collection in structured notes and 'exotic' instruments. Its elected treasurer Robert Citron, who was heading Orange County's trading desk, was dealing with several brokerages, including Merrill Lynch.

Other municipalities and educational institutions also lost hugely in derivatives trading in the mid-1990s when structured instruments such as death-backed bonds, worthless warrants, heaven and hell bonds, exploding options, sushis, down-unders and kiwis flooded the US market. The profit-to-loss ratio enjoyed by the derivatives dealers in the United States in early 1990 was 2,000:1, but that dramatically changed after the Gibson disclosure.

First Derivatives Loss in India

In India, the first time media reported derivatives loss of a company was in 2006 when the Food Corporation of India—which lends price support to safeguard the interest of farmers, distributes food grains and is responsible for ensuring national food security—suffered a loss in its swap transaction with a British bank. Being a state-run company, it did not hide its losses, but hundreds of small and medium companies that bought such products from banks were tight-lipped about their transactions till such time the potential loss was enough to wipe out their entire net worth. That was in early 2008.

Lawyers and risk management experts hired by the companies that burnt their fingers in 2007–08 started accusing banks of 'mis-selling' and enticing companies to 'speculate' instead of hand-holding them to genuine hedging. The banks, in turn, called these lawyers 'ambulance chasers'—a derogatory phrase that typically refers to attorneys in the United States who solicit business from accident victims or their families.

In March 2008, P. Chidambaram, as finance minister, made a statement in India's Parliament that banks operating in India had ₹127.86 trillion of derivatives on their books as on 31 December 2007. The 'outstanding notional principal amount' of derivatives, according to him, was 291% higher than the corresponding number on 31 December 2005.

By itself, the amount was not important as it was the notional amount of all derivatives transacted such as overnight indexed swap or dollar/rupee forwards. This number included two legs of transactions that could actually be reversing or closing out any risk that a bank had. Typical products that were permitted by the RBI till that time were forwards, currency swaps, interest rate swaps and foreign currency options.

Banks in India carry a market risk on their foreign exchange contracts but that is largely controlled by the net open position limit that the RBI prescribes for each bank. The larger risk that the banks carry is the credit risk. Since they are not allowed to keep a cross-currency book, they always need to enter into a mirror contract with an overseas bank when they sell cross-currency options to their customers. So, a customer can back out from the second leg of the contract but a bank cannot. Here lay the main problem.

Hundreds of Indian companies that had bought these complex cross-currency options and structured products to seemingly protect themselves from foreign exchange risk started crying foul when significant losses started staring at them. Banks that sold such products geared up for legal battles with clients-turned-adversaries, predominantly small and medium Indian companies, many with unsophisticated internal risk management practices, who were questioning the very legality of such products.

On one side of this battle were new-generation private banks such as HDFC Bank, Yes Bank, Kotak Mahindra Bank Ltd, Axis Bank and ICICI Bank; quite a few foreign banks operating in India such as Barclays, Deutsche Bank, J. P. Morgan, HSBC, BNP Paribas, Crédit Agricole S. A., Citibank, Standard Chartered, Bank of America, Royal Bank of Scotland; and a few public sector banks, including SBI, backed by powerful law firms such as Amarchand & Mangaldas

& Suresh A. Shroff & Co., and AZB & Partners. On the other, was a growing list of small companies, some publicly traded, as well as the well-regarded law firm of J. Sagar Associates, a crack team of investigators at auditor KPMG and independent consultants such as A. V. Rajwade, a leading expert when it comes to derivatives.

At that time, India's accounting laws did not require companies to report notional losses on account of derivatives contracts and hence none had an exact idea of the losses. The numbers floated in media reports were possibly hugely exaggerated.

The banks and their lawyers claimed the derivatives—a financial term used to describe an instrument whose value is a function of an underlying commodity, bond, stock or currency (also simply called underlying)—were legal. They are used as a risk management and mitigation tool. But the lawyers and consultants advising the affected companies said the products that were sold violated the country's Foreign Exchange Management Act, which regulates all foreign currency transactions, and the RBI guidelines.

Hedging or Speculation?

At the core of the battle was a debate over whether these were sold for hedging or speculation.

The issue first came to light in late November 2007 when software company Hexaware Technology Ltd set aside

$20–25 million (about ₹80–100 crore at the prevailing exchange rate) to cover exposure from unauthorized deals entered into by an employee which involved derivatives. The company later reported a net loss of ₹81 crore for the quarter that ended in December 2007, after the actual damage on account of these transactions ended up being ₹103 crore.

Sundaram Brake Linings Ltd, Rajshree Sugars and Chemicals Ltd and Sundaram Multi Pap Ltd, among others, hired law firms to fight it out with the banks.

According to Berjis Desai, managing director of J. Sagar Associates, whose firm advised around a dozen affected companies, such transactions are worse than betting on horse races or playing slot machines in Las Vegas. 'Banks can say that the contracts are fine but, under the Indian Contract Act, wagering is not permitted. Nobody can punt on any currency under RBI norms,' Berjis told me at that time. But Cyril Shroff, managing partner of Amarchand & Mangaldas & Suresh A. Shroff & Co., claimed there is enough jurisprudence on derivatives contracts all over the world and they are not wagering contracts.

Deepankar Sanwalka, head of the forensic wing of audit and consultancy company KPMG India, too, said some of these transactions were in violation of the RBI's derivatives guidelines. 'The issue is not as simple as some of the banks are projecting. The documentation of such contracts is not always watertight and if the firms decide to go to court, the contracts can be null and void,' Deepankar told me while I was writing a report for Mint in 2008.

The derivatives involved include swaps and options—a sort

of insurance that companies with exposure to dollars or other currencies buy as a protection against any adverse movement in these currencies that can hurt their income (for exporters) or increase their liabilities (for companies that have borrowed overseas).

Theoretically, a swap is a financial transaction in which two counter parties agree to exchange a stream of payments over time at an agreed price. An option is an agreement between two parties in which one grants to the other the right to buy or sell an asset under specified conditions.

Thus, in case of a currency swap, both parties have the right and obligation to exchange currencies. In case of options, the buyer has the right but no obligation, and the seller, the obligation but not the right to exchange currencies.

A Black Swan Phenomenon

Bankers claim there was nothing wrong in such transactions. Both the buyer and the seller understood the products well, but who would have anticipated that the dollar would touch 100 yen? It's a 'black swan phenomenon', they say. A black swan is a large-impact, hard-to-predict and rare event beyond the realm of normal expectations.

There are two sets of RBI guidelines that banks, consultants and lawyers swear by—comprehensive guidelines for derivatives, a thirty-page document, dated 20 April 2007, and a fifty-three-page master circular of risk management and inter-bank dealings, released on 2 July 2007.

The RBI insists that such transactions must be 'suitable' and 'appropriate' for the end users. Besides, every derivatives contract must have an underlying transaction. RBI norms also say that when companies enter into such derivatives contracts to reduce their costs, such transactions must not increase 'risk in any manner' and should not 'result in net receipt of premium by the customer'.

In private, some bankers admit that there could be a few companies that used the same 'underlying' for many derivatives transactions that they have entered into with different banks without their (the banks') knowledge but they vehemently contest allegations of mis-selling. All phone calls made from banks' treasury are normally recorded and one can hear the tape and decide who enticed whom. They also claim all derivatives contracts follow the guidelines of the International Swap Dealer Association; and they proceed only after getting the board resolution from a company and a confirmation that their risk management policy is in place.

Bankers blame the dollar's weakness against global currencies for the turn of events. Between April 2007 and March 2008 when the lit fuse on the derivatives time bomb got shorter, the euro had appreciated 17.8% against the dollar, the yen more than 16% and the Swiss franc some 21%, making most of the bets against currency movement go horribly wrong. Thus, a company that transformed its dollar liability into a yen or Swiss franc liability through complex derivatives faced significant losses.

Typically, these have 'knock-out' and 'knock-in' clauses.

While these options protect a company's yen or Swiss franc exposure against dollar depreciation, this is only till a certain level; once the dollar's weakness crosses this, the knock-out clause is triggered, leading to losses.

Similarly, if the dollar rises and touches the knock-in level, the customer makes money. If the dollar continues to depreciate and losses increase, the companies can either terminate the deals midway or wait till they are mature, hoping that by that time the currency movement would have been reversed.

After 2008, most banks have stopped selling such products as companies' appetite for such products has gone down, but risk management consultants say the demand was never there and banks led the companies up the garden path. A few banks settled their disputes with companies by sharing the losses whereas others advised their clients to get into new contracts by shifting currencies or close the contracts to cut losses. Yet a few others are fighting court cases challenging the contention of companies. HDFC Bank is one of them.

Reputation Risk

HDFC Bank was penalized ₹15 lakh. By no means is this big money for the bank but such regulatory actions tarnish the image of a bank. In the financial world, they call it reputation risk. HDFC Bank couldn't escape this despite its hatred for risks. What went wrong?

Is selling derivatives compatible with the bank? 'Yes, it

is, as it meets customers' need to hedge risks,' Paresh replies. Financial markets offer a range of products and no bank can sit in judgement on whether or not products add value to a customer. They can only have policies on which product is appropriate to which type of customer.

Could it have been a little more measured in its approach? Did it avoid some of the most over-leveraged, most complex structures? The bank claims that from a pure risk point of view, it never ran the book. When it comes to non-rupee-related derivatives, Indian banks are allowed to do this only on a back-to-back basis. So, HDFC Bank, like many others, didn't take any market risk on the product; it was taking only credit risk.

None of the customers actually lost big money but they were afraid that they would lose. The rates moved and there was high volatility in cross-currency markets. So, while an actual crystallized loss might have been very little or a modest amount, the companies had a much bigger potential loss staring at them as they were extrapolating volatility. Risk management socialites and lawyers saw an opportunity in this. Once they rushed to seize it, a fear psychosis gripped the companies and that did the banks in.

'We didn't flirt with the worst of the lot, and not even ten out of over a hundred derivatives customers accounting for less than 5% of such deals challenged their contracts or sued the bank,' Paresh told me. There have been about eight cases, and a couple of them came as a legacy from Centurion BoP. At least some of the companies that moved the court did a flip-flop. The Bangalore-based home textile manufacturer, retailer and distributor Himatsingka Seide Ltd first filed a case against HDFC Bank for alleged mis-selling. But when the market moved back in its favour, the company asked for the transaction to be unwound and paid off its dues. (I did not reach out to the company for its comments.)

No Out-of-Court Settlements

GS, country head for internal controls and compliance risk management, said the bank has not gone for any compromise settlement: 'We steadfastly refused to do any out-of-court settlement because we believe we didn't do anything wrong.' HDFC Bank has won an arbitration award in a case filed against Centurion BoP by apparels and garments maker Sportking Group of Ludhiana. The company had challenged the award in the Bombay High Court, which has since been dismissed by the court.

The RBI has taken quite a few steps to ensure that the market doesn't indulge in complex derivatives trades anymore. The change in regulations, which came in 2011, allows transactions in only plain vanilla derivatives and combinations of vanilla derivatives. The banking regulator has also made it necessary for corporate governance in companies to be at a certain level if they want to transact in structured derivatives. A tacit acceptance that such trades were indeed allowed earlier.

GS cites an instance where a customer filed a case against the bank after making a loss but the company had earlier gained. He wouldn't name the customer though. 'They were so happy that after a few months they came and said that they wanted to do one more transaction. They repeated the transaction and when they lost money they sued the bank. While the case was being filed, currency again moved and when they came back "in the money" they wanted to withdraw the case,' he told me. In the money simply means one's derivatives contract is worth money and not in losses. His point is that a customer understands the transaction as long as he is making money but professes not to when he loses.

GS claims the bank has improved its risk monitoring systems and reworked on its derivatives offerings. Has there been a tightening of the internal norms? 'Yes.' Is there any room for improvement? Here also his answer is 'yes'. That's typical of HDFC Bank. No admission of guilt; no aggression; a measured response to everything related to risks.

The IPO Scam

The so-called derivatives scam is not the only episode where HDFC Bank was tarred with the same brush as many other banks. It got involved in another scandal, in which a few unscrupulous market intermediaries cornered a sizeable portion of shares kept for retail investors by opening 'fictitious' demat accounts with banks. The RBI penalized it for not displaying prudence in the opening and operations of certain deposit accounts and failure to comply with the so-called 'know your customer' (KYC) norms in certain accounts. It was also reprimanded for not exercising due diligence while opening such accounts. The demat or dematerialized accounts are for individual Indian citizens to trade in listed stocks or debentures in electronic form.

The IPO scam, unearthed in April 2006, involved depositaries, depositary participants and many market operators who allegedly used or abetted certain entities in creating 59,000 fictitious demat accounts to corner shares of many IPOs meant for small investors. Apparently, in 105 IPOs between 2003 and 2005, scamsters cornered shares meant for retail investors by creating multiple identities. Typically, 35% of any share issue is kept for retail investors. In a booming market, companies rush to raise money through public floats and most shares are listed at a hefty premium. For instance, in 2005, there were sixty-three IPOs and fifty-four of them were listed at a premium. In that year, the bellwether equity index Sensex rose by 46.7%. In 2004, there were thirty-two IPOs and twenty-seven of them offered handsome gains on the listing day. The Sensex rose by 13.08%. In 2003, eight out of ten IPOs witnessed listing day gains and the Sensex rose by close to 73%.

Investigations by India's capital market regulator, the Securities and Exchange Board of India (Sebi), revealed that certain entities had illegally obtained IPO shares reserved for retail applicants through fictitious demat accounts. They then transferred the shares to financiers, who sold the shares on the first day of listing.

Roopal-ben Panchal

Roopal-ben Panchal of Ahmedabad, allegedly the linchpin of the operation, had opened hundreds of fake demat accounts and raised finances on the shares allotted to her through branches of an old private bank. Media reports suggest she advertised free photo shoots in local newspapers and used those pictures to create fake demat accounts to trade in the shares.

Sebi found that the National Securities Depository Ltd as well as the Central Depository Services (India) Ltd 'failed to exercise oversight over the depository participants' and directed them to take 'all appropriate actions, including revamping of management'.

It also found HDFC Bank's due diligence lacking and in its interim order on the IPO scam in 2006 said, 'It emerged that HDFC Bank had failed to exercise due diligence and has opened demat accounts in the name of fictitious/*benami* entities.'

Sebi's 252-page interim order was quite castigating. The regulator had said that during the verification, HDFC Bank had confirmed that it has complied with the KYC norms with respect to its demat account clients. 'In the light of the findings of the inspections, the confirmation by HDFC Bank appears to be totally divorced from reality as established,' Sebi said in its order in 2006.

According to Sebi, '286 savings bank accounts opened by the key operator (Purshottam Budhwani) with HDFC Bank is clearly proof enough for the plan of action to open multiple dematerialised accounts and channelise the funds in the manner they would bury the audit trail.' Budhwani had these accounts under different names with joint account holders in various HDFC Bank branches in Mumbai.

Budhwani, according to Sebi's investigation, is one of the key operators who cornered the retail portion of IPOs from companies such as Suzlon Energy Ltd. 'The role of HDFC Bank raises serious concerns on its compliance, while suggesting it had truck with Purshottam Budhwani in so far as it had actively lent its system to be misused by wily operators,' it said.

Sebi banned HDFC Bank from opening fresh demat accounts but later revoked the ban. In 2009, HDFC Bank settled with the markets regulator through the so-called consent process by paying ₹1 lakh. A settlement through the consent process means neither admission nor denial of the charges.

An internal Sebi note, to which I had access, said, 'KYC norms have been followed but not in the true sense of what it stands for as per Sebi regulations so we would like to put in as "KYC norms followed but not followed".' This sounds like either a puzzle or a poem.

The RBI slapped a penalty on HDFC Bank in two phases—₹5 lakh first and ₹25 lakh later. Many other banks too were fined 'for violation of regulations on KYC norms, for breach of prudent banking practices and for not adhering to its directives/guidelines relating to loans against shares/IPOs'.

As the issue is sensitive and the regulators are involved, HDFC Bank does not talk about this. I don't blame them. Purely from a process point of view, if one were to look at what KYC requirements are—the 'ticking-the-box' that one needs to do in terms of ensuring that the people actually exist, they have ration cards and photographs, and so on—the bank met the process. Where it slipped up and didn't do what it should have done is to go beyond the obvious. 'This customer does exist but given this profile, should he or she be investing in an IPO?' The bank didn't ask this question.

'The Bank Is No Investigative Agency'

GS said that a bank deals with documents and it's not an investigative agency. That's fine. But there were 215 savings accounts opened by XYZ and the second holder in all these accounts was the same. Shouldn't HDFC Bank have been more careful? Incidentally, these 215 accounts were opened over six years, on thirty-two occasions, and in various branches. Budhwani was the common name appearing in all 215 accounts.

Technically, they were not *benami* accounts because the bank had the documents and the people involved actually existed. This was a case of name lending. The individual account holders existed but they were used by somebody else. A smart Budhwani ensured every original election ID, address and ration card was produced but the people who sold their identities to him for little money didn't know that the shares allotted to them fetched much more than what they were given.

HDFC Bank should perhaps have gone beyond the documents and checked where these people actually stayed and if they had the means to invest in the stock market. In the end, the bank was as much a victim as the market and the gullible people who lent their identities.

The 2002 RBI circular said banks had to comply with the KYC norms but they also needed to ensure that their procedures weren't so straightjacketed as to deny a person the normal banking facilities that he or she was entitled to. A few rogue investors took advantage of the system.

Although a settlement through consent doesn't mean admission of guilt, HDFC Bank has introduced additional checks and balances, one more layer of document verification, to plug the loopholes.

The IPO scam also speeded up the process of converting branches into sales outlets and pushing all processing into back offices. This system has got a significant advantage because, when a customer walks in, if the branch manager knows the person well, he or she can get influenced and accept the documents even if they are not up to the mark. As volume grows, the branch manager may find it difficult to meet all the customers and may starts delegating responsibility to junior colleagues. Under pressure to bring in more and more accounts, a branch can be flexible in checking the documents and verifying the originals. But when these documents come to a back office, the process is much more streamlined. And the back-office employees can actually go and check if they find anything suspicious.

The bank had also shown the door to a dozen employees in Ahmedabad and Mumbai. Budhwani was issued 1,000 cheque leaves and that helped him apply for so many IPOs. The bank's system did not catch this, but it should have as HDFC Bank has a process whereby if the number of cheque leaves exceeds a threshold, the issue is flagged to a senior person. The senior person in this case did not find anything wrong in issuing so many cheque leaves. He had to go.

'Those were very painful days,' Rajan told me.

Paresh said, 'The fact that we tightened the processes and took some action means that there was some room for improvement. However, in the light of the events as they unfolded, was there a major failure of the processes? A complicity in helping the fellow to do this? No, certainly not. There wasn't a scent of any moral turpitude or collusion.'

But had the senior person noticed the red flag that the system raised, it would have been a different story.

Chapter 12

The Common Sense Banker

On 15 July 1994, a gentleman in corduroy trousers and a T-shirt, wearing leather sandals, entered Ramon House. He definitely did not look like a banker, even in his Friday casuals.

'I am Aditya Puri,' he introduced himself to Goretti, then Vinod's secretary, and gave his tickets to her for flight confirmation. He was scheduled to fly back to Kuala Lumpur that night. Goretti knew who he was. She had just sent an application to the Foreign Investment Promotion Board for the government's nod on the NatWest stake in HDFC Bank. The application form named Aditya as the managing director of the bank.

He joined on 12 September 1994, at Sandoz House.

If you go out with Aditya for lunch, make sure you have a wallet on you. He does not carry one. Nobody in the bank laughs at this any more. Aditya's work–life balance (read:

eating lunch at home and leaving the office at half past five in the evening) is always tilted in favour of life but still he ends up doing the right thing at the right time. His refusal to carry a mobile phone or a BlackBerry, to check e-mails, and his habit of wearing a tie with a half-sleeved shirt, or of eating *roti* and *dal makhani* at roadside *dhabas* or eateries in a suit, make Aditya different from his peers.

How much of this is put on and how much genuine?

People who know him well find all this natural. He is an earthy Punjabi who does what his heart tells him and does not bother about what others say. Which is why, instead of heading to Europe for a holiday in the summer, he prefers to spend time at his farmhouse at Lonavala, a hill station in Pune, to unwind.

He grows strawberries, mulberries, guavas and Italian lemons there, and plays with his favourite dog, Bushka, a mix of a Great Dane and a Doberman. This is one place he loves to show off to his close colleagues and friends. Every few months he rearranges the furniture to make the house look different.

It's his love for a good life—not for banking—that made him a banker. At his first job as an executive assistant to the finance director of automobile company Mahindra & Mahindra, Aditya was jealous of his cousin Vikram Kochar, a Citibank trainee, who used to live in an air-conditioned and carpeted apartment with his batchmates on posh Carmichael Road in Mumbai. There was a cook and a butler on call. On top of that, the young men were to be trained in Beirut.

'What the hell am I doing living as a paying guest in Colaba, surviving on a toast and half a cup of tea in the morning, and catching a train to Kandivali [a western suburb in Mumbai where Mahindra & Mahindra's factory is located] every day?' Aditya wondered.

He asked Vikram to get him an interview with Citibank. After all, how different can banking be from accounting? Both are driven by common sense. He got the job, the comforts and a hefty pay hike.

Aditya nearly lost it once, though. Seeing him leaving office rather early almost every day, his boss at Citibank asked him whether everything was all right with him. Aditya was then working in Kolkata. 'Yes, of course, I am working very hard. I am in office until dark,' Aditya told him. That was in December when evening descends around five o'clock in Kolkata. His boss advised him to look at his watch before leaving.

Aditya does not wear a watch. And normally does not stay in office beyond half past five in the evening even when he is the boss.

He has always been a straight talker. In the early 1980s when Victor Menezes, then head of Citibank in India, asked him to go to New York, Aditya opted for Saudi Arabia instead, where he could save more money. There was a 60% hardship allowance for Saudi Arabia.

A Banker by Accident?

Those who know Aditya's lineage find it hard to believe that he is a banker by accident. After all, how many can claim to have two family members who were central bankers? His grandfather, Shambhu Lal Puri, was on the board of the Reserve Bank in British India and Shambhu Lal's brother K. R. Puri was the twelfth governor of the RBI between August 1975 and May 1977. Before this, he was chairman and managing director of Life Insurance Corporation of India. His family was also one of the early shareholders of PNB and the Sunlight of India Insurance Co. in Lahore.

Originally from Sargodha, an agricultural trade centre in the northwest of Pakistan, Aditya's great-grandfather Rai Bahadur Lala Brij Lal Puri shifted to Chandigarh, Sector IV, after Partition. They used to have a summer house in Shimla, which is now a hotel called Bridge View.

Aditya's father, Tapishwar Puri, the spoilt son of a rich family, joined the British Air Force and was the aide-de-camp to the first Indian to head the Air Force, Subroto Mukherjee.

An Air Force kid, Aditya's schooling was all over India. He led a cushy life. Wherever he went, there were clubs and friends and if he had nobody to play with, orderlies could always make a cricket team for him. Chandigarh was a very organized city then and more than three cars on the road meant a traffic jam. Aditya did his B.Com from Panjab University, Chandigarh, and his chartered accountancy from the Institute of Chartered Accountants of India, New Delhi, before joining Mahindra & Mahindra.

His rather casual approach to work camouflages Aditya's appetite for challenge. Today HDFC Bank's strongest point is its retail business, but its managing director's core competence was never retail. Aditya was an institutional banker throughout his career. He could change his area quickly in sync with the organizational demand because, banking, according to him—whether corporate or retail or investment—is all about common sense. Something he has in abundance.

It may sound very simple but definitely is not an easy task. If one is successful one tends to stick to one's comfort zone. The biggest reason for the downfall of any bank is success itself because it tends to go the same way it has been historically successful in.

One can go off the beaten track only if one has one's ears to the ground, has common sense and is street smart. Aditya has the big picture but he's not an economist or someone who thrives on complicated theories.

According to Satwalekar, former head of HDFC Standard Life Insurance Co. Ltd, who was on the bank's board for eight years, the biggest thing about leadership is asking questions and not necessarily providing the answers. 'That makes your people think. Look at the retail portfolio of all banks and NBFCs [non-banking finance companies] in 2008—whoever was aggressive got decimated. The exception is HDFC Bank as they were always very clear in their mind on what could and could not be done. Aditya would ask the right questions and make his people see what was required. The top line was not a target for him. Value creation through profitability was the objective,' says Satwalekar.

In one aspect though, Satwalekar does not find Aditya fully transparent. 'He gives the impression of being an extremely aggressive guy, but if you look closely his banking is as conservative as it can be. He is an extremely conservative banker. You see his risk management strategy. Who is his senior most guy there? Paresh Sukthankar. Paresh by nature is risk averse. Aditya has got a bunch of aggressive people to go out in the front and get business. But the gatekeeper is someone who dislikes risk as much as himself and in whom he has complete trust,' says Satwalekar.

Common Sense Banker

Common sense and curiosity are far more important than anything else in banking which has been on a roller-coaster ride in India since the birth of the first set of new-generation private banks in 1994. Technology, products and profile of competition have been changing and, to understand the change, one has to be like a school kid or a teenager while heading an institution.

Aditya has done that remarkably well, and very differently. Nobody knows this difference better than Arun Maira, member of the Planning Commission, Aditya's neighbour in Samudra Mahal on Worli Sea Face in Mumbai in the 1980s. Arun was an executive director of Tata Engineering and Locomotive Co. Ltd (Telco; now Tata Motors Ltd) then and Aditya was with Citibank, looking after corporate banking. Arun's responsibility was getting Telco into new markets.

At that time, he was working on a proposed joint venture with General Motors Co. to develop a pickup truck suitable for southern regions of the United States and the Middle East.

General Motors would assemble the truck at one of its factories and distribute it. Arun had earlier worked on a similar project in Malaysia in the 1970s, but it did not do well.

General Motors was pushing for a very stiff price formula as it believed that the rupee would depreciate and, therefore, Telco would gain a lot even though they would not have to pay much in dollars. Arun asked for Aditya's view on the rupee.

Aditya's projection was quite different from what every other person in the financial services business was saying. 'He was just talking from common sense. He wasn't a fancy financier,' Arun told me.

Aditya, according to him, is a bit of a rebel and, like a Punjabi peasant, he is proud of himself. 'He likes to have his simple but certain opinions about things, a good earthy Punjabi trait, if I can say so. People like me who went to St Stephen's [College, Delhi], Doon School [in Dehradun] or Oxford [University] may not always appreciate his views but that's him. Rebel may not be the right word. He's different,' says Arun.

After an overseas stint when Arun came back as the chairman of The Boston Consulting Group in 2000, HDFC Bank was six years old and India was in a frenzy of work. People in the finance and corporate sectors in India were working much harder and longer than people in the United States from where Arun had just come.

Amid all these, he observed that Aditya would wake up in the morning, have a cup of tea with his wife, and then go to the golf course. He would come home, go to the office, come home again at one o'clock for lunch, go back to work and was back home after five o'clock to be with his wife and children. 'One would feel tempted to say that Aditya was not taking his job seriously but results of the bank were there to show what he was doing,' Arun admits.

Arun also knows Deepak well. In fact, one of HDFC's first big projects was with Telco in Pune. The Tata Group company didn't have enough money to build a big colony like it had done in Jamshedpur, though it had land. Hasmukh-bhai came up with a proposal that HDFC could lend money to the Telco workers to build houses.

HDFC lent to the Telco employees and the company took responsibility of repaying by deducting money from their salaries every month—a unique arrangement in those days. Deepak had just come back from the United States and Arun was a young general manager, in charge of the Pune factories.

Deepak asked Arun to join his board but expressed helplessness in not being able to offer much money as RBI rules did not allow the bank to pay commission to its directors. Aditya advised him not to jump at the offer unless he was convinced that money was not important. Arun listened to him.

'Deepak is someone very sound and conservative in his approach who wants to do the right thing. Aditya has the same approach but he is different from others,' observes Arun. For instance, Deepak's business habits are similar to common business habits such as playing bridge with friends, but Aditya spends time only with his family. Deepak spends long hours in office, Aditya does not. Even if his chairman calls, he may say he does not have the time.

'If you are calling because you are the boss and it's something about work, Aditya would say, "Let's talk tomorrow." Deepak would say, "Your friend is quite a character." Deepak could have initially been irritated because he has a style of how he gets his work done and he suddenly finds a character with whom he can't work like that. Aditya is a character,' Arun told me.

He Is a Character

He is indeed a character. Samir recollects this story:

One day, Aditya said, '*Chalo, main sabko khana khilata hoon. Aa jao, gaadi mein baith jao, acchi jagah lekar jaata hoon.*' He promised to take them to a place where the food would be something they would have never eaten before. He had a Maruti Esteem at that time. Since the others did not know which place he was talking about, he told those who weren't in his car to meet him near the Siddhi Vinayak Temple at Worli.

They all drove and got off near the temple, wondering where to go. There was this small *dhaba* with the typical benches and tables. Aditya sat and said, 'Let's eat here.' The place was full of taxi drivers and others had to wait to get a seat.

'We had *naan*, *paratha* and other Punjabi dishes. The food was great. We had a great time even though I didn't like the glare—all of them were looking at us in our suits and ties,' Samir says.

Aditya once went to an awards function in a Hyundai Getz, packing his entire family in it, something no CEO would do even if he were not winning an award. He was footloose. Now, of course, Aditya has changed—his preferred vehicle for official use is a brownish peach-coloured E-Class Mercedes and there's an Audi for personal use.

Aditya loves his whisky and food but not the five-star types. Mughlai food and *kheema* at Olympia in Colaba and Malvani food at Sindhudurg in Dadar are his favourites. He likes Madras Café at Matunga a lot—*dosa* and coffee on Sunday mornings. And *batata vada* and *pav* on his way to Lonavala, ninety-six kilometres away from Mumbai.

But the simplicity vanishes when it comes to business. And, he can be really uncanny. I am told he often asks his office boy Suryakant to do rounds on the fifth floor of Bank House, the bank's headquarters in Lower Parel, Mumbai, where most group heads sit, at half past nine in the morning to see who has arrived on time. At times, he himself does it.

A few years ago, a register was kept at the foyer for latecomers to sign. Rumours have it that most big guys used to scribble their names in such a way that nobody could make out who had come late.

Aditya can be ruthless. Samir recalls another incident, which also reveals Aditya's business philosophy. One day, a cheque came for clearing from a gentleman who was often seen in Aditya's cabin at Sandoz House. Samir was aware that the boss knew him well. The gentleman did not have the required balance in his account. He was a current account holder and people like Samir who were on the front desk could always take the call of sanctioning a temporary overdraft, depending on whether the person was financially solvent.

Samir cleared his cheque and then triumphantly walked into Aditya's room and said, *'Boss, aapke dost ka cheque maine clear kia.'*

Aditya looked at Samir and said, *'Mera koi dost nahi hai. Main yahaan bank chala raha hoon, bas.* Now go and get the money yourself from him. If you don't get the money, I'm going to debit your account for it. There are no friends in business.'

Samir was sweating when he came out. The quick word went around the bank: *'Boss ka koi dost nahi hai, yaad rakhna.'*

To get a loan a little cheaper or to get a little more interest on deposits, if a corporate customer ever told Samir *'Main Aditya se baat karta hoon,'* Aditya in turn would tell the unfortunate fellow, *'Tu mere logon se baat kar, main yeh sab nahi dekhta hoon.'*

Aditya would tell them all decisions are made in the bank by a set of people who are empowered. 'You are my friend, but please talk to my people if you need anything.'

Satwalekar was at the receiving end of Aditya's 'nobody-is-a-friend-in-business' philosophy when he was heading the life insurance company. HDFC Bank was one of its key distributors. 'Every year, we had to go and re-negotiate because [Aditya] Puri's team would come back to us and say, "Hey listen, MetLife is offering us this thing, Bajaj Allianz is offering us this much. How much are you giving us? Don't tell us about the HDFC brand and HDFC Group. All that doesn't matter. We have to make money for our shareholders. Tell us what you are going to give us."'

Satwalekar is pretty sure that ICICI Prudential Life Insurance Co. Ltd did not have similar issues with ICICI

Bank. 'When I met him [Aditya] he would be very nice, but when it came to putting pressure to extract a few pennies more, he would be relentless.'

Building Relationships

Aditya is shrewd both in strategy and in building relationships. In corporate banking, he would make it a point to meet the small guys who give the business. Before getting into any meeting with a company, he would invariably ask his colleagues, *'Dhanda kaun deta hai?'*

Typically, in an organization, the letter of credit is issued by a junior guy. For Aditya, he is as important as the CEO of the company. He would walk up to him and say, 'Hello, I'm Aditya Puri, I'm the MD of HDFC Bank; thank you very much for giving us the business.'

That's one of his main principles—no matter how high one may climb the ladder, one must be sure to acknowledge whoever is giving the business.

Aditya would wait for hours for a petty officer in a company who is supposed to be dealing with the bank. Others would get impatient but he would say, 'No, sit, nothing doing—he is giving us business, right? So wait.'

He does not waste time being friendly with those who do not give business, however big the company. Piyush, who now heads DBS in Singapore, recalls his Citibank days in Mumbai in the 1980s when he used to report to Aditya.

Citibank was probably the only bank that did not have dealings with one of the large industrial groups in India in those days. 'Piyush, if I get into a relationship with this group, it would be a one-sided relationship. All the banks run around them. It would be an unequal relationship where they would call the shots. We should run business on equal relationships,' Aditya told Piyush.

Many bankers equate maintaining good relationships with maintaining a good credit portfolio. They lend money to maintain relationships. While giving money, the banker becomes the company's best friend but if it does not do well, the bank turns into its worst enemy. The most important ability for a banker is how to say 'no' without damaging a relationship.

Shirish swears by Aditya's ability to do this with ease. Shirish had worked with him in India in the 1980s. He was the chief risk management officer and Aditya was the head of corporate business, both at the same office, in Sakher Bhavan at Nariman Point. 'He can tell a client that he can't lend because it doesn't make sense and then they have a drink and the guy goes away baffled, trying to figure out what happened!' says Shirish about Aditya.

Eye for Detail

As a banker, the most remarkable thing about Aditya is probably his eye for detail. Sashi told me an incident that illustrates this. Once in 2007, they were in New York for the bank's third ADS offering. On a Manhattan street, there was a Chase Manhattan ATM with a sign saying it's the fastest ATM.

'Can you just click that?' Aditya asked him. Sashi clicked a picture of it with his mobile phone camera. 'We need to understand about this fastest ATM,' Aditya said.

Sashi sent a message and the photograph to Rahul Bhagat, head of retail liabilities, marketing and direct banking channels at HDFC Bank, asking him to check it out. Rahul checked with ATM-maker NCR Corporation and got back to Sashi and Aditya saying it could be just a marketing gimmick. Aditya did not agree.

'When you go to Singapore, I want you to meet NCR there. Chase Manhattan won't make that statement without genuinely having it faster. Go ahead and talk.'

In Singapore, Sashi got to know of a software called the Customer Power that has the ability to reduce the number of clicks a customer uses to transact at an ATM. It has intelligence and saves 40% time. This means more customers can use it and the bank needs fewer ATMs.

'There is cost savings; and the time saved can be used to cross-sell other products,' Sashi told Aditya.

'Even though it is expensive, go ahead and do it from the strategic perspective,' Aditya told him.

'Frankly, that has yielded fantastic results. The investment is large but we're saving on operating expense on an annual basis. Earlier we used to do about 250 transactions per day per ATM. Now it has gone up to 350,' Sashi said.

Aditya has this simple logic—to understand technology, one does not need to be a techie. As Ram explains, Aditya is one guy who, without knowing the technology, knows what technology has to deliver. He would say, 'a car is a car and one just needs to know how to drive.'

Crosses and Arrows on a Piece of Paper

Samir recalls how HDFC Bank discovered the big business of supply chain management. 'We used to dread the small notes that used to come from the MD's office. Aditya would spend more than half the day reading magazines, business reviews and would pick out one or two essential things. We would regularly get these small notes from his office. One day, I got a piece of paper with some supplier/dealer information written on it. There were crosses and arrows going all over. I couldn't understand anything.'

'Do you know you are missing the biggest opportunity of financing?' Aditya asked Samir.

'What's that?' asked Samir.

Aditya spoke about how the bank should link all the suppliers and dealers of large companies and set up this massive financing opportunity. HDFC Bank went to Tata Motors, the first to link up. Within three years, it built a business worth

₹5,000 crore and was the only bank that had effectively done the entire financing linkage for a large number of companies.

All of that just came on a piece of paper in 1997. 'We all read, but the ability to read between the lines is what sets him apart,' says Samir.

Every month, Aditya reads 2,000 branch reports—their business plans, the scope, and competition. If one customer's accounts balance drops, he would say, 'the customer must have opened an account with another bank and it must be checked out. What's the other bank offering?'

He reads all reports and at least 500 mails a day. There is no computer on his table; Goretti and his second secretary Govind hand over the printouts to him. About a dozen sharp pencils are always on his table. Aditya uses them to scrawl his remarks on the reports and mails.

By half past five when he leaves the office, there's not a single piece of paper on his table. When he is on leave, all papers and e-mail printouts are sent home and they come back by the end of the day.

Piyush used to report to Aditya in the late 1980s in Mumbai. They developed a very close working relationship—Aditya ran the business and left the middle- and the back-office work to Piyush.

The first thing that strikes Piyush is Aditya's ability to simplify the most complicated things. He'll take the most complex situation and distil it down to a couple of things.

The second is his ability to prioritize. Once he focuses on what he sees as important, he does not let extraneous items cloud the agenda. Other things can wait or be taken care of by others, but he will focus on those couple of things that matter.

'Unlike a lot of other people who have twenty balls in the air and end up dropping some balls or killing themselves trying to keep all twenty in the air, Aditya knows which three balls matter as he can prioritize. He doesn't focus on the balance seventeen. I don't know anybody else in my working experience who has that ability to just focus on the crucial things, prioritize and deliver,' says Piyush.

Work–Life Balance

This is also the key to his work–life balance—Aditya just does not let his life get complicated by the things that are not important.

Initially, Piyush used to come to work at half past eight in the morning and spend time with Aditya to figure out what he needed to do. After a few months, Aditya refused to see him before nine o'clock. Even though he would be in office, he would say the first half an hour of the day is for him. He would use the time to do the big-picture thinking.

Piyush worked for him for three years from 1988 to 1991 in Citibank, Mumbai, when Aditya was heading institutional banking. 'When you run into trouble, come to me. If you don't come to me, I assume you're doing your job,' was Aditya's style of work.

He used to leave office by half past five in the evening and tell Piyush's wife Ruchira, 'Your husband is inefficient. He is in office till eight-thirty–nine. I am out at five-thirty.'

'The reason for that is you make me do all the dirty work; you do all the good work and go away,' Piyush would retort.

'I do what I am good at, what I'm supposed to do.'

Amit of Times Bank is well aware of this side of Aditya's personality. 'He is a man who does extraordinary things in an ordinary way. He doesn't try to do complex transactions in a complex way. He never delegates. He empowers,' Amit gushes about Aditya.

There is a big difference between delegation and empowerment. Aditya empowers people. He doesn't keep checking *'iska kya hua? uska kya hua?'* with his colleagues. Only in empowerment, there's trust and that gives confidence to the empowered person. In delegation, this doesn't happen.

Aditya is one of the most phenomenal operational managers that Shirish knows: 'He picks up a lot of information, which is natural when you go to cocktails and dinners. This guy has the ability to analyse the information very quickly and figure out some trends around it.'

Shirish says, 'He would tell me, "You know yesterday, I was at this cocktail party and there was one guy who was asking questions about such and such a topic. I think you should take a look at this. Something didn't sound right to me."

'Then, we'd start reading into it and a year down the line, it would be clear that there was a problem that Aditya could read into and make the connections ahead of all of us.

'You can't fool him. He had no consumer experience. So he hired people to do consumer banking. Initially, it didn't go very well; he got rid of those people. I was chatting with him one day and he told me that he has figured out this business and it's not very complicated. These guys make it too complicated. What you really have got to have is a lot of common sense about how to run it. Then you pick the right people and leave it to them.'

That's his style. He'll pick the right people and once he agrees to hire a person, he trusts him implicitly. If he is not the right person for the job, Aditya will get rid of him very quickly but in a nice way. He'd say, 'I think you should try your hand at something different.'

'The most valuable lesson I have learnt from him is that you can't be doing someone else's job,' Shirish told me.

Giving a Long Rope

Aditya's style is to give people a long rope. If he trusts, he trusts completely. Neeraj was trusted by him. When he left, Aditya didn't replace him. He had two people under him but neither of them got Neeraj's job and nobody was brought from outside. He didn't want to lose either by promoting one; if he had brought in an outsider he ran the risk of losing both. He himself took over the retail portfolio.

Aditya loved to be flanked by these two people—Rahul, head of retail liabilities, and Pralay Mondal, head of retail assets, till Pralay left in mid-June 2012 to join Yes Bank, another new-generation private bank, set up ten years after HDFC Bank.

Rahul is every inch a *sahib*, speaks with a clipped accent and likes golf. An alumnus of Doon School and with a major in history from St Stephen's College, Rahul is very bullish on mobile banking. An art aficionado and a regular at book launches, he acted in Satyajit Ray's *Seemabaddha* when he was eight.

An IIT-ian, Pralay had a fleet of cars but used a battered WagonR on the days he drove. He had a fantastic collection of colourful ties and Aditya always had him around when he met foreign delegates.

Another *pucca sahib* and a colourful character is Navin Puri, head of branch banking. Navin, known as the 'other Puri' in the bank, and Rahul, always lunch together. Their cabins on the fifth floor at Bank House are also adjacent to each other. Aditya calls them remnants of the Raj. Tall Rahul and bulky Navin are Laurel and Hardy in the bank. Navin has light blue eyes and is often seen in blue shirts. He lends his secretary Joyce to Aditya when Goretti or Govind is on leave.

They are great pals but their two divisions—retail products and branch banking—do not necessarily collaborate always. They compete and want to outdo each other. Aditya also has his own contribution through creation of what others call 'constructive tension' between different business groups. Sashi thinks Aditya does that to shatter complacency.

Once, things came to such a pass that the middle-level executives of both the business groups virtually stopped talking to each other. The retail liabilities products group devises products and the branches sell them—it is absolutely critical for the two to work in close coordination but they were two silos.

To break the ice, Aditya called them for an informal outing at Lonavala over a weekend. In the evening, three groups were formed led by Sashi, Arvind Kapil of the direct sales group and Ravi Narayan of branch banking. The three walked Aditya's dogs—Scooby, a highly energetic Mudhol hound, was given to Sashi; Arvind led Pogo, a mix of a Doberman and an Alsatian; and Ravi, Bushka. There were thirty-odd people and none of them really knew how to walk a dog. So, they had to share tips and help each other manage the three unruly pets. By the time they came back to Aditya's house after the walk, everybody was talking to each other. The party started in right earnest and by nine o'clock Aditya ran out of the stock of booze. It was business as usual in the office next week.

Aditya has a unique way of keeping politics out of work. If anyone ever comes to him and complains about a colleague, he simply picks up the telephone and calls the colleague, 'Come here, your friend is saying this about you. Let's discuss.'

So, either the person has to have the guts to openly speak his cause of complaint or he will die over there and never go back to the boss with false complaints! Everyone knows that if one goes and tells the boss anything about a colleague, one has to substantiate, one has to have the guts to face that person.

Ram says Aditya made sure that he got the right people and gave them complete freedom. 'Whenever I used to say, "Why don't you meet this big chief coming from IBM or HP?" he would say, "Why should I meet him? You are the MD of IT. You meet him." That is the kind of confidence he had in us and in empowerment. But, he had his eyes on the ball.'

Abhay finds him a fantastic reader of the human mind who

understands colleagues' motives and behaviour very well. He thinks the key to Aditya's leadership is being able to deal with different people differently. 'If there was a book telling you how to be a perfect manager, everyone would have been a great manager just by mugging it up. You can't have one fixed rule; you have to be flexible. Aditya does that. If I and X colleague of mine were handled the same way, either I would have left by now or my colleague.'

Abhay's field is not really related to banking. It has more to do with capital markets. 'The only reason why I haven't left or even tried looking for another job in the past so many years is personal rapport. Aditya is very flexible, though it doesn't come across like that. If you ask anyone, they'll tell you he's a hard taskmaster; Aditya is very disciplined but he isn't dogmatic, he's open to dissent,' says Abhay.

Anything Negative?

Is there anything negative about him? Yes, there is.

Vinod says if anyone upsets Aditya that is the end of the relationship. Aditya won't do any harm but he will give the cold shoulder and make the person feel unwanted.

Samir says in the early years he always thought that HDFC Bank was a little behind in doing highly innovative stuff. It wasn't a risk-taker at all. When its peers were launching something or the other all the time, Aditya would always say he wants to be the best, not necessarily the first. 'Let somebody do something, let us learn from that, let us see how everything happens,' was his refrain.

Aditya can really be abrasive too. In a meeting, if you haven't prepared something despite him telling you to do it or you have missed something right under your nose, he can be brutal and cut you to pieces. He would say, 'You haven't done your job; I think you are useless, you should just be out of this place.'

And every time he would do that, it would be for such a valid reason that one would want to hang oneself. 'How could I have missed that?' one would wonder.

Aditya always does his homework for every meeting and presentation. He spends extensive time on numbers and has a grasp of detail. In a flash, he knows the mistakes that need rectification.

By design or by default, Abhay says, 'Aditya sometimes just does not call a spade a spade. He'll get someone else to do that. This is the only thing that has puzzled me in all these fifteen years. In an open meeting once, I told him if he had something to say, he should tell me directly, not lean on someone else's shoulder to fire the gun.

'The general perception in the bank is that he doesn't tolerate dissent but I don't think so. I believe that if your point makes sense and if you back it up with logic and rationale, he will buy it. There have been times when he has said, "I buy your point but I'm the MD," and I think that's fair enough. There are rare occasions when he has used that argument.

'There have also been times when he has said, "I agree, but what to do, such is life," hinting at constraints in implementing a plan even if it makes sense. This speaks volumes about his leadership.'

Harish says, 'At times, Aditya exudes a lot of aggressiveness towards customers who tend to believe in him. He promises something but later when he realizes it can't be done, he finds it difficult to go back and say so.'

Anil of 3i finds Aditya very decisive, which is good and bad. 'He takes a decision very quickly, which is why his table is always clear, which is why he can go home at five. He takes a lot of decisions and in a very short period of time too. The decision making is centralized and is very quick, which makes it a one-man organization,' says Anil.

Anil doesn't know how well the bank treats its people below a certain level. 'There is a core top management team that is very well taken care of. But outside it's a factory,' he says.

Neeraj finds Aditya a bit impatient at times. 'He's a people's guy—he can motivate but he doesn't have time for softer things. For him, it's about action, business and, if not business, golf or some activity. He won't stop and talk to people about the small things of life—that is left to us.'

Aditya has no patience for non-performance or slow decision making. When all are killing themselves for twelve to fourteen hours a day, he will take critical decisions in ten minutes. If he doesn't give a decision within ten minutes, even if he does not say a 'no', it's 'no'. If he says he will get back, it generally means 'no'.

Aditya would rather take a decision, even if it is wrong, than not take a decision at all. If he is surrounded by good people then it works. If he takes a decision without understanding all the risks involved, he needs somebody around him with courage to tell him that.

Importantly, Aditya is also willing to reverse the decision if it's not right. He can say he has made a mistake. 'So what? Let's change it.'

He has become successful and therefore a little larger than life; so people who work for him are less challenging to him and may be scared to tell him he is not right. That's a danger in Aditya's style of functioning.

Shirish finds Aditya is willing to admit his mistakes. As a risk manager, once Shirish shared his apprehensions about a company, which made Aditya upset. The next morning, as Shirish entered his room, he found Aditya waiting for him. 'He said I was right and he was wrong and offered an apology for what he had said. Sometimes Aditya makes decisions and says things very quickly but he reflects on it and if he thinks he has made a mistake, he's not shy to walk up to anybody and admit to it,' Shirish told me.

Why Do People Leave HDFC Bank?

From the original team—the dirty dozen—Shailendra was the first to leave. Rajan left to come back. Samir, Luis and Ram left for good. Neeraj, not part of the original team, left after a few years. Shailendra, Samir and Neeraj left for bigger roles as they knew that as long as Aditya was around, none of them had any chance to be the boss. Luis and Ram left for different kinds of assignments.

How does Aditya react when his dear colleagues leave?

In 2006, Samir got a call from a head-hunter for the top job of British bank Barclays. He asked Aditya, *'Milke aaoon kya?'*

After he met the people at Barclays, he confessed to Aditya that the offer of managing director was up his alley and he was tempted because he had never headed an organization.

'MD bana rahein hain kya?' Aditya asked him.

Samir replied in the affirmative.

'I'm around for a lot many years; if you've the ambition of becoming an MD and are getting a good opportunity and decent pay package, then go and have that experience because you won't have that experience here for a long time.'

Samir went back to Barclays, negotiated, and showed Aditya the offer letter. Aditya recommended some changes such as the inclusion of a severance package in case they shut shop. Aditya's foresight was immensely valuable. Indeed, Barclays shut its retail shop.

Abhay did look for a job once, but just once. It was a large corporate house and a very prestigious offer. Before saying 'yes', he wanted to talk to his boss. They were in Barbados, watching the cricket World Cup.

Over beer, Abhay explained the offer and the money. Aditya heard everything and asked, 'How many times have I called you outside working hours?' The answer was twice. And those times were when Aditya needed Abhay for something really important. He told Abhay that this group would call him on Sunday afternoons to make presentations. 'I want you to first think about whether you're ready to face that. If you're willing to do that, then we'll discuss how good your offer is.'

That got Abhay thinking. He knew he wouldn't be able to do that. 'I didn't go any further after that. For a long time, they kept coming back to me, asking what the problem was. I couldn't tell them the real reason because that sounded very stupid.

'Aditya hadn't really talked to me from the finance or economics point of view. He just made one simple statement and that disarmed me completely. He knew the sort of person I was and didn't even make any counter offer.'

Neeraj raised the subject while on a road show in Paris. Standard Chartered had approached him in February–March 2005. A foreign search company from the United Kingdom was talking to Neeraj.

'Are they serious?' Aditya asked Neeraj.

'They could be.'

'Find out whether they are serious.'

After meeting half a dozen times, Neeraj got some understanding about the offer and went back to Aditya. Aditya tried to talk him out of it without directly saying 'no'. 'It's useless as in the matrix structure in a foreign bank, nobody would report to you,' he told Neeraj. He even spoke to Ashok Sud, then head of corporate banking in Standard Chartered in India, in front of Neeraj on a speakerphone. Ashok had worked with Aditya in Mahindra & Mahindra.

Ashok's voice was loud and clear; he was not reporting to the CEO.

Christopher Low was CEO of Standard Chartered in India at that time.

'What are they offering you?'

Neeraj explained. 'It's too little. You should get a better deal.'

Neeraj did some negotiations and improved the package, slightly. It was significantly better in terms of cash but poorer in terms of stock. As the package was not improved much, Neeraj stopped answering their calls.

Then he got a call from London. Mervyn Davies was on the line.

'Hello, my people have been calling you. I am told you aren't finding it attractive. I want to meet you.'

Mervyn was the group CEO. He would be in Singapore for a board meeting and called Neeraj there.

When Neeraj informed Aditya of this, Aditya told him they had not improved his package and asked what was the point in meeting again.

But Neeraj found it difficult to say 'no', especially because Mervyn had called him personally.

Mervyn, a charmer, had arranged an exclusive lunch for Neeraj. He called the human resources director to the meeting with Neeraj, made some changes in the offer letter, and signed it off.

When Neeraj showed it to Aditya—his colleague, well-wisher and boss rolled into one—he was in a fix.

The next day, Aditya told Neeraj he'd had a long chat with his wife Smiley and she advised him to let Neeraj go. 'You are not fair to him,' she told Aditya.

Never Under Stress

Goretti has never seen Aditya under stress. Even if he is, he does not show it. He always says there is a solution to every problem. 'I have never seen him flinging his hands or scratching his head. He walks the same way as he used to eighteen years ago. I have never seen him rushing or pushing around or screaming at the corridors,' Goretti says. Even in the worst of time, like during the derivatives and IPO scam and the fall of Lehman Brothers, Aditya laughs loudly. Even in stress, he smiles and there's a dimple on his cheeks!

And he is mischievous and loves to play all sorts of pranks. Once one of his close friends playfully asked Aditya what he would be sending him on his birthday. 'Flowers,' said Aditya.

Goretti was asked to get the biggest cauliflower from the Dadar market, one that could feed two dozen people. It was sent in a nice box with a birthday card.

The next year, Aditya decided to gift his friend a rooster. The rooster was kept in a huge basket, covered by a nicely decorated net so that it could breathe. The bird was terrified and didn't make any noise. When his friend, a Marwari and a strict vegetarian, opened his gift, that rooster ran all over the house.

That's Aditya, at his best and worst. He knows how to humour people and get the best out of his colleagues and corporate contacts and give returns to investors.

Chapter 13

Whose Bank Is It Anyway?

*G*reat by Choice: Uncertainty, Chaos, and Luck—Why Some Thrive Despite Them All, the 2011 sequel to Jim Collins' 2001 bestseller *Good to Great*, identifies seven characteristics that make companies truly great over an extended period. Through painstaking research over nine years, Jim and his co-author, Morten T. Hansen, a management professor at the University of California, Berkeley, tried to find out how a company achieves lasting success in an environment of change, uncertainty and chaos.

Jim began his research and teaching career on the faculty at Stanford Graduate School of Business, where he received the Distinguished Teaching Award in 1992. In 1995, he founded a management laboratory in Boulder, Colorado, where he conducts research and consults with executives from the corporate and social sectors.

In an article in *Fortune* ('How to Manage through Chaos',

17 October 2011), the duo said that from an initial list of 20,400 companies only seven could make it to the final list through eleven layers of cuts. The project started in 2002, the year the bull market crashed and a year after the attack on the Twin Towers of the World Trade Centre in New York that shook the United States' false sense of security. Ahead of that the Internet bubble burst.

'Why do some companies thrive in uncertainty, even chaos, and others do not?' the duo introspects.

What are their findings? The successful leaders aren't the most 'visionary' or the biggest risk-takers; instead, they tend to be more empirical and disciplined. They rely on evidence over gut instinct and prefer consistent gains to blowout winners. Successful companies are definitely not more innovative than others. They don't always adopt internal changes as a response to a changing environment.

Jim and Morten call them '10Xers' for beating their industry indices by ten times or more in terms of shareholders' returns.

The entire theory is built around the stories of the great Norwegian explorer Roald Amundsen and British naval officer Robert Falcon Scott—two men who set out separately, in October 1911, to become the first explorers to reach the South Pole. Roald won the race by setting goals for each day's progress and by being careful not to overshoot on good days or undershoot on bad ones—a disciplined approach shared by the 10Xers. Robert, in contrast, overreached on good days and fell apart on bad days.

Roald and Robert were thirty-nine and forty-three years

old, respectively, and with comparable experience. They started their respective journeys for the Pole within days of each other, both facing a round trip of at least 1,400 miles into an uncertain and unforgiving environment, where temperatures could drop twenty degrees below zero even in the summer.

In October 1911, the two teams made their final preparations in their quest to be the first in history to reach the South Pole. For one team, it was a race to victory and a safe return home, and, for the other, a devastating defeat that ended in the death of all five members. Roald reached the destination thirty-four days ahead of his rival.

What separated these two men?

Roald and Robert had exactly the same ratio—56% of good days to bad days of weather. As they faced the same environment in the same year with the same goal, environment couldn't be the cause of one's success and the other's failure. The outcomes were different because they displayed very different behaviours.

In an interview with *Forbes* in 2011, Jim said, 'The 10X winners didn't generally out-innovate everyone else; they combined creativity with discipline so that the discipline amplified the creativity rather than destroying it . . . Hand in hand with this is that the leaders who led successfully in the face of turbulent disruption and rapid change were not generally more visionary, more risk-taking, or more blessed by luck than their direct comparisons.'

According to him, one should not place big bets without empirical validation. Firing an uncalibrated cannonball before firing bullets to validate a concept is taking excessive and unnecessary risks. Fire the bullets first to gain empirical validation and then fire a cannonball. This allows one to get the exponential results of concentrated bets, while also limiting one's risk. When one engages in inherently risk-oriented activities, such as entrepreneurship, the key is in managing the risks, to achieve 'big hairy audacious goals' and to stay above the 'death line'. Never forget, the only mistakes one can learn from are the ones one survives.

Market Hates Volatility

Jim's book reminds Helios Capital's Samir Arora of the HDFC Bank story. 'Market doesn't like volatility. It always rewards steady, predictable growth. Aditya Puri controls himself in good times and doesn't lose control in bad times. Since 1994 there have been quite a few crises but in none of them HDFC Bank has been exposed,' says Arora. He owns HDFC Bank stock from day one.

Arora isn't the only one who hates volatility. Satwalekar believes that in the financial sector, the biggest strength of an entity is the steadiness, the lack of volatility. 'I do respect a lot of the things ICICI Bank has done but it has been too volatile for a financial sector stock. HDFC Bank is different,' he says.

Performance of some of the foreign banks in India is also volatile. Typically the CEO, an expat, comes in for a three-year term. He cleans up the balance sheet in the first year, grows it in the second and repeats in the third year what his predecessor had done. Then he gets a promotion and moves on. The experience of some of the state-run banks where the chairman's tenure is not very long is similar. The incoming chairman typically invests the first year in cleaning up the balance sheet—undoing the incumbent's doing—but he leaves behind the same legacy, like his predecessor, in his strive for growth: rising bad assets that eat into the bank's profitability. And the cycle continues.

'For HDFC Bank, there has been no volatility in the earnings or growth and therefore no volatility in the market price. It's never worried about the market share. You'd need to create value over a long term. Buying a market share today is the easiest thing one can do but later it becomes extremely expensive. HDFC Bank hasn't bought the market share. It has bought solidity,' Satwalekar told me. He was on the bank's board for the first eight years till 2002.

Even Kamath, non-executive chairman of ICICI Bank, which competes with HDFC Bank, admits that. 'For the last fifteen years, HDFC Bank has shown steady growth—unrelentingly so. They have been performing well, in a very measured way. By measured, I mean predictable; they do things which are tried and tested and they do them exceptionally well.

'When you record this sort of growth, a few things strike you. One is, clearly, the leadership. It's always a function of two components—how the board looks at growth and momentum in an enterprise and the level of executive management. As you move further down, it percolates to how well you have built your team. In all these respects, HDFC Bank has done very well. The HDFC Bank story is a very good story for anyone looking at banking—a mini tutorial for building a business in a developing country.

'They have followed a measured growth trajectory where growth is substantially high and yet the path is well defined. Its valuation is basically a reflection of the belief that this growth is sustainable,' says Kamath.

Growth Outliers

It's for the same reason that HDFC Bank as well as Infosys (Kamath is also the non-executive chairman of Infosys) figure in an elite group of ten companies identified by *Harvard Business Review (HBR)* which have consistently performed better than others around the world over a decade. Calling this group as growth outliers among 4,793 listed companies with market capitalization of at least $1 billion, *HBR* in its January–February 2012 issue said that some of the things these companies do 'don't match up well with some conventional ideas about growth'.

In an *HBR* article titled 'How the Growth Outliers Do It', in the same issue, Rita Gunther McGrath said they searched for listed companies that have grown by at least 5% each year over a ten-year period ending 2009. The results showed that only ten companies—three from the United States, two each from India and Spain, and one each from Japan, China and Slovenia— grew their net profit by at least 5% during this period. And only five grew both revenues and net profit every year.

Rita, a professor at Columbia Business School, wrote in the article:

Data suggest a need to rethink our assumptions about corporate performance. Steady, consistent growth is difficult to achieve even at modest rates, never mind the double digits that corporate leaders are fond of promising.

Her analysis challenges some of the conventional beliefs. It was found that a company's growth rate is not determined by the industry it is in, that the larger a company gets, sustaining growth doesn't get harder, that consistently higher growth rates need not happen only in fast-growing markets or single geographic regions, or that growth doesn't necessarily slow down as companies age.

Rita wrote:

Our outliers are in wildly different industries, including pharmaceuticals, beer, construction, and banking. All outperformed their industry. Moreover, most of them are in very competitive industries, without the protections that patents or trade secrets provide. [. . .]

No single geographic region dominates the outlier group, which represents both high-growth emerging economies and mature economies. Nor did the degree to which the companies had globalized seem to be a factor. Although Infosys and ACS both planned from the beginning to focus on overseas opportunities, Yahoo Japan conducts business almost entirely in Japan, HDFC Bank operates only in India, and Atmos Energy focuses on the U.S. market. Tsingtao Brewery earns 50% of its revenue from exports, but it didn't venture outside China to manufacture until 2007. Krka Group [headquarters in Novo Mesto, Slovenia] is mainly a regional player, manufacturing generic pharmaceuticals throughout Eastern Europe.

HDFC Bank has been growing at a compounded annual growth rate of at least 25% every year in deposits, advances, net interest income and net profit over the past decade. This is more than the industry average. Its growth rate is almost double that of the industry leader, SBI, whose balance sheet is, of course, more than four times that of HDFC Bank. It has consistently outperformed the industry with 40% credit growth, 33% net profit growth and around 18% return on equity over the past twelve years. The industry growth rate in each of these areas is 23%, 21.5% and 14%, respectively.

The nine-year average return from the stock is 27%, higher than the 18% shown by India's bellwether equity index, the Sensex, but lower than the 29% shown by BSE's banking index, Bankex. (I am talking about nine years, and not ten, since Bankex data is available for only nine years.)

In the last twenty-one quarters till 31 March 2012, while the net profit growth rate for the banking sector has been erratic—between as high as 61% in June 2009 and as low as 2% in June 2011—HDFC Bank's earnings growth rate has been between 30% and 45%. It has outperformed the sector in eighteen of the last twenty-one quarters.

Bouts of Stress

It isn't an easy task to be consistent and record a rather monotonous 25% growth rate quarter after quarter. There have been bouts of stress, particularly in the beginning, as certain senior employees of HDFC Bank didn't get along well with each other. Then, there have been issues on which the bank and its promoter didn't see eye to eye.

The tension between Harish and Samir, two of Aditya's key men in corporate banking, is well known among their colleagues. Neither of them would talk about this but it got to such a level that Harish, the corporate banking boss, volunteered to give up his role. Aditya was worried that Harish might leave the bank.

'Tu kya karega?' he asked Harish when he confided in Aditya his desire to get out of corporate banking.

'I won't leave the bank. I will do something new,' he assured Aditya.

Harish started the financial institutional group in 2002–03 to focus on mobilizing money from government business. He gave up chasing assets (advances) and started dealing with only liabilities (deposits).

The tension between Vinod, Deepak's man Friday, and others in the initial years is the stuff folk tales are made of. It started with Aditya snatching his secretary, Goretti. Vinod had brought her from Mather & Platt. Aditya joined the bank in September 2004 at Sandoz House, whereas Vinod, Goretti and a few others still remained at the Ramon House office. One day when Aditya called Goretti to take charge of his office as his secretary was making a mess of things, she politely told her managing director to get Vinod's okay. 'I don't take permission from people; I instruct them what to do,' Aditya told her.

Vinod was a tough and stingy person who would count every penny. Many even considered him Deepak's spy. 'The feeling with some of the bank people was that I had planted Vinod to oversee them. He was a finance guy, a conscientious book-keeper. He had to be strict. He wasn't liked by some people but at no stage did they ask for him to be taken away,' Deepak told me.

Aditya describes Vinod as 'the original Brit'.

Vinod's first impression about Aditya is 'a typical Citibanker, a roaring lion'.

Vinod saw two different cultures in the bank—of Citibank and Bank of America, the two US banks from where most employees came. They were poles apart. The Bank of America people were modest, down to earth and friendly; the Citibank boys were aggressive, demanding and arrogant. Vinod formed the third culture, a strict disciplinarian who would need to know how a penny is spent, prefer to hire furniture on rent for senior employees instead of buying it, and be happy if they took flats in suburbs where he himself lived, instead of in fancy localities where the rent is very high.

'I am not in the right place. Let me quit,' Vinod once told Deepak.

'You better get used to the Citibankers. I am also doing the same,' Deepak replied.

Vinod listened to his friend's advice. Initially, there was confrontation between Vinod and Aditya, eight years his junior, but after about eighteen months they got to know each other well and started liking each other.

Vinod would always sit to Aditya's left at every meeting and kick him under the table whenever Aditya would shout. Occasionally, Aditya has shown his bad temper. Vinod used to tell him to check his blood pressure. Aditya didn't let Vinod go when he turned sixty in 2001. He was given three extensions for three years each, rare in the bank.

Fighting the Promoter

The tension between HDFC and the bank has primarily been on two counts: one, compensation for the bankers and two, sale of home loans by the bank.

'Senior team compensation was a key issue and the subject of many meetings. My sole objective was for the bank's value to go up. This would not have been possible without Deepak Parekh's support,' Anil Ahuja told me. He was on the HDFC Bank board for six years between 1999 and 2005 as a director from Chase Capital Partner, which had bought the bulk of NatWest's stake in the bank.

'I never got into the HDFC compensation structure; never tried to compare it. If you go down that path, you are asking for trouble. This is a banking company and the compensation package will be different here. If you don't pay, people will walk out of your door,' Anil says.

In a bank, the top team of half a dozen people drives the

business strategy and the core team has to be retained. To do that, HDFC Bank worked out one of the best stock option programmes in the market. This wasn't easy to pass through the board.

Between March 2000 and March 2012, over the past twelve years, HDFC Bank has given 345.16 million stock options to its senior employees. This is after taking into consideration a stock split. In July 2011, the bank split its ₹10 face value stock into five. The options were not granted at a discount but at the prevailing market price of the shares at the time of each grant. So, the gains for individual employees are a function of the future performance of the bank and its shares. Aditya has got 5.47 million, Paresh and Harish 2.04 million each, Jaggia 1.6 million, Ashish 1.55 million, Abhay 1.5 million and Kaizad 1.3 million. In August 2012 when the bank turned eighteen, the price of its share was ₹596.37 apiece, carrying a face value of ₹2.

The bank's investors were keen that it must sell home loans to complete the suite of retail products but HDFC had reservations on this 'duplication of business' which, it felt, would create confusion in the market. Besides, banks don't make money on housing loans as they are cheaper than other retail loans, it argued.

'If the bank started giving home loans and HDFC started giving car loans, consumer loans and personal loans, it would have caused tremendous confusion in the market,' Keki says.

In fact, well before it promoted the bank, HDFC did make a foray into the consumer loans business in the early 1990s, partnering with GE Countrywide Consumer

Financial Services Ltd, a unit of General Electric Co. of the United States. It used to finance white goods, office equipment, two-wheelers, used cars, furniture, jewellery and travel. Later, it withdrew from this space by selling its stake to GE.

The solution was found in 2002–03. HDFC Bank got into the mortgage business but not directly; it was decided that the bank would source home loans for HDFC and buy them back partially.

Keki claims that housing loans are the least profitable among retail products as they are relatively cheaper. And it's a specialized business. 'It isn't credit alone. There are other technical and legal aspects with regard to property and, therefore, home loans [require] an expertise which many banks don't have,' says Keki.

The bank had a two-fold interest in home loans—firstly, it wanted to complete its product range so that it could meet its customers' need for mortgages, and secondly, it wanted on its books home loans that qualified for priority sector lending.

Both Keki and Renu, the managing director of HDFC, worked hard to find the solution. After rounds of discussions and tough negotiations, it was decided that the bank would source housing loans for HDFC as it has a strong distribution network. It would also have the right to buy back up to 70% of the loans. Simply put, if the bank arranges a loan of ₹100 for HDFC, it can buy back ₹70.

So both HDFC and HDFC Bank sell the same (HDFC's) home loan product and there is no confusion with the branding of home loans or with customers. All loans originated by HDFC Bank are first processed and booked by HDFC on its books and the bank earns a selling commission. After that, the bank has the option (right, not the obligation) to buy up to 70% of the loans originated by it.

Both HDFC and the bank say it's a 'win–win' arrangement, leveraging their respective strengths—the former's expertise in mortgages and its economies of scale and the latter's distribution and customer base.

The pricing was also decided upfront. The bank would buy it at 1.25 percentage points lower than what the home loan taker was paying to HDFC. This payment is for the processing and collection services. In effect, if the interest rate on the loan were 11%, the bank would buy it at 9.75% even though the customer would continue to pay 11%.

What does the bank gain from this arrangement? Under RBI norms, Indian banks need to give 40% of loans to the so-called priority sector consisting of agriculture and small businesses. Relatively smaller home loans are also treated as priority loans. Buying back such loans from HDFC helps the bank meet the priority loan target.

The bank also gets virtually risk-free income on the loans it has bought back as HDFC is a servicing and collections agent. By being a single-product company, HDFC has expertise and very low costs in processing, servicing and recovery of loans. The bank does not have this expertise or scale. Over thirty-four years, HDFC's total loan loss, or the money written off, has been only 0.04% of its mortgage portfolio.

HDFC makes money by keeping a 1.25 percentage point margin on the loans sold. The bank too makes money—if it's buying loans at 9.75%, subtract its cost of fund from this, and the difference is its profit. A home loan customer is not in any way concerned about this internal arrangement.

Whose Brand Is Bigger?

Yet another area of hush-hush discussions in the corridors of the parent and the offspring is about whose brand is bigger now. Everyone in the bank agrees that it wouldn't have been successful had it not got the 'HDFC' name. But that was in 1994. Now the eighteen-year-old seems to be adding to the umbrella brand and is not a parasite any more. In valuation parlance, this phenomenon is called equity migration.

Renu feels the bank has a positive rub-off on the HDFC brand as it has followed the basic tenets of integrity, transparency and customer service in line with the HDFC philosophy.

In private, many in the bank say it's contributing significantly to the HDFC brand compared to the promoter.

It could be true. How many times does one deal with HDFC? One may take a home loan or two and instruct one's bank to transfer money from the account every month to repay the loan. But one is dealing with the bank frequently at different service points—for keeping deposits, taking loans, using credit and debit cards, ATMs, buying mutual funds and insurance. 'Frequent interaction of customers with the bank leads to a high recall and enhances the overall brand recall,' Renu says.

The HDFC brand is responsible for the success of the bank but the incremental value is being created more by the bank than by HDFC. Use of one brand across the spectrum is always risky. If any one of the entities does not do well, the overarching brand suffers. The HDFC brand hasn't suffered despite minor loss of reputation by the bank on two occasions—it was penalized by the regulator. The bank has been solidly contributing to it.

Ranjan Kapur, country head of WPP India, the parent of well-known advertising agencies such as J. Walter Thompson USA Inc. (commonly called JWT), Young & Rubicam and Ogilvy & Mather, talks about the brand: 'What is a brand? It's an asset whose transfer takes place at an emotional level. Initially, it had got transferred from HDFC to the bank—the parent's value, integrity and so on. Then the child grew up, stood on its feet and became equal to its parent. Now it is a brand in its own rights—it is neither dependent on HDFC nor confused of its identity. Each one is now equally strong a brand and transferring assets back and forth. One is lifting the other. It's unfair to compare who is bigger as they are in different spaces, banking and mortgage. In future anyone can become a liability or an asset to the other but at this point both are equally strong.'

Ranjan was on the board of HDFC Bank for two years— between January 2004 and March 2006. 'I admire the bank for its governance and ability to grow without being aggressive. I used to call [Aditya] Puri "Mr 31%" as he would always grow at 31%—not half a per cent less or more,' Ranjan told me.

Ramanujam Sridhar, CEO of Integrated Brand Comm

Pvt. Ltd, a communications consulting company headquartered in Bangalore, says HDFC is the leader in performance and imagery: 'Newer, more aggressive players like ICICI Bank have entered the market but haven't been able to match the service quality of HDFC which has been a strong financial services brand. The key thing to be remembered is the equity of the HDFC brand which the bank has used to great advantage.' He admits that the mother brand continues to be strong and each feeds on the other's equity and success.

He refers to the Japanese principle of 'stretching' a brand. Companies such as the Mitsubishi Group and Yamaha Corporation straddle industries and verticals with varied degrees of success in the respective industries though the overarching brand is crucial to success. Virgin is yet another diversified brand.

Ramesh Jude Thomas, president and chief knowledge officer of Equitor Management Consulting Pvt. Ltd, a brand value advisory, believes HDFC Bank has outgrown the parent primarily because a banking licence opens up opportunities far beyond mortgage business. However, mortgage finance is such a universal need that a strong pedigree in this area can easily extend itself to almost any financial services undertaking.

The first example that comes to Ramesh's mind is Caterpillar Inc. The company has exploited the gene of 'providing a firm foothold' to move into more consumer-driven businesses, including footwear. These, in turn, strengthen the mother business by maintaining integrity of the original DNA.

Another example is Samsung Electronic Co.'s mobile handset division—it's the most recent business line of the company and accounts for less than a fourth of its revenues, but handsets are what the company is known by. Similarly, Disney's theme park revenue is about 28% of its overall revenue. The media networks, films and merchandise have outgrown the theme parks but they were incubated by the theme park pedigree. Now it is running in the opposite direction—a Disney game influences park traffic.

The diversified Tata Group companies pay a licensing fee to Tata Sons Ltd, the holding company, for using the 'Tata' brand but other Indian business groups are wary of even discussing a licensing fee for fear of pushback from powerful CEOs. Ramesh says the Tata licensing programme is meant to get business heads to recognize two significant realities—the Tata brand is an arm's length asset belonging to Tata Sons and not to any individual listed entity; and the mere absence of the right to use this name will impair performance and valuations of many of the group companies by several dollars.

HDFC doesn't have any agreement to charge royalty for lending its brand to the bank but it does have an agreement with the bank that if HDFC's shareholding falls below a certain level, the bank would have to change its name. Keki says they haven't done any study on this. There have been informal internal discussions on licensing fees, but Deepak, insiders say, always puts his foot down.

'Will you charge your son? You set up HDFC Bank, haven't you? So, where is the question of collecting money for it?' he asks.

'Deepak is a giver; he is not a taker,' Satwalekar says.

'Who will charge royalty to whom?' Ranjan of WPP asks.

'Both brands are equally strong and they are adding value to each other.'

Here is what Deepak has to say on the brand issue: 'All the HDFC Group companies need to contribute towards enhancement of the mother brand to make it resilient, which will benefit everyone during rough periods. They should be careful or refrain from doing anything that will eat into the mother brand.'

Merger on the Cards?

The market has been speculating on a possible merger of HDFC with the bank ever since ICICI, the project finance institution, merged with ICICI Bank in 2002. The context of that merger is different though. ICICI was crumbling under huge asset–liability mismatches. Survival in a changing environment was becoming increasingly difficult for it as the inherent cost advantage that such institutions were enjoying by virtue of their access to long-term cheap funds was disappearing and commercial banks were getting into project financing in an aggressive way. The regulator was pulling down the wall that separated financial institutions from banks.

Two years later, in 2004, IDBI too merged with IDBI Bank, for similar reasons.

But HDFC is a different story. It's a highly successful housing finance company. Most commercial banks that entered the mortgage business have a distinctive cost advantage over

HDFC by virtue of their access to low-cost savings and no-cost current accounts, but HDFC continues to be profitable in an expanding mortgage market in Asia's third largest economy. The merger is not imperative for its survival.

'We have a ₹1.67-trillion balance sheet. If we were to merge with a bank, then we would need huge reserve requirement. That's the biggest issue,' Keki says.

In September 2012, under RBI norms, banks were to invest 23% of their deposits in government bonds or SLR and keep 4.5% of their deposits with RBI in the form of CRR, on which they do not earn any interest. Besides, they need to have 40% of their loan exposure to the so-called priority sector—where the size of loans is smaller and hence the transaction cost is higher and return is relatively lower.

'If the regulator excuses us from these pre-emptions for five years or allows us to maintain SLR and CRR on incremental deposits and not on the existing balance sheet, it would make tremendous sense for both HDFC and the bank,' Keki told me.

Holding Company

Can HDFC become a holding company? Keki feels the holding company concept makes immense sense but it requires a number of legislative changes, particularly from the fiscal side. HDFC is a housing finance company and it also holds equity in the bank, life insurance and general insurance companies, an asset management company and a venture capital fund. It is playing a dual role but technically it's not a holding company.

Conceptually, in a holding company structure, the holding company does not have any function except for owning the equity in group companies. This means, the mortgage business has to be separated from the holding company and made a subsidiary.

HDFC makes money in the mortgage business and re-invests that in the bank, insurance and asset management businesses. If it becomes a holding company by spinning off the mortgage business into a subsidiary, then the profit will get crystallized in that subsidiary and the holding company will get only dividends. At the time of paying dividend, the subsidiary will have to pay dividend distribution tax.

If HDFC as a holding company used that dividend to pay dividend to its own shareholders then the dividend distribution tax paid by the subsidiary to the holding company can be set off against the dividend paid by the holding company to its own shareholders. However, in case the dividend received by the holding company is used for further investment in other subsidiaries, then no such set off is permitted. So, there is tax leakage in the holding company.

'If the law is changed and tax exemptions are given when a holding company pays dividends to its shareholders and invests in its subsidiaries, the holding company structure makes sense,' Keki says.

At the moment, all options are open, depending on how the regulations frame out. The bank can become bigger overnight through a reverse merger with HDFC if the RBI relaxes the reserve requirements. HDFC can also become a holding company if the tax issues are sorted out.

Such a structure also has implications for public sector banks. They always need capital to grow business as well as maintain the floor for the government's holding. For every loan of ₹100, a bank needs a capital of at least ₹9, and the government holding cannot come down below 51% under banking laws.

Public sector banks have their own subsidiaries and some of them are capital guzzlers. For example, SBI has its insurance arm. Since the insurance business eats up capital, SBI requires more capital than others. If SBI's shareholding is split into two parts, being held partly by a holding company and partly by the government, then the government can infuse capital only in the bank and the insurance company's needs can be taken care of separately by the holding company.

This makes sense, particularly when the government is cash-starved and struggling to bridge its widening fiscal deficit. The RBI has set up an internal panel to look into these issues. The budget for the fiscal year 2013 also announced a plan for a holding company for public sector banks which will raise money from the market, but nobody knows the status of either the RBI report or the budget announcement.

Aditya or Deepak?

Who has built HDFC Bank—Deepak who had the vision and chose Aditya to fulfil it or Aditya who got together the team and runs the business? Aditya is the longest serving managing director in the Indian banking industry.

'It's Aditya's bank. Would it have been possible without Mr Parekh? No. This is because every leader or CEO who builds an enterprise needs an understanding head. Deepak may not have been the chairman of the bank but as chairman of HDFC, his influence is enormous. What is required of such a leader is to give space to the CEO to grow and develop and that space Deepak has definitely given Aditya. But if you look at purely building this bank, it certainly is Aditya's bank,' Kamath told me.

Shirish of Citibank thinks Deepak and Aditya in equal measure were absolutely critical for the success. 'I don't think any other two people could have taken HDFC Bank to this level. . . . Deepak's credibility and ability to connect with the business sector and Aditya's phenomenal managerial skill are a deadly combination. Aditya has got a unique ability of being above and yet being very involved.'

In 1977, HDFC started in virgin territory. The mortgage business did not exist in India before the housing finance company came into being: Hasmukh-bhai created the industry. But banking did exist when HDFC Bank set up shop. In fact, the entire Indian banking industry was privately run till July 1969 when then Prime Minister Indira Gandhi nationalized fourteen banks despite stiff opposition by her finance minister Morarji Desai.

It wasn't an easy task for HDFC Bank. But it succeeded because the timing was correct. Could this bank have happened in 1960 or 1970? No, it couldn't. After the economy opened up in 1991, the canvas for a bank got broader and there was a vast open space to function in. When it came into being, there wasn't another HDFC Bank in India. It had to be created. And the best two people to create it were Deepak and Aditya.

The combination was able to take competition in a crowded sector and create a space for itself. It's one of the three banks in Asia that stands out in a crowd, the other two being Mizuho Corporate Bank (Malaysia) Berhad and Hang Seng Bank Ltd of Hong Kong. 'It has been able to ride the growth of the Indian economy in a very disciplined way without any of the excesses that some banks tend to get into,' Piyush of DBS says.

Renu attributes the bank's success to its excellent team built by Aditya who, she says, 'is a great leader and has the capacity to innovate and think about new products and businesses ahead of others'. 'HDFC being a trusted brand also provided huge goodwill and comfort which is fundamental to the bank's success,' she says.

'How do we have an institution which is world class, privately owned and functioning as a corporate entity subjected to the best governance and international regulatory standards?' asks Bimal Jalan, former RBI governor, who has been on the board of HDFC since January 2008. It can be done if there is no interference in day-to-day management and operations of a bank by regulatory authorities or government.

Earlier, Indian psychology was that in a developing country and protective market, one can't compete. But instances such as the creation of HDFC Bank have dismembered this belief and proved that one can compete in the Indian scenario, provided one allows the institution to be run by professional managers under the guidance of a competent board.

Who chose HDFC Bank's CEO Aditya, who has contributed substantially to the bank's growth and credit-worthiness? He was chosen and appointed by the board of the bank on merit, after careful consideration, and given full management responsibility for running the bank as per best international standards. This management freedom, subject to accountability, is critical for excellence.

Bimal cites the example of the Election Commission and the Comptroller and Auditor General of India (CAG). The Election Commission gives India the largest free and fair election in human history because it is not controlled by the Home Ministry. The CAG couldn't have been objective had it been reporting to the Finance Ministry. Would HDFC Bank have been so successful if its managing director had been selected through a bureaucratic process? Could it have performed so well had its board been interfering in day-to-day management?

Aditya is a highly competent banker, and he could succeed because he had a free hand to run the bank, with accountability for performance, but without any interference. HDFC, the promoter, holds a 23.1% stake in the bank; the foreign stakeholders a little less than 50%. The ADS holders, about 20%, have no voting rights. Neither HDFC nor others interfere in any way. They keep an eye on the performance and nothing else. They don't enjoy power without responsibility the way ministers and bureaucrats do with respect to public sector banks.

The biggest lesson from the HDFC Bank story is that once the market is opened to competition, people must be allowed the freedom. They are capable of delivering the best globally. Promoters of the new set of private banks that will open shop soon should also take note of this. A few new banks that were peers of HDFC Bank did not survive because they did not respect corporate governance or the freedom they enjoyed and because they did not work for the benefit of their customers and investors.

HDFC Bank is not merely a story of entrepreneurship. It's a testimony to what new India can do—what can happen when passion for excellence merges with high corporate governance. It has not done anything unique. Doing very ordinary things in ordinary ways with extraordinary execution and redefining the distinction between real risks and perceived risks are what make HDFC Bank different from the rest.

Abbreviations

A

ADS: American depositary shares

AIIMS: All India Institute of Medical Sciences

ATMs: automated teller machines

B

BoB: Bank of Baroda

BoP: Bank of Punjab

BSE: Bombay Stock Exchange

C

CAG: Comptroller and Auditor General of India

CASA: current account/ savings account

CBDT: Central Board of Direct Taxes

CEO: chief executive officer

CFO: chief financial officer

CGA: controller general of accounts

Citil: Citicorp Information Technology Industries Ltd

CRR: cash reserve ratio

D

DBS: Development Bank of Singapore Ltd

F

FERA: Foreign Exchange Regulation Act

Fincon: financial control unit

FMCG: fast-moving consumer goods

G

GAAP: generally accepted accounting principles

H

HBR: Harvard Business Review

HDFC: Housing Development Finance Corporation Ltd

HFC: housing finance company

HSBC: Hongkong and Shanghai Banking Corporation

I

I-Sec: ICICI Securities Ltd

ICICI: Industrial Credit and Investment Corporation of India Ltd

IDBI: Industrial Development Bank of India

IDFC: Infrastructure Development Finance Co. Ltd

IFC: International Finance Corporation

IIM-A: Indian Institute of Management, Ahmedabad

IIT: Indian Institute of Technology

IPO: initial public offering

IT: information technology

J

JLGs: joint liability groups

K

KYC: 'know your customer'

M

MCX: Multi Commodity Exchange Ltd

MD: managing director

MFIs: micro finance institutions

MIS: management information system

MNC: multinational company

N

Nabard: National Bank for Agriculture and Rural Development

NatWest: National Westminster Bank PLC

NBFCs: non-banking finance companies

NGOs: non-government organizations

NIM: net interest margin

NPAs: non-performing assets

NRIs: non-resident Indians

NSE: National Stock Exchange

NYSE: New York Stock Exchange

O

OCI: overseas citizenship of India

P

PNB: Punjab National Bank

R

RBI: Reserve Bank of India

S

Samba: Saudi American Bank

SBI: State Bank of India

SBICI: SBI Commercial & International Bank Ltd

SCM: supply chain management

Sebi: Securities and Exchange Board of India

SHG: self-help group

SLR: statutory liquidity ratio

SMEs: small and medium enterprises

T

Telco: Tata Engineering and Locomotive Co. Ltd

Tisco: Tata Iron and Steel Co. Ltd

U

UTI: Unit Trust of India

UBS: United Bank of Switzerland AG

Y

YMCA: Young Men's Christian Association

List of Persons

A

A. Balasubramaniam

A. C. Muthiah

A. M. M. Sarma

A. Rajan (Rajan)

A. S. Thyagarajan

A. V. Rajwade

Abhay Aima (Abhay)

Aditya Puri (Aditya)

Agha Hasan Abedi

Akira Kurosawa

Ambi Venkateswaran (Ambi)

Amit Judge

Anand Dusane

Anil Ahuja (Anil)

Anil Jaggia (Jaggia)

Anil Nath

Arun Arora

Arun Maira

Arvind Kapil

Aseem Dhru

Ashima Bhat (Ashima)

Ashish Parthasarthy (Ashish)

Ashok Jain

Ashok Sud

Ashok Wadhwa

Asim Ghosh

Atul Sud

Azim Premji

B

B. M. Munjal

B. Ramalinga Raju

Baba Kalyani

Benjamin Frank

Benjamin J. Sottile

Berjis Desai (Berjis)

Bharat Shah (Bharat)

Bhavesh Zaveri (Bhavesh)

Biju Patnaik

Bimal Jalan (Bimal)

C

C. K. Venkatesh

C. N. Ram (Ram)

C. Rangarajan

Chain Roop Bansali

Chanda Kochhar (Chanda)

Charles Steadman 'Charlie' Sanford

Chetan Shah (Chetan)

Christopher Fitzgerald

Christopher Low

Cyril Shroff

D

D. D. Rathi (Rathi)

D. N. Ghosh

D. R. Mehta

Darshanjit Singh

Deepak Maheshwari (Maheshwari)

Deepak Majithia

Deepak Parekh (Deepak)

Deepak Satwalekar (Satwalekar)

Deepak Vaidya

Deepankar Sanwalka (Deepankar)

Derek Wanless

Deven Pandit

Devendra Ahuja

E

Edward Gerald Corrigan

F

Francis Bruce Pike

G

G. Subramanian (GS)

Gayatri Krishna Rao (Gayatri)

Gerald Clive 'Gerry' Dobby

Goretti Soares (Goretti)

Govind

H

H. N. Sinor

Harish Engineer (Harish-bhai / Harish)

Harjit Sawhney

Hasmukh Thakordas Parekh
(H. T. Parekh /
Hasmukh-bhai)

Hemendra Kothari

I

I. M. Kadri

Imran Khan

Inderjit Singh

India Jane Birley

Indira Gandhi

Ishaat Hussain (Ishaat)

J

J. K. Basu (JK)

Jaithirth 'Jerry' Rao (Jerry
Rao)

James Goldsmith

Jemima Khan

Jim Collins (Jim)

Jimmy Tata

John Shepard Reed (John)

Joyce

K

K. Manohara Raj

K. P. Singh

K. R. Puri

K. V. Kamath (Kamath)

Kaizad Barucha (Kaizad)

Keki Mistry (Keki)

Keshub Mahindra

L

Lakshmi N. Mittal

Louis Pratico (Lou)

Luis Miranda (Luis)

M

M. Narasimham

M. Narendra

Mahesh Priolkar

Mandeep Maitra (Mandeep)

Manmohan Singh (Singh)

Manohar Rajaram Chhabria

Mehli Mistry (Mehli)

Mervyn Davies (Mervyn)

Morarji Desai

Morten T. Hansen (Morten)

Murli Deora

N

N. G. Pillai

N. Vaghul

Nandan Nilekani (Nandan)

Nani Javeri (Nani)

Nasser Munjee

Navin Puri (Navin)

Neeraj Dhawan

Neeraj Swaroop (Neeraj)

Nilesh Shah

Nimesh Kampani

P

P. Chidambaram

P. K. Srivastava

P. S. Subramanyam

P. V. Ananthakrishnan

P. V. Narasimha Rao

Paresh Sukthankar (Paresh)

Partha S. Bhattacharyya

Pervez Musharraf, General

Piyush Gutpa (Piyush)

Pradip Pain (Pradip)

Pralay Mondal (Pralay)

Purshottam Budhwani

R

R. Balasubramanian

Rahul Bhagat (Rahul)

Rai Bahadur Lala Brij Lal
Puri

Rajeev Lall

Rajender Sehgal

Rajesh Hukku

Rama Sridhar

Ramakrishna Dalmia

Ramanujam Sridhar

Ramesh Gelli

Ramesh Gowani

Ramesh Jude Thomas
(Ramesh)

Rana (Gurvirendra Singh)
Talwar

Rana Kapoor

Ranjan Kapur

Rashesh Shah

Ravi Kant

Ravi Narain

Ravi Ruia

Renu Sud Karnad (Renu)

Rita Gunther McGrath
(Rita)

Roald Amundsen (Roald)

Robert Alexander

Robert Citron

Robert Falcon Scott (Robert)

Roopal-ben Panchal

S

S. A. Dave

S. P. Talwar

S. S. Nadkarni

S. S. Tarapore

S. S. Thakur (Thakur)

Sahu Shanti Prasad Jain

Sahu Shital Prasad Jain

Samir Arora (Arora)

Samir Bhatia (Samir)

Samir Jain

Samit Ghosh

Samudra Sen

Sandeep Jhavar

Sanjay Dongre

Sanjay Sakhuja

Sashi Jagdishan (Sashi)

Satpal Khattar (Satpal)

Satyajit Ray

Saurabh Jambhekar

Shailendra Bhandari
(Shailendra)

Shambhu Lal Puri

Shankar Dey

Shantilal Parekh

Sharad Marathe

Sharad Pawar

Shaukat Aziz (Shaukat)

Shirish Apte (Shirish)

Subroto Mukherjee

Sudhir Joshi (Sudhir)

Suranjan Ghosh

Suresh Prabhu

Suryakant

Susan Philips

T

T. Chandrasekhar

Tapishwar Puri

Tarini Vaidya

Thakordas Parekh

Tony Singh

U

Uday Kotak

Ujwal Thakar

Uma Krishnan (Uma)

V

V. Leeladhar (Leeladhar)

V. S. Rangan

Victor Menezes

Vijay Mallya

Vikram Kochar

Vikram Talwar

Vineet Jain

Vinod Yennemadi (Vinod)

Vivek Vig

W

William L. Flaherty

Y

Yaga Venugopal Reddy

List of Institutions / Groups / Locations

Tamal Bandyopadhyay

Tamal Bandyopadhyay

Glossary

A

accretive merger: An acquisition that results in a rise in the price-to-earnings ratio of the acquiring company.

ambulance chasers: A derogatory phrase that typically refers to attorneys in the United States who solicit business from accident victims or their families.

American depositary share (ADS): A US-dollar-denominated equity share of a foreign-based company available for purchase on an American stock exchange. An ADS is issued by depository banks in the United States under agreement with the issuing foreign company; the entire issuance is called an American depositary receipt and an individual share is referred to as an ADS.

articles of association: The regulations governing the relationships between shareholders and directors of a company.

asset classification norms: Norms introduced by the Reserve Bank of India (RBI) in the mid-1990s as a prudential measure to strengthen banks' balance sheets. Banks' loan accounts are classified into four categories: sub-standard assets, doubtful assets, loss assets and standard assets. To strengthen their balance sheets, banks need to set aside money not only for their bad assets but also for their standard assets, marginally though for the latter.

asset management company: A company that invests its clients' pooled fund into securities that match its declared financial objectives. Such companies are called mutual funds in India and they run different schemes for investments in debt and equities.

asset–liability mismatch: A mismatch that occurs when an institution's assets and liabilities do not match. They should match in terms of tenure as well as amount.

audit and compliance committee: An operating committee of the board of directors charged with oversight of financial reporting and disclosure.

B

back office: The section of a company that provides administrative and support services. A financial services company is logically broken up into three parts: the front office, which includes sales personnel and corporate finance; the middle office, which manages risk and information technology resources; and the back office.

bad assets: Assets on which a bank does not earn any interest. Additionally, it needs to set aside money to provide for such assets.
An illiquid asset is also called a bad asset when its secondary market disappears.

balance-of-payment crisis: Also called a currency crisis, this occurs when a nation is unable to pay for essential imports and/or service its debt repayments.

bank guarantee: A guarantee that enables the customer (debtor) to acquire goods, buy equipment or draw down loans, and thereby expand business activity. Banks offer such a guarantee for a fee.

bank-on-wheels: A banking kiosk in a mobile van that goes to various places in rural India offering banking services at one's doorstep.

Bankex: An equity index traded on the Bombay Stock Exchange (BSE Ltd) that tracks the performance of the leading banking sector stocks. It consists of fourteen stocks.

Banking Regulation Act: The 1949 Act enacted to safeguard the interest of depositors and prevent abuse of power by promoters of banks. It has been amended many times to make the laws contemporary. This Act, however, does not supersede the Companies Act. This means that a listed banking entity is governed both by the Banking Regulation Act as well as by the Companies Act.

bellwether equity index: A security or indicator that signals the market's direction. The Sensex is BSE's bellwether equity index.

bill discounting: The process by which a bank buys the bill—a bill of exchange or a promissory note—before it is due and credits the value of the bill after a discount charged to the customer's account. The transaction is practically an advance against the security of the bill and the discount represents the interest on the advance from the date of purchase of the bill until it is due for payment.

black swan phenomenon: A concept derived from the 'black swan' event or theory, a metaphor that describes an event that is a surprise (to the observer) and has a major impact. The theory was developed by Nassim Nicholas Taleb to explain the disproportionate role of high-impact, hard-to-predict, and rare events that are beyond the realm of normal expectations in history, science, finance and technology.

blue chip: A nationally recognized, well-established and financially sound company. Blue chips generally sell high-quality, widely accepted products and services.

bonus share: A free share given to current shareholders in a company.

book building: The process of generating, capturing and recording investor demand for shares during an initial public offer.

book runner: The main underwriter or lead manager in the issuance of new equity, debt or securities instruments.

bulk deposit: Typically, any single deposit that is about 0.25% of the total deposits of a bank. So, for a bank with a ₹1,000-crore deposit base, anything above ₹2.5 crore are bulk deposits. The definition varies from bank to bank and generally relatively large deposits are called bulk deposits and banks pay higher interest rates on such deposits.

business correspondent: A financial organization such as a securities company or a bank that regularly performs services for another company that does not have the requisite facilities or the access to perform the services directly. Business correspondents earn commission for their services.

business process outsourcing: The process of hiring another company to handle one's business activities.

business process re-engineering: The analysis and redesign of workflow within and between enterprises.

C

CASA: Low-cost current and savings accounts. Banks do not pay any interest on current accounts (CA) and pay relatively low interest on savings accounts (SA). Till 2011, interest on savings accounts was mandated. The higher the CASA, the lower the cost of fund for a bank.

cash management: Functions for processing receipts and payments, that is, managing the cash flow between a company and its suppliers. For example, a Mumbai-based company selling its products across India gets a payment as a cheque drawn on some bank's branch in Ludhiana, Punjab. When the Mumbai company deposits the cheque in its account, the cheque goes back to Ludhiana for clearing and the money could take up to a week to be credited. In a cash management system, the company deposits the cheque with the bank's branch or a partner bank in Ludhiana and gets the money almost immediately. The bank either charges a commission, or gets to keep the money for a day or two.

cash reserve ratio (CRR): The portion of deposits a bank needs to keep with the Reserve Bank of India (RBI), on which it does not earn any interest.

certificate of deposits: A savings certificate entitling the bearer to receive interest. It bears a maturity date, a specified fixed interest rate and can be issued in any denomination.

circuit breaker: Any measure used by stock exchanges during large sell-offs to avert panic selling. It works the other way too, when a stock price rises too much.

circular trading: A fraudulent trading scheme where sell orders are entered into by a broker who knows that offsetting buy orders, the same number of shares at the same time and at the same price, either have been or will be entered.

clearing corporation: An organization associated with an exchange to handle the confirmation, settlement and delivery of transactions, fulfilling the main obligation of ensuring transactions are made in a prompt and efficient manner. It is also referred to as a 'clearing company/firm' or 'clearing house'.

collateral: A borrower's pledge (in a lending agreement) of specific property to a lender, to secure repayment of a loan.

collection agent: A person who contacts debtors on behalf of a client.

compensation committee: Also known as remuneration committee, it is a committee of the board of directors that sets appropriate and supportable pay programmes in the organization's best interests and aligned with its business mission and strategy.

compounded annual growth rate: The year-over-year growth rate of an investment over a specified period of time. It is calculated by taking the nth root of the total percentage growth rate, where n is the number of years in the period being considered.

compromise settlement: The resolution of a dispute by mutual agreement to avoid a lawsuit.

consent process: A process by which a company or an individual involved in an alleged wrongdoing settles a dispute with the capital market regulator by paying some money. Such a settlement neither establishes the guilt of the company involved nor does it say the company has not done anything wrong.

control premium: An amount that a buyer is willing to pay over the current market price of a publicly traded company to gain control over it.

controller general of accounts (CGA): The principal accounts adviser to the Government of India, responsible for establishing and maintaining a technically sound management accounting system.

corporate social responsibility: The continuing commitment by a business to behave ethically and contribute to economic development while improving the quality of life of the workforce and their families as well as of the local community and society at large.

cost-to-income ratio: An efficiency measure, similar to the operating margin, defined by operating expenses divided by operating income. Unlike the operating margin, lower the cost-to-income ratio is the better. The cost-to-income ratio is most commonly used in the financial sector, and can be used for benchmarking by a bank when reviewing its operational efficiency.

credit counselling centre: A centre run by banks to counsel a potential defaulter or one who has already defaulted in clearing bank dues by giving them advice on how to avert defaults and iron out their problems in repaying bank loans.

credit score: A number representing the creditworthiness of a person, that is, the likelihood that a person will pay his or her debts.

credit scoring model: A model based on credit scores used by lenders, such as banks and credit card companies, to evaluate the potential risk posed by lending money to consumers.

cross-selling: The practice of selling among or between established clients, markets and traders, or selling an additional product or service to an existing customer. For an instance, a bank can sell an auto loan to an existing home-loan buyer.

currency swap: A foreign-exchange agreement between two parties to exchange aspects (the principal and/or interest payments) of a loan in one currency for equivalent aspects of an equal in net present value loan in another currency.

current account: The difference between a nation's total exports of goods, services and transfers, and its total imports of them. The key component of a current account is the balance of trade figure. In economics, the current account is one of two primary components of a nation's balance of payments, the other being the capital account.

A current account in a bank is a form of demand deposit from which withdrawals are allowed any number of times. Generally, such accounts do not offer any interest and carry an overdraft facility.

D

data warehouse: A database used for reporting and data analysis. The data stored in the warehouse are uploaded from the operational systems (such as marketing, sales etc.). The data may pass through an operational data store before being used in the data warehouse for reporting.

death-backed bond: A security backed by life insurance which is derived by pooling together a number of transferable life insurance policies. Similar to mortgage-backed securities, the life insurance policies are pooled and repackaged into bonds to be sold to investors.

delinquency: A default in repaying bank loans. Typically, a loan becomes 'delinquent' if the borrower does not pay interest/principal for a quarter or ninety days.

demat: A dematerialized account for Indian citizens to trade in listed stocks or debentures in electronic form rather than on paper. The Securities and Exchange Board of India (Sebi) has made a demat account mandatory in order to trade in stocks.

depositaries: Organizations where the securities of an investor are held in electronic form.

derivative product: A contract between two parties that specifies conditions (especially the dates, resulting values of the underlying variables and notional amounts) under which payments are to be made between the parties.

direct sales agents: Individual sales agents who reach out to and deal directly with clients. Typically, private and foreign banks employ such agents to sell loans.

direct tax: A tax paid directly to the government by the persons on whom it is imposed (such as income tax).

dividend distribution tax: The tax levied by the Government of India on a company according to the dividend paid to the company's shareholders.

due diligence: An investigation or audit of a potential investment. Due diligence serves to confirm all material facts with regard to a sale.

E

'eat well, sleep well' dilemma: An adage that refers to the risk/return trade-off—the type of security an investor chooses depends on whether he or she wants to eat well or sleep well.

economic liberalization: On-going economic reforms in India that started on 24 July 1991.

F

face value: The nominal value of a security stated by the issuer. For stocks, it is the original cost of the stock. For bonds, it is the amount paid to the holder at maturity.

financial inclusion: The delivery of banking services at an affordable cost to vast sections of disadvantaged and low-income groups.

fiscal deficit: The shortfall created when a government's total expenditure exceeds the revenue that it generates in a fiscal year. This deficit or gap is taken care of by borrowing money from the market.

fiscal stimulus: The proposition that by borrowing money and spending it, the government can raise the overall state of the economy, raising output and lowering unemployment. The Government of India did this in 2009 in the wake of an unprecedented credit crunch following the collapse of US investment bank Lehman Brothers Holdings Inc.

float money: The money that a bank enjoys for a short period without paying interest for it. For instance, the money that remains with the bank between the time a bank draft is made and the time it is encashed, on which the bank pays no interest. Smart banks do business that ensures a steady flow of float money.

Foreign Exchange Management Act (FEMA): The Act passed in the 1999 winter session of the Indian Parliament to replace the Foreign Exchange Regulation Act. This Act seeks to make offences related to foreign exchange civil offences.

Foreign Exchange Regulation Act: The 1973 legislation passed by the Indian Parliament, under the Indira Gandhi government, that came into force with effect from 1 January 1974. The Act imposed stringent regulations on certain kinds of payments, such as dealings in foreign exchange and securities and transactions that had an indirect impact on foreign exchange and the import and export of currency.

G

gala: An industrial shed. Typically, small and medium enterprises operate in a *gala* which is nothing more than an industrial floor where heavy-duty machinery works.

generally accepted accounting principles (GAAP): The standard framework of guidelines for financial accounting used in any given jurisdiction, generally known as accounting standards.

greenfield project: A new project that is not constrained by prior work (metaphorically, creating a business opportunity where none existed before). In construction, greenfield projects refer to construction on unused land where there is no need to remodel or demolish an existing structure. Such projects are often coveted by engineers.

gross NPAs: The bad assets of a bank which have not been provided for. *See* net NPAs; non-performing assets (NPAs).

growth outlier: A company whose growth is abnormally higher than that of its peers.

gurukul **system:** An ancient Indian system of education where the '*shishya*' (student) resides with the '*guru*' (teacher) for the duration of learning; thus, knowledge was imparted in the natural environment of the *guru*'s home and its surroundings.

H

heaven and hell bond: A bond with principal redemption related to the change in the spot exchange rate from issuance to maturity.

high-net-worth customer: A classification used by the financial services industry to denote an individual or a family with high net worth (wealth).

high-value cheque: A cheques with a high denomination; they get cleared on the same day, if deposited before 11 a.m.

holding company: A parent corporation that owns enough voting stock in another corporation to control its board of directors (and, therefore, its policies and management).

I

'in the money': A state where one's stock option is worth money and one can sell or exercise it.

Indian Contract Act: The Act relating to contracts in India, passed in 1872. Based on the principles of English Common Law, it is applicable to all Indian states except for Jammu & Kashmir. The law determines the circumstances in which an agreement made by the parties to a contract shall be legally binding on them.

initial public offering (IPO): A stock market launch where shares of a company are sold to the general public, on a securities exchange, for the first time. Through this process, a private company transforms into a public company.

inter-corporate deposit: An unsecured loan extended by one company to another.

interest rate derivative: A financial instrument based on an underlying financial security whose value is affected by changes in interest rates. Interest rate derivatives are hedges used by institutional investors such as banks to combat the changes in market interest rates.

interest rate swap: The exchange of one set of cash flows (based on interest rate specifications) for another.

Internet banking: A facility that allows customers (of a financial institution or individuals) to conduct financial transactions on a secure website operated by banks.

IPO scam: A well-structured game played by the absolute opportunists consisting of intermediaries, financiers and bank employees, who make a lot of money by controlling shares meant for retail investors in an initial public offer.

The IPO scam, unearthed in April 2006, involved depositaries, depository participants and many market operators who allegedly used or abetted certain entities in creating 59,000 fictitious demat accounts to corner shares of many IPOs meant for small investors. Apparently, in 105 IPOs between 2003 and 2005, scamsters cornered shares meant for retail investors by creating multiple identities.

J

joint liability group (JLG): An informal group consisting of preferably of four to ten individuals, but can be up to twenty members, coming together to get bank loans either singly or through the group mechanism against mutual guarantee.

K

'knock-in': A financial option contract that is valid only when a certain price is met; so if a price is never reached, the contract is considered to have never existed.

'knock-out': A financial option contract with a built-in mechanism to expire worthless should a specified price level be exceeded.

'know your customer' (KYC): A norm enforced by all regulatory authorities in financial services. Banks, mutual funds and all other intermediaries should 'know' the customers whose money they deal with. A customer's identity can be established by his or her driving licence, passport and/or permanent account number (PAN), among other documents.

L

lead manager: An investment banker appointed by companies going public. For bigger public issues, companies appoint more than one lead manager. The main responsibilities of a lead manager are to initiate the offer processing, help the company in road shows, create the draft offer document and get it approved by the capital market regulator and stock exchanges, and list shares at the stock market.

M

market capitalization: The market value of a company's outstanding shares. Market capitalization is calculated by multiplying a company's outstanding shares by the current market price of one share.

micro finance institutions (MFIs): Organizations that 'micro finance' or offer tiny loans to micro entrepreneurs, small businesses and poor people who lack access to banking and related services owing to the high transaction costs associated with serving these client categories.

multi-channel banking: The concept of multiple or alternative modes of banking. Banking via bank branches is the first, and perhaps most conventional, channel of banking. Increasingly, banks are offering multi-channel banking facilities such as Internet banking, telephone banking, automated teller machines and even doorstep banking where a banker goes to a client's house with products. Typically, high-net-worth customers have the privilege of banking in their homes.

N

nationalized bank: A government-controlled bank that is governed by the Nationalization Act. The first set of banks was nationalized in 1969.

net interest margin (NIM): A measure of the difference between the interest income generated by banks or other financial institutions and the amount of interest paid out to their lenders (e.g. deposits), relative to the amount of their (interest-earning) assets. It is similar to the gross margin of non-financial companies.

net NPAs: The net of provision for bad assets. A profitable bank can provide handsomely to bring down its net NPAs. *See* gross NPAs; non-performing assets (NPAs).

net open position limit: An aggregate limit of a bank's currency risk exposure.

non-banking finance company: A financial institution that provides banking services without meeting the legal definition of a bank, that is, one that does not hold a banking licence. Non-banking finance companies are not allowed to mobilize deposits from the public.

non-government organizations (NGOs): Legally constituted organizations created by natural or legal persons which operate independently from any form of government.

non-performing assets (NPAs): Credit facilities or loans for which the interest and/or instalment of principal has remained 'past due' for at least a quarter or ninety days. *See* gross NPAs; net NPAs.

O

open offer: A secondary market offering that is similar to a 'rights' issue in which a shareholder is given the opportunity to purchase stocks. The pricing of an open offer is determined by a formula of market regulators. Any entity that wants to buy at least 25% in a listed company is required to make an open offer.

over-the-counter derivatives: Contracts that are traded (and privately negotiated) directly between two parties, without going through an exchange or other intermediary. Products such as swaps, forward rate agreements, exotic options—and other exotic derivatives—are almost always traded in this way.

overdraft: A deficit in a bank account caused by drawing more money than the account holds. An overdraft facility allows money to be withdrawn even when the available account balance goes below zero.

overnight indexed swap: An interest rate swap involving the overnight rate being exchanged for a fixed interest rate. Overnight indexed swaps are popular among financial institutions for the reason that the overnight index is considered to be a good indicator of the inter-bank credit market and less risky than other traditional interest rate spreads.

overseas citizenship of India (OCI): A scheme by which a person of Indian origin in a foreign country who was (or was eligible to become) a citizen of India on 26 January 1950 or thereafter, except who is or has been a citizen of Pakistan and Bangladesh, can register as an 'overseas citizen of India'. Foreigners of Indian origin whose present nationality is such that their country of nationality allows dual citizenship in some form or other are eligible to apply and if accepted are provided with an OCI card. The status provides no political rights, but essentially travel benefits and parity with non-resident Indians in financial, economic and educational fields.

P

par issue: A public issue where shares are offered at their face value without any premium.

pay-ins: A pay-in of securities refers to the transfer of stocks from a client's demat account to a broker's/clearing member's account; a pay-in of funds is the transfer of money by a broker to an exchange towards settlement dues for that particular day.

pay-outs: A pay-out of securities is the transfer of stocks from a broker's pool account to a client's demat account; a pay-out of funds is the transfer of money from an exchange to a broker towards settlement dues for that particular day.

personal loan: A consumer loan granted for personal use as opposed to business or commercial use.

point-of-sale terminal: A computerized replacement for a cash register.

price-to-book: A ratio used to compare a stock's market value to its book value.

priority loan: A loan given to the priority sector of farmers (agriculture) and small-scale industries. Under RBI norms as of 2012, banks are required to give 40% of their loans to small and medium enterprises and people from socially backward classes.

private equity: Equity capital (or shares) of a company not quoted on the market or publicly traded on an exchange.

private equity company: Investors and funds that make investments directly into private companies and even listed entities. Typically, they cash out by selling their stakes in the market when the private company goes for a public issue. Private equity firms characteristically make longer-hold investments in target industry sectors or specific investment areas where they have expertise.

project finance institution: An institution that gives project loans. The erstwhile Industrial Credit and Investment Corporation of India Ltd and Industrial Development Bank of India were such institutions.

prudential regulation: A regulation of deposit-taking institutions and supervision of the conduct of these institutions that limit their risk-taking. The aim of prudential regulations is to ensure the safety of depositors' funds and keep the financial system stable.

public equity: Stocks and shares of a company that are traded on a public exchange.

public float: The portion of a company's outstanding shares that is in the hands of public investors, as opposed to company officers, directors or controlling-interest investors.

R

real-time gross settlement: A fund transfer system where transfer of money or securities takes place from one bank to another on the basis of 'real time' and 'gross' amounts.

receivables: Claims that are expected to be collected in cash.

relationship manager: A professional who works to improve a company's relationships with partner companies and customers. They play a key role in banks, particularly for getting business from high-net-worth customers.

reputation risk: A type of risk related to the trustworthiness of business. When a bank is penalized by the banking regulator and a company is penalized by the market regulator, they suffer from reputation risk.

retail banking: Banking in which institutions execute transactions directly with consumers, rather than with corporations or other banks. Home loans and auto loans are part of retail banking.

return on equity: The amount of net income returned as a percentage of shareholders' equity. Return on equity measures a corporation's profitability by revealing how much profit a company generates with the money shareholders have invested.

risk appetite: The level of risk that an organization is prepared to accept. It represents a balance between the potential benefits of innovation and the threats that change inevitably brings on.

risk–reward trade-off: The principle that potential return rises with an increase in risk. Low levels of uncertainty (low risks) are associated with low potential returns, whereas high levels of uncertainty (high risks) are associated with high potential returns.

run on the bank: A rapid loss of deposits that occurs when a large number of customers (rush/'run' to) withdraw their deposits from a bank at the same time as they believe that the bank might become insolvent. A run on the bank is also known as a 'bank run'.

S

S&P/CNX Nifty Index: The Standard & Poor's CRISIL NSE Index 50, popularly called Nifty, is a stock market index, and one of several leading indices for large companies listed on the National Stock Exchange of India, index-based derivatives and index funds. It consists of 50 stocks. All Sensex stocks are part of Nifty stocks.

savings account: A bank account that offers the account holder a cheque facility and pays interest on money deposited.

securitization: The financial practice of pooling various types of contractual debts such as residential mortgages, commercial mortgages, auto loans or credit card debt obligations and selling these consolidated debts as bonds, pass-through securities or collateralized mortgage obligation to various investors.

self-help group (SHG): A financial intermediary usually composed of ten to twenty local women. Most SHGs are located in India, though they can also be found in other countries, especially in South Asia and Southeast Asia. SHG members make small regular savings contributions over a few months until there is enough capital in the group to begin lending.

Sensex: A free-float market capitalization-weighted stock market index of thirty well-established and financially sound companies listed on the BSE, Asia's oldest bourse.

settlement fund: The transferable assets available to meet obligations or debts of a transaction or trade. The Securities and Exchange Board of India requires stock exchanges to have a system of guaranteeing settlement of trades or set up a clearing corporation to ensure that the market equilibrium is not disturbed in case of payment default by members of the exchanges. Typically, exchanges have a trade guarantee fund (or a settlement fund) to ensure timely completion of settlements of contracts. Members of the exchanges contribute to the settlement fund.

small and medium enterprises (SMEs): Companies whose personnel numbers as well as turnover fall below certain limits. In India, a micro enterprise is one where a company's investment in plant and machinery does not exceed ₹25 lakh; a small enterprise is one where the investment is between ₹25 lakh and ₹5 crore; and a medium enterprise is one where the investment is between ₹5 crore and ₹10 crore.

statutory liquidity ratio (SLR): A ratio of the amount that a commercial bank is required to maintain in the form of cash or gold or government bonds before providing credit to its customers. As of 2012, the SLR is 23% of bank deposits.

stock options: A privilege, sold by one party to another, that gives the buyer the right, but not the obligation, to buy (call) or sell (put) a stock at an agreed-upon price within a certain period or on a specific date.

strategic partner: A party with which a strategic partnership is reached. A strategic partnership in this context is a formal alliance between two commercial enterprises, usually formalized by one or more business contracts but falls short of forming a legal partnership or agency or corporate affiliate relationship.

supply chain management (SCM): The management of a network of interconnected businesses involved in the provision of product and service packages required by the end customers in a supply chain.

sweep facility: The facility of automatically transferring money from a customer's savings bank account to a term deposit once it crosses a certain limit, say ₹5,000. This way, customers earn higher interest while banks earn customers' loyalty by offering a facility to earn more. Few banks, however, offer this facility.

T

teller: An employee of a bank, or similar institution, whose job includes helping the bank's customers with their banking needs, such as depositing a cheque or making a withdrawal.

three-in-one: A facility that links savings and demat accounts to online trading accounts.

trade finance: International trade transactions involving exports and imports. While a seller (the exporter) can require the purchaser (an importer) to pre-pay for goods shipped, the purchaser may wish to reduce risk by requiring the seller to document the goods that have been shipped. Banks may assist by providing various forms of support such as by offering letters of credit.

transactional banking: A banking process that allows for the safe and efficient movement (transaction) of cash securities in the global financial system.

turnaround time: The time required to complete a task; in this context, from the date (time) a transaction is submitted (received by the bank) to the date (time) it is completed.

U

unsecured loan: A loan that is issued and supported only by the borrower's creditworthiness, rather than by any collateral.

W

wagering: A sort of gambling; betting on the outcome of an external event.

warrant: A derivative security that gives the holder the right to purchase securities (usually equity) from the issuer at a specific price within a certain time frame.

wholesale banking: The provision of services by banks to large corporate clients, mid-sized companies, real-estate developers and investors, international trade finance businesses, institutional customers (such as pension funds and government entities/agencies) and other banks or other financial institutions as opposed to retail banking that involves products such as home loans and auto loans.

Y

yield: The return on an investment. This refers to the interest or dividend received from a security and is usually expressed annually as a percentage based on the investment's cost, its current market value or its face value.

Glossary of Hindi Usage

Chapter 1

'Abhi aake desh ke liye kuch karo.' ['Now come and do something for the country.']

Chapter 3

'Bharat . . . bhi aa raha hai.' ['Bharat is also coming.']

'Kya kar raha hai aaj kal?' ['What are you doing these days?']

'Aaj kal toh main corporate banking mein hoon.' ['I'm involved in corporate banking.']

'Kya karna chahta hai?' ['What do you want to do?']

'Main khush hoon . . .' ['I'm happy . . .]

'Warden Road mein rehta hoon,' ['I live on Warden Road.']

'. . . kya karna hai' [what to do]

Chapter 4

'Bank bandh ho gaya.' ['The bank's closed.']

Chapter 6

'. . . "Teri unchi English mere ko samajh me nahi aati hai; mere ko ye bata ki ladoo kidhar hai." ' ['I can't follow your sophisticated English; simply tell me where is the money.']

'Paisa kidhar hai woh dikha, mujhe aur kuch nahi samajhta hai, seedha baat pe aa. Mujhe tu global gyan mat de.' ['Show me the money; I don't want to listen to anything else. Don't give me global knowledge.']

Chapter 10

'Bharat yatra' ['India voyage']

Chapter 12

'Chalo, main sabko khana khilata hoon. Aa jao, gaadi mein baith jao, acchi jagah lekar jaata hoon.' ['Let's go, I'll take everyone out for a meal. Come, sit in the car, I'll take you to a nice place.']

'Boss, aapke dost ka cheque maine clear kia.' ['Boss, I've cleared your friend's cheque.']

'Mera koi dost nahi hai. Main yahaan bank chala raha hoon, bas.' ['I don't have any friends. I'm running a bank here.']

'Boss ka koi dost nahi hai, yaad rakhna.' ['Remember, the boss has no friends.']

'Main Aditya se baat karta hoon,' ['I'll talk to Aditya']

'Tu mere logon se baat kar, main yeh sab nahi dekhta hoon.' ['Go and talk to my people, I don't deal with such matters.']

'Dhanda kaun deta hai?' ['Who is giving the business (the money)?']

'iska kya hua? uska kya hua?' ['what happened to this?' 'what happened to that?']

'Milke aaoon kya?' ['Should I go and meet them?']

'MD bana rahein hain kya?' ['Are they making you the MD?']

Chapter 13

'Tu kya karega?' ['What will you do?']

A Bank for the Buck

343